Antler on the Sea

THE YUP'IK AND CHUKCHI
OF THE RUSSIAN FAR EAST

Anna M. Kerttula

Cornell University Press

Ithaca and London

First published 2000 by Cornell University Press
First printing, Cornell Paperbacks, 2000

Library of Congress Cataloging-in-Publication Data

Kerttula, Anna M.
    Antler on the sea : Yup'ik and Chukchi of the Russian Far East / Anna M. Kerttula.
        p. cm.
    Includes bibliographical references and index.
    ISBN 978-0-8014-3681-9 (cloth : alk. paper)
    ISBN 978-0-8014-8685-2 (pbk. : alk. paper)
        1. Chukchi. 2. Yup'ik Eskimos—Russia (Federation)—Chukotskii avtonomnyi okrug.
    3. Ethnology—Russia (Federation)—Chukotskii avtonomnyi okrug. 4. Chukotskii
    avtonomnyi okrug (Russia)—Ethnic relations. I. Title.

DK759.C45 K47 2000
957'.7—dc21   00-034036

Cornell University Press strives to use environmentally responsible suppliers and materials to the fullest extent possible in the publishing of its books. Such materials include vegetable-based, low-VOC inks and acid-free papers that are recycled, totally chlorine-free, or partly composed of nonwood fibers. For further information, visit our website at www.cornellpress.cornell.edu.

Title page illustration, *Processing the Reindeer,* courtesy of Sergei Kalentonau.

Cloth printing   10   9   8   7   6   5   4   3   2   1
Paperback printing   10   9   8   7   6   5   4   3

To Oscar Alexander Kerttula,
my grandfather,
with me always in spirit

Contents

Illustrations

Illustrations

Acknowledgments

I extend my deepest gratitude to the people of Sireniki for being such gracious hosts during my fieldwork; without them this book would have remained only a dream. Special recognition is due Kawawa, Klava, Valerii, Sergei, Nina, and Lena, who fed me, clothed me, and made me a part of their family. These people are still like family to me; my gratitude for their kindness and generosity knows no bounds.

I owe a debt of gratitude to the late Timofei Panauge for giving me insight into the hunter's world; without his help I would have only stood on the shore.

Others in Sireniki who were instrumental in this work deserve mention: Vitiia Menkov, Panauge, Boriia Mumykhtikak, Tania Barzova, Tiotia Olia, Serezha, Olia, Lida Iurievna, Lilia, Sveta Zabusova, Tat'iana Danilovna and Svetlana Aleksandrovna, Irina Efimovna, Lebedev, and Sasha Kalinin.

A special debt of gratitude goes to my close friend Ada Gyrgaltagina and her family, who instilled in me a love for the tundra and a new worldview. "Thank you" cannot begin to repay my debt.

The people of Sireniki are to be commended for their patience and perseverance. I hope this book does them justice.

The book manuscript was carefully read and sensitively critiqued by Aram Yengoyan, Roger Sanjek, Bruce Grant, Ray Kelly, Sergei Kan, Igor Krupnik, Jane Burbank, Daniel Sheveiko, Michael Tubman, and Bev Haywood. Thank you all for your advice and suggestions.

I thank my parents, Helen Joyce Campbell Kerttula and Jalmar Martin Kerttula, who never failed to support my dreams. They have my love, gratitude, and undying respect for being open enough to let me pursue my path to anthropology.

The fieldwork on which this book is based was supported by a grant from the Hewitt Foundation through the University of Michigan Program to Promote International Partnerships. The writing was supported by Joyce and Jalmar Kerttula and Elvi Maria Martin Kerttula Rebarchek, my paternal grandmother.

To my life partner, John Echave, thank you for sharing with me your wonderful photographs, superior editorial skills, and undying support.

A. M. K.

A Note on Translation and Transliteration

I have followed the Library of Congress system of transliteration of Russian terms and names (with diacritics omitted), with the exceptions of the word *yaranga* and names familiar to U.S. readers in other forms; thus Yevgeny Yevtushenko rather than Evgenii Evtushenko. All translations from Russian to English are my own, unless I have indicated otherwise. The translation and transliteration of Yup'ik words are from two sources. The words *siqeneq* (sun) and *sighinəq* (antler) were supplied by Michael Krauss of the Alaska Native Languages Center, University of Alaska, from the *Dictionary of St. Lawrence Island / Siberian Yup'ik Language* (1987). All other Yup'ik words come from the *Eskimossko-Russkii, Russko-Eskimosskii Slovar'* (1988), which I have transliterated in accordance with the Library of Congress system.

Most Russian plurals are formed by the addition of -*i* or -*y* to the ends of words in the nominative case, as English uses -*s*. Except for Russian words that have become so familiar that they are listed in English-language dictionaries, such as "kulak" and "kolkhoz," I have used the Russian plurals for Russian words; for example, *yaranga, yarangi; kollektiv, kollektivy; baidara, baidary; internat, internaty.*

Antler on the Sea

PROLOGUE

Fieldwork In Sireniki

> The whole key and rhythm of my life had been altered for-
> ever by a handful of experiences that left no communicable
> mark. And even now, as I wait for the right words, I wonder
> how accurate, how honest, these descriptions will be, and to
> what extent I am working them up a little afterwards.
>
> EDMUND CARPENTER, IN HUGHES,
> "UNDER FOUR FLAGS," 1965

I arrived in Sireniki, a small coastal village on the western side of the Bering
Sea, in 1989, just as winter was setting in. On October 15 I boarded a large
blue-and-orange helicopter in the town of Provideniia and set out for the village. Sitting next to me was Iurii Grigorevich, the regional native education administrator, who was coming to Sireniki on his *komandirovka* (work assignment) to conduct an audit of the school. After several minutes, I became aware
that he was staring at me, undoubtedly because of my unfamiliar clothing. Finally, over the roar of the helicopter, he asked an almost inaudible question:
"Are you the new schoolteacher?" As I think back to that question, I realize
with some irony that I should have answered, "No, I'm the new student."

My path to Sireniki started in 1984 when I was invited by the Institute of
Circumpolar Health (ICH) at the University of Alaska to tour medical facilities in the Soviet Far East and Siberia. Knowing that I was interested in doing anthropological fieldwork in Chukotka, the far northeastern part of Russia,
our Soviet sponsor, Academician Iurii Nikitin, arranged for me to meet with

social science colleagues at the Academy of Sciences in Novosibirsk. I hoped to persuade them to allow me to do Western-style fieldwork in Chukotka among the Yup'ik,[1] but at that time I was told that extensive fieldwork would be impossible.

Five years later, I received a phone call from ICH informing me that one of their research partners, Dr. Aleksandr Grigorevich Volfson, at the Institute of Biological Problems of the North in Magadan, was looking for an Alaskan research partner to do ethnographic fieldwork in Chukotka. I contacted him and he agreed to work with me.

I was interested in working with Siberian Yup'ik people and there were only two communities in Chukotka whose populations were primarily Yup'ik. I had the choice of Novo Chaplino or Sireniki. I chose Sireniki because Novo Chaplino was closer to the larger town of Provideniia and easily accessible by road. That seemed an indication that Sireniki would be a more "traditional" village. Although the assumption proved to be inaccurate, Sireniki's isolation proved to be an asset in a different way: the isolation intensified the community's sense of identity and protected me from daily interference by regional authorities. Several months after the ICH called me, I found myself in Nome, Alaska, aboard a chartered small plane that flew me to Provideniia.

In Provideniia my Russian guide to the village was waiting. Leonid was a geneticist from my sponsor, the Institute of Biological Problems of the North, Magadan. My research partner, Dr. Volfson, had died a few weeks earlier of pancreatic cancer. Leonid had the misfortune, in his estimation, of having made a deathbed promise to Volfson that he would meet me in Provideniia and accompany me to the village. Leonid being a self-proclaimed sophisticated urbanite, his idea of a good assignment was not a winter visit to an Arctic village. But his sense of obligation to his good friend led him to our meeting in Provideniia and his *komandirovka* to accompany me to Sireniki.

As the helicopter descended on the hillside village by the sea, I could see through a small circular porthole tiny wooden houses interspersed with whitewashed two-story apartment buildings of an architectural style familiar in the Soviet North. In spite of the Soviets, this village had a reassuring familiarity, a kinship with the Alaskan Inuit and Yup'ik villages I had spent much of my childhood visiting when I traveled with my father. This moment was the culmination of years of studying Chukotka from the Alaskan side, diligently practicing Russian, and hoping that one distant day I might actually do fieldwork in this land. Now, thanks to glasnost, here I was.

Once in Sireniki, Leonid introduced me to the mayor and the head of the state farm, and made arrangements for me to live and work in the village, all the while trying to convince me that the village was an uncomfortable and poor place to work, especially for someone of my background and "social position."

He urged me to return with him to Magadan and develop my project there. This was perhaps a natural reaction for a Ukrainian who had no knowledge of the American school of anthropology and its tradition of extensive fieldwork. He also didn't know of my tenacity. Leonid spent the week until the helicopter came back nervously smoking and assiduously trying to change my plans. Then on the Friday before the next scheduled helicopter, the village organized its fall slaughter of reindeer.

Realizing this was a major event, I got up very early and rode with the first brigade of workers to the reindeer corral. I participated in chasing the wandering reindeer into the corral and the beginning of the slaughter. About one in the afternoon Leonid showed up. I was busily pulling the hide off a recently killed animal. When I looked up at Leonid, he was pale with shock and disgust. I was covered to my elbows in blood, my hands deep inside the reindeer's belly. He shook his head in dismay and asked me what I was doing. "I'm learning how to skin a reindeer," I replied. He simply walked away, got on the truck, and drove off. He left on the helicopter the next morning, with promises to call me from time to time to make sure I was still alive and to see if I had come to my senses. Leonid gave me my first insight into how *priezzhii* (Newcomers)[2] looked upon the indigenous people of the Far North. I think Leonid believed me to be the strangest woman he had ever met.

Being from an Alaskan farming family, I instinctively began to work when the reindeer slaughter started. I was unaware of it at the time, but my willingness to participate was my entrée into the Chukchi and Yup'ik world. Although more or less everyone in the village took some part in the slaughter, Newcomers did not do the actual butchering. They considered such work dirty and primitive, certainly no work for a woman. By enthusiastically working in the slaughter, I immediately separated myself from other Newcomers; and although I was still considered different, I was less different. As a result, native people were willing to open up and talk with me. This single event did more to create a frame of reference in which people could communicate to and about me than anything else I could have done. On Soviet Workers' Day my work was publicly recognized and I was honored with a certificate and a book from the state farm.

To be honest, my work in Sireniki consisted of living. I conducted interviews, collected data, and researched village records and regional archives, but mainly I lived. I was befriended by some people and families and not by others. I participated in as many activities as were open to me: sea mammal hunting, reindeer herding, fox farming, fishing, gathering, teaching, visiting, cultural activities, weddings, funerals, baptisms, state farm meetings, and standing in line. I held a regular job in the skinning *kollektiv*. My work in the *kollektiv* introduced me not only to the craft of scraping and tanning reindeer

[3]

hides and walrus hides but also to a circle of women, many of whom became good friends. The hours we spent together working, gossiping during tea breaks, and sharing stories provided some of my greatest insights into the daily lives and concerns of the women in the village.

The two most powerful experiences I had in the village were spending a summer in a *yaranga* (a tent covered with reindeer skin) on the tundra with my friend Ada, her mother, and her children, and traveling with the hunters during the spring walrus hunt. These two activities not only provided untold pages of data for my research but gave me personal insight into the tundra and the sea. These events changed my own consciousness, allowing me new insight into the way others construct their worlds.

The people of Sireniki assumed that I was an intern on her *praktikum* (internship), and many came to view me as the village chronicler. Many Soviet and foreign journalists had written about life in Sireniki in a way that focused on the negative. Soviet journalists high on their newfound freedom wrote about poverty, poor working conditions, and alcoholism among the northern indigenous peoples. Foreign journalists romanticized the traditional lives of the people and the devastating effects of Sovietization—alcoholism, poverty, high mortality rates. One Japanese film crew even supplied the alcohol in order to photograph alcohol abuse. Local people rightfully considered this behavior unethical; they recognized that the outside world was being given a distorted picture of their lives. On more than one occasion, people spoke about how important it was for me to "really understand" their lives so I could "set the record straight."

Although I tried on numerous occasions, it was impossible to explain to everyone the theoretical underpinnings of my work and that I wasn't just an observer but an analyzer as well. Saying that I was an ethnographer was of little use, for although people were familiar with the various Soviet ethnographers who visited the village yearly, these researchers rarely stayed more than a few months and didn't participate in village life to the extent I did. When an outsider would ask someone from the village who I was and what I was doing there, the most common answer was that I was on my *praktikum*. Today I believe this was the right word—I was indeed an intern of Sireniki life.

The day I left Sireniki, Ada handed me a single bead strung on a leather thong. It was not until months later, while reading the work of the early ethnographer Vladimir Bogoraz, that I understood the full meaning of the gesture. A single bead strung on a leather thong was given between trading partners as a sign of their faith in each other and the wish for a safe return. I carry that bead with me in all of my travels. It ensures my safe passage home to Sireniki; it is a talisman that connects the events of this lifetime with the events of a past lifeway; and most important, it is a symbol of the deep friendship formed between two people so different and yet so alike, so far apart and yet so near.

This book is as accurate a chronicle of Sireniki life from 1989 to 1991 as I can write. I never expected to be writing ethnohistory, but that is in effect what this book has become. I only hope I have lived up to my hosts' expectations and that it indeed "sets the record straight" for the people of Sireniki as they were in those formative glasnost years.

Chukotka Peninsula

[1]

The People of Sireniki

The Soviets Come to Chukotka

> My father's father told me of how he had a premonition of
> the Revolution. He told me the sky turned red and he looked
> up to see the numbers one, nine, one, and seven written
> across it. He later remembered this premonition when he
> saw 1917 written in a journal and he told me about it.
>
> KAWAWA, A YUP'IK WOMAN

After the Bolshevik Revolution, the new Soviet government attempted to compensate for the past abuses of the tsarist empire by officially recognizing the equal rights of all national minorities. In 1917 the Soviet state adopted the Declaration of the Rights of the Peoples of Russia, which provided for "the free development of national minorities and ethnic groups living on Russian territory" (Vakhtin 1992). Article 22 of the Constitution of the Russian Soviet Federated Socialist Republic (RSFSR), promulgated in 1918, established equal rights for all citizens and forbade repression of the national minorities (Puchkova 1993). Throughout the 1920s the Soviet government tried to preserve, protect, and even encourage non-Russian minority cultural development by creating guidelines for indigenous peoples' interaction with the larger state apparatus.

The Bolsheviks, who were primarily the urban Russian proletariat and constituted the power base of the new state, were at a decided disadvantage in their efforts to govern the multiethnic, predominantly agricultural state that was the Russian Empire. In order to legitimize the Russian-dominated proletarian revolution among the non-Russian, primarily peasant, agricultural pop-

Bering Sea coastline of Chukotka between Provideniia and Sireniki, as captured from a *baidara*. (Photo by John Echave.)

ulation, in 1923 the Communist Party formalized a policy, *korenizatsiia*, or nativization, to socialize and industrialize the non-Russian population. In accordance with this policy, non-Russian peoples were given the right to study socialism in their own language and within their own cultural contexts. *Korenizatsiia* was the Russian proletariat–dominated Communist Party's formal recognition of its lack of support among non-Russian peoples, primarily in the larger, more densely populated central Asian regions. It was their attempt to bring the diverse population of the non-Russian Republics into the Soviet sphere of influence (Liber 1991).

In this effort the Communist Party made compromises with the non-Russian territories. Through the program of *korenizatsiia* the Party created separate republics and autonomous regions with some, albeit circumscribed, political autonomy; supported the creation of a separate Communist party within each non-Russian republic; legitimated indigenous languages and cultures; and promoted non-Russians into high Party positions. *Korenizatsiia* was essentially a policy to appease the non-Russian citizenry through a rhetoric

Smokestacks and apartment buildings in Provideniia. (Photo by John Echave.)

that pointed out the abuses of Russian chauvinism under the tsar while displaying the benevolence of the Soviet government and the Communist Party by promoting local language, culture, and economic development.

Along with the social policies of *korenizatsiia* came economic modernization. Soviet policy makers believed that industrialization of the more rural-based republics would draw the indigenous peoples out of their "primitive" economic systems into the socialist proletariat and create a cadre of native elites who could be useful to the larger Soviet bureaucracy. Huge capital investments in the non-Russian republics were made in the 1920s in an attempt to industrialize these regions' economies and urbanize their populations.

Urbanization, however, did not bring the expected cultural homogenization or internalization of the socialist ideology. Instead, it solidified each cultural group's own identity. With the strengthening of local economies and the raising of literacy rates in local native languages came pride in and identification with one's natal culture.

By the 1930s, Russians accounted for only 52 percent of the All-Union

Communist Party (Liber 1991). Although the Party was not a democratic institution, and therefore the power base of its Russian founders was not truly threatened by the sharp increase in non-Russian members, the central government became increasingly paranoid about the power forming among the non-Russian elites at the periphery. *Korenizatsiia*, far from homogenizing the Union, had actually institutionalized identification with the ethnic group and its local political organizations.

The Russian center never intended to transfer actual political power to the periphery. When the non-Russian republics and autonomous regions tried to exert their local autonomy, the Soviet government abandoned its *korenizatsiia* policy in hopes of avoiding a civil conflict between the non-Russian republics and the RSFSR. By 1945, there was an ideological shift in the country toward Russian control. Russian was declared the official language and culture of the Soviet Union; all higher education took place in Russian, all government business was conducted in Russian, and programs aimed at promoting local language, culture, and political strength were ended.

During the 1930s and 1940s many of the state institutions and legal safeguards of national minority rights were liquidated. Industrialization in the non-Russian republics was carried out with blatant disregard for the interests of indigenous peoples (Puchkova 1993). The non-Russian cadre of native elites was lost to Stalin's purges. What was originally criticized as Russian chauvinism was now hailed as the pinnacle of social evolution.

Because the Russians viewed the indigenous peoples of the Far North as extremely "primitive" and "backward," they directed their efforts toward "civilizing" rather than industrializing the local populations. "Civilizing" entailed primarily material changes—apartment houses, roads, hospitals, schools—but also included changes in personal hygiene, economic organization, social organization, literacy, and educational attainment.

In a position to aid this process were, surprisingly, a number of tsarist political exiles. These men, having been exiled from tsarist Russia, had lived for many years with native peoples in Siberia. After the Bolshevik Revolution they found themselves in the interesting position of being de facto ethnographers. Most notable were Vladimir Bogoraz-Tan and Vladimir Iokhel'son, who later joined the Jesup North Pacific Expedition of the American Museum of Natural History, and Lev Shternberg. As the senior ethnographers of their time, they wrote the seminal ethnographic works on the Chukchi, Koriaki, Iukagiry, and Nivkhi (Giliaks) (Dikov 1989; Freed et al. 1988; Slezkine 1991; Vakhtin 1992). These remarkably insightful individuals suddenly found themselves close to the center of power. From this position they lobbied the Soviet government to create the Committee for the Assistance of the Peoples of the Northern Borderlands—shortened to Committee of the North—to "define and to preserve the territories necessary for the life and cultural development of each ethnic group" (Dikov 1989; Kolarz 1969; Slezkine 1992; Vakhtin 1992). This committee gained its power by being administratively attached to the People's Commissariat of Nationalities (Narkomnats).

The original members of the Committee of the North had the intention of protecting the indigenous minority populations from further exploitation by Europeans. For the first five years of its existence the committee's members were able to exclude nonindigenous peoples from the northern areas, with the exceptions of health officials, teachers, and state farm administrators. In 1923 Bogoraz proposed that "reserved territories" be set aside for the exclusive use of the indigenous inhabitants, in order to protect them from mixing with the Russians and causing their own ultimate extinction (Vakhtin 1993b). By the 1930s, however, the Committee of the North had an increasing number of "progressive" members whose interests were motivated more by socialist politics and economic production than by a desire to protect minority cultures.

The new majority was interested in advancing class struggle among indigenous peoples. Its basic assumption was that the northern indigenous peoples were in the evolutionary stage of "primitive communism" and therefore needed assistance up the "evolutionary ladder" if they were to reach the state of socialism. This was an immense simplification of the basic Leninist view of historical materialism based on the writings of Karl Marx and Friedrich Engels. In 1844 Marx met Engels and the two began sharing their ideas on historical materialism. In his essay "The Premises of the Materialist Method," Marx describes the developmental stages through which forms of ownership evolve, from tribal ownership to ancient communal and state ownership to feudal or estate property (Marx 1977). Then in 1877 Lewis Henry Morgan published *Ancient Society*, which outlined his theory of human social evolution (Leacock 1974). Marx and Engels agreed with Morgan that society was not static but evolving, and social forms come into existence at particular historical periods as a result of specific socioeconomic conditions. Engels borrowed Morgan's ideas, and in 1884 published *Origin of the Family, Private Property and the State*. Lenin praised Engels's work as "one of the fundamental works of modern socialism" (Reed 1972). Engels's theory of the evolution of society from "savagery" to matriarchy to patriarchy, accompanied by the evolution from tribal ownership to capitalism to communism, became the basis for Soviet social ideology and policy toward northern minority peoples.

At first a local system of administration was instituted. Tribal general assemblies and tribal soviets were elected by the tribal executive committees of the various local indigenous cultural groups. The drawbacks of tribal administrations were many; in many areas there was no connection between ethnicity and territory, and eventually the tribal administrations were abolished and their duties assigned to the metropolitan areas. During this time Chukotka came to be administered from Khabarovsk, a city more than 3,000 kilometers to the south (Vakhtin 1992).

Assisting in what the committee originally perceived as a gradual process was a Leninist-inspired program called the *kul'tbazy* (cultural bases) with a mobile component, the *krasnye yarangi* (red tents). The program was created to help educate the northern minorities about socialism and help them achieve it. A *kul'tbaza* was a political, cultural, and scientific research center that included a boarding school, kindergarten, hospital, and veterinary station. The first *kul'tbaza* in Chukotka was opened in 1928 in Lavrentiia. By the end of its original five-year plan the first *krasnye yarangi*, envisioned as "traveling foundations of political enlightenment," were formed (Dikov 1989).

One of the Yup'ik men in Sireniki, Kolia Galgauge, spoke fondly of his time with the *krasnye yarangi*. Kolia spoke of his travels by dogsled to the Chukchi living on the tundra to deliver newspapers, magazines, and mail and to give the children lessons in Russian, undoubtedly accompanied by lessons in socialism. He was very proud of his achievements and told me of the many Chukchi adults who had thanked him profusely for his teaching efforts when they were children.

While I was there a young Sireniki man, Misha Zavin, traveled from the House of Culture to the reindeer brigades. The House of Culture was a Soviet institution consisting of a recreation building with several administrators who organized village social events and political meetings, and brought "high culture"—dance, theater, poetry readings, and videos—to the rural areas. Misha spoke of his mission as a "modern red tent." He explained that he delivered the mail, brought magazines, newspapers, and books, and entertained the herders with his video movies, "just like they used to." Although I never heard him give a lesson in socialism—and I am sure if he had given any, no one would have been interested—Misha's work certainly drew much of its structure from its predecessor, the *krasnaia yaranga*.

One of the primary goals of the *kul'tbazy* and the *krasnye yarangi* was to increase local literacy in native languages and to educate indigenous peoples about socialism in "culturally sensitive ways." Perhaps the imagery of the *krasnaia yaranga*, combining the color of the revolution, red (*krasnaia*), with the name of the skin house used by the nomadic Chukchi and Koriak reindeer herders (*yaranga*), best symbolized the goals of the committee.

Although the Committee of the North tried to soften the impact of the evolution of a hunter-gatherer society to a socialist proletariat society, by the late 1920s the central government grew impatient. As Yuri Slezkine points out: "In Stalin's paradise there was no place for the native Northerners, whose otherness was understood as nothing but backwardness" (1992:57). Thus began the

"Great Transformation" to socialism, the effort to push indigenous "backward" cultures "across a thousand years" in only a few (Kovalenko 1986; Slezkine 1991). Articles written by "Soviet social scientists" about this period read like laundry lists of "achievements": "well-built comfortable housing, heated with anthracite . . . furnished with beds, chairs, tables . . . cloth trousers, jackets, coats, leather and rubber boots . . . airmail regularly delivers newspapers, magazines, and letters to remote tundra villages" (Antropova and Kuznetsova 1964:832).

As part of this Great Transformation, the new governmental programs in the North followed the general policies of the Soviet state concerning all non-Russian minorities, including principles from the *korenizatsiia* program. The efforts to bring socialism to Chukotka were originally carried out by "enthusiastic" young Russian teachers, men and women who had little knowledge of local language and culture. The first teachers recommended the creation of a cadre of people who were familiar with local languages and customs to work in these northern regions. In 1925, nineteen students from various northern indigenous groups entered the *rabfak* at Leningrad University for special education as disseminators of socialism. *Rabfaki*, or Rabochie Fakul'tety (Workers' Departments), were departments set up in various universities after the revolution for the purpose of educating workers and peasants. The state's goal was to train "politically conscious" cadres of proletarians to fill key managerial positions for the work of constructing socialism. Such people were especially needed in the northern regions, where the Russian population was minimal.

Special institutes were built exclusively to study indigenous peoples and to provide for their higher education. Some were the Institute of the Peoples of the North in Leningrad, the Khabarovsk Pedagogical and Technical Institute, the Anadyr Pedagogical Training School, and a technical institute in Provideniia, which later included an institute for training future administrators, economists, and accountants for collective farms. New departments in the Chukotka regional institutes were set up to educate a group of young native specialists who would return home and spread the teachings of socialism among their people.

This cadre consisted primarily of native members of Komsomol (the Communist Youth League) willing to spread socialism among indigenous peoples. These would-be educators were so inadequately prepared, however, and their reception by many of the indigenous groups was so unfavorable that the transformation to socialism was slow (Slezkine 1992). Finally in 1928, exasperated by the leisurely rate of improvement among northern peoples, the Central Executive Committee of the RSFSR, through an addition to the Criminal Code, "Crimes That Constitute Survivals of Tribalism," made "backwardness" illegal (Slezkine 1991).

This revised code opened the door for the forceful eradication of many traditional social practices. In the end, bride service was defined as slavery, bridewealth as an illegal fine, and polygamy as a crime. Industrious herders were redefined as kulaks (wealthy peasants) and shamans as exploiters; both were criminals subject to punishment under the law.

Another part of the Sovietization program was the mandatory schooling of indigenous children. To this end, *internaty* (boarding schools) were set up to focus on training children in "civilized behavior." They were originally designed to give children of nomadic groups access to systematic education. Eventually they evolved as part of a Russification policy for the education and training of the children of all of the native groups, nomadic and settled. Parents were required to send their children to boarding schools from kindergarten through high school. The separation of children from their families had disastrous effects on native cultures.

In 1992 a group of Koriak in Kamchatka told me that as late as the 1960s the Soviets sent huge military helicopters to the tundra in search of truant children. They told of armed men in helicopters circling their small encampments, children running every which way to hide, frantic parents screaming for the soldiers to leave them alone, and children being carried onto the helicopters. Although they told these stories with nervous smiles, punctuated by raucous laughter, the devastating effects of the situation were not lost on them. Children were separated from their families for months at a time and educated in schools that focused on the Russian language and culture and devalued indigenous cultures and practices. Many such children never became fully reintegrated into their own cultures.

No one in Sireniki ever recounted such extreme measures in their region, but they, too, were subject to the *internaty*, and were well aware of the cultural consequences. One Yup'ik woman told me that when she completed her education at the *internat* and returned home, she was barely able to speak her native language. She spent many years relearning Yup'ik in order to converse with her mother. Many other students in their late teens were never able to speak their native language fluently again.

A Chukchi woman told me of the rigorous training in hygiene she and others underwent as late as the 1970s, being taught how to wash and brush their teeth, how to clean their clothes and their rooms, and how and what to eat. She confessed that when she returned home she found it difficult to accept what she had come to perceive as the lower standard of living and inferior customs in the village.

In the early years of socialist development, attempts were made to teach in native languages. In Sireniki, Yup'ik elders remembered learning the Yup'ik alphabet with Latin letters. In 1937 the Latin script was changed to Cyrillic script (Kolarz 1969; Vakhtin 1992). Most of the elderly still complained that they preferred the Latin alphabet's transliteration of Yup'ik. When I brought a book from St. Lawrence Island, Alaska, that was written in Siberian Yup'ik in the Latin script, after a few minutes of adjustment many elderly Yup'ik were able to read it easily.

By the 1960s social scientists were lauding the numerous successes in the North: "The overcoming of the extreme political, economic, and cultural backwardness of these peoples was a bright page in the history of the nationality policy of the Soviet state" (Gurvich 1961:22). The early policies of the government and the Party, however, had little actual effect on the "political, economic, and cultural backwardness" of Sireniki, and probably little on Chukotka as a whole. Igor Krupnik notes that the "rhythm of life among the northern peoples did not appreciably change until the 1950's" (1993:64). Although collectivization started in the 1930s with the reorganization of local hunting groups into hunting artels (workers' collectives) and herding cooperatives into collective farms, it was not until after World War II that the Soviet state began to exert its power effectively.

On the Chukotka Peninsula the Great Transformation actually took place from the 1950s through the 1970s. With the advent of the Cold War, the Soviet Union and the United States stationed troops close to the Bering Sea, and with the military came civilian infrastructure. During that period Chukotka was opened to extensive timber and mineral exploration and exploitation, which also demanded infrastructural support. These developments brought a great influx of nonindigenous peoples to Sireniki, as well as to other areas.

Accompanying the nonnatives came industrialization and acute material transformations. Indigenous peoples came under intense pressures to change if they were going to survive. Regionally centralized communities were built and villages were relocated in the name of "economic viability." Nonindigenous enterprises were organized: fox farms, dairy and swine farms, lumber mills, greenhouses. Administrative control over marine resources, especially fishing and whaling, was centralized in state-owned companies, limiting local people's access to their own natural resources. Chukchi herders were forcibly collectivized, and schoolchildren were taught in Russian about the Soviet Union.

Local people were not just passive recipients of Soviet colonialism, however; they actively participated in their own transformation. Many local people joined the Communist Party, became Party secretaries, and accepted Russian education and collectivization without resistance. From the 1950s to the present, the people of Sireniki have been in a dialogue with Soviet institutions and individuals. To unwrap this process we have to know who the actors are.

[15]

Sireniki's People

> I have read in books that the name Sireniki comes from the
> Yup'ik word for sun, *siqeneq*, and that Sireniki means sunny
> valley. This is not true. Sireniki comes from the word for
> antler, *sighinəq*. When I was young there was a mound of
> antlers on the hill not far from the village. People would go
> to those antlers to receive answers to their questions. It was
> from that mound of antlers that Sireniki got its name.
>
> KAWAWA, 1991

When this story was first told to me, its significance was not apparent. It was only later that I recognized it as a metaphor for post-Soviet Sireniki, where two symbolic and cultural systems, tundra and sea, Chukchi and Yup'ik, were brought together and in the process were transformed.

In 1991, at the conclusion of my field research, the total population of Sireniki was approximately 770: 343 Yup'ik (44 percent), 221 Chukchi (29 percent), and approximately 200 Newcomers (27 percent). Of the 200 Newcomers, approximately 50 were military personnel, regular soldiers and border guards. I did not collect detailed statistical data on these groups because asking questions about potentially sensitive subjects might have created suspicion about my work.

Sireniki was unique in that it was the only prehistoric Yup'ik village in the region still inhabited (Krupnik 1993; Vakhtin 1984), although not exclusively, by Yup'ik peoples. The Chukchi residents were a fairly recent addition to the village. Before the 1950s, the Chukchi lived a nomadic life of reindeer herding on the tundra surrounding Sireniki. In the 1950s they were required to relinquish most of their family herds to the collective farm (uncooperative male heads of families were imprisoned), leaving herds too small (approximately 200 reindeer or fewer) to sustain families on the tundra. Thereafter, many Chukchi were forced to settle in coastal villages such as Sireniki.

Newcomers were drawn to the village by the promise of higher pay and better jobs than they could get in their native republics. These people often worked in the North for fifteen to twenty years, then retired to their home towns, where living was perceived as easier and more "civilized."[1]

Although Newcomers were not a numerical majority, because of their education, professions, and political connections they rapidly came to control the social and political power in these regions. They were able to direct social policy toward their own Russified Soviet goals, ignoring the voices of the indigenous majority. These structural changes in the social and economic organiza-

The village of Sireniki and its Soviet-style buildings. (Photo by Anna M. Kerttula.)

tion of the region brought together three distinct social-cultural groups, Yup'ik, Chukchi, and Newcomers, and led to the development of a pluralistic village.

In order to understand fully the implications of this pluralism on the cultural transformations that occurred in Sireniki, it is first necessary to understand how each of the three main cultural groups define themselves.

The Yup'ik

> Kawawa and I were having tea this afternoon when Panauge saw us from the street and walked into the kitchen. "I heard some-one stole the track off Ankalin's *buran*," he said. "Tell him I have a track that he can have." Then he turned to me and explained, "We are Yup'ik. It is the Yup'ik way to help one another. That's why I'm offering him my track, because we are Yup'ik."
>
> EDITED DIARY ENTRY, 1990

[17]

Sasha plays in the sandbox outside his Sireniki home. (Photo by John Echave.)

Fully developed maritime societies that are indisputably Inuit / Yuit have occupied many of the coastal communities of the Chukotka Peninsula, possibly
for over three thousand years (Ackerman 1984; Arutiunov and Fitzhugh 1988;
Dikov 1989; Okladnikov 1965). In 1991, evidence of Yup'ik prehistory dotted
the Sireniki landscape. On the village hillside overlooking the Bering Sea,
stone *yaranga* rings covered by almost a century of vegetation were still visi-
ble. The beach ridge lining the shore was an ancient site that with every new
storm revealed stone, bone, and ivory artifacts used by the ancestors of the
Yup'ik people.

The earliest historic records of the Yup'ik come from the diaries of the
seventeenth-century explorers of the Bering Sea. During his 1644 expedition
to Siberia, Mikhailo Staduchin met with Chukchi traders who told him of the
people who lived on an island where they killed "Sea-horses" (walruses) for
their "teeth" (tusks). In the 1640s Semen Dezhnev wrote: "There are two islands upon which were seen people of the Tschuktschi [Chukchi] Nation, thro'
whose lips were run pieces of the teeth of the sea-horse [labrets]." Since
Chukchi did not wear labrets, we assume that Dezhnev was writing about the
Yup'ik of the Diomede Islands (Muller 1967). Other explorers wrote similar
statements about the Yup'ik: Gavriil Sarychev in the 1780s, F. P. Wrangell in
the 1820s, and the famous Captain James Cook, who sailed in the Bering Sea
in the late eighteenth century. None of these travelogues, however, gives us

Kavauge and Typykhak, Yup'ik hunters, await the launch of the whaleboat. (Photo by John Echave.)

much insight into the social organization or daily lives of the Yup'ik people at the time of their early contact with Europeans. In fact, as Michael Chlenov and Igor Krupnik point out, the early explorers failed to distinguish between the Yup'ik and the Coastal Chukchi because of their lack of ethnolinguistic skills (1983).

The first comprehensive ethnographies of the Yup'ik people in Chukotka were by G. A. Menovshchikov. Menovshchikov was a member of the first cadre of young Soviet students sent to "eliminate illiteracy" among the indigenous peoples of the northern regions in the 1930s. During his tenure as a teacher at the school in Sireniki, Menovshchikov helped to develop the first "Eskimo" alphabet in the Latin script (Dikov 1989:223). Many elderly Yup'ik in Sireniki remembered Menovshchikov fondly. They spoke of their teacher as a kind and generous man who shared his rations of tea, sugar, and tobacco with the local residents; and they remembered his speaking and teaching the lessons in Yup'ik.

After his work in Chukotka, Menovshchikov became a member of the Institute of Linguistics at the Academy of Sciences of the USSR in Leningrad. Menovshchikov's publications provide insightful analysis of the social organization, material culture, and language of the Yup'ik in the Soviet Union.

Before Sovietization, the Yup'ik people were semimobile hunters and gath-

Yup'ik *babushki* wait for transportation to Sireniki. (Photo by John Echave.)

erers living in small villages, primarily exploiting sea mammals, though some families kept small herds of reindeer. Families generally occupied a single site, or *yaranga*, in a village, and labor was divided by gender: men hunted and women gathered and processed raw materials. The Yup'ik supplemented these activities by trading with Chukchi reindeer herders in Chukotka and with Yup'ik and Inupiat peoples in Alaska.

Indigenous trading was a classic relationship of exchange of material goods across ecological zones. The items traded were basic to the survival of both groups. The Chukchi primarily supplied reindeer skins to the Yup'ik, who needed them for clothing to survive in the subzero temperatures of the Arctic winters; the Yup'ik provided seal and walrus meat, oil, and skins to the Chukchi, who needed the dietary fat and the strength of the sea mammal hides for ropes, the soles of their skin boots, and the floors of their tents.

Charles and Jane Hughes (1960), G. A. Menovshchikov (1962), and D. A. Sergeev (1962) suggest that patriclans (the Hugheses' term) were the main form of social organization among the Yup'ik of Chukotka (before Sovietiza-tion) and the Yup'ik of St. Lawrence Island, Alaska. The evidence for patriclan organization was territories used exclusively by kin groups, exogamous mar-riage practices, terminology differentiating maternal and paternal kin, and kin collective subsistence activities. Chlenov disputes this conclusion; he says the Siberian Yup'ik were organized into small endogamous settlements on the basis of patrilineal kin groups resembling a "kindred" (Yup'ik patrilineages included mother's kin), but did not possess the key element of strict exogamy necessary for clan organization. As small settlements were combined into larger settlements in the 1930s, even patrilineal group endogamy became diffi-cult to maintain, and the contemporary pattern of marriage and social organi-zation eventually evolved.[2]

At a glance, the Yup'ik looked very Sovietized; they bore little resemblance to their ancestors. They wore factory-made clothing, rode motorcycles, hunted with rifles and outboard motors, lived in Soviet-constructed apartments, spoke Russian, and ate *pel'meni* (meat dumplings). But if one penetrated the mate-rial surface of Sireniki, one uncovered the Yup'ik culture.

As Panauge demonstrated, the Yup'ik people had a definite sense of being members of a unique cultural group. As such, the Yup'ik shared more than a nationality designation on their internal Soviet passports—they shared core concepts about the way their world was constructed. One such concept in-volved the Yup'ik's intimate identification with the sea.

Their main economic activity was sea mammal hunting, and sea mammals continued to be their primary source of food. For the Yup'ik, sea mammals were the very definition of good food. Their relationship with the sea was not exclusively economic, however, but spiritual as well. It was this connection to the sea, above all else, that distinguished the Yup'ik from the other groups in Sireniki.

Another aspect of being Yup'ik was speaking the Yup'ik language. Although, according to the linguist Nikolai Vakhtin (1984), only people over the age of 40 could be considered fluent in the Yup'ik language, and only two elderly women spoke the Sireniki dialect, people considered the ability to speak Yup'ik es-sential to the preservation of their culture.

In the early 1980s, when Vakhtin was collecting his data, young people in the age group 11–20 were able to understand the general theme of a conversation in Yup'ik but could not join in. By 1990, when these people were in their 30s, some had gained more competency in the language, but younger people who were now in the 11–20 age group were unable to understand even the gist of a Yup'ik conversation. Unfortunately, as recently as 1998, the last two women who spoke the Sireniki dialect of the Yup'ik language died. For all intents and purposes, this language and all of the cultural and symbolic thought that went along with it died with them.

None of the people in Sireniki remembered being "forbidden" to speak Yup'ik at boarding school, as students in many early Alaskan schools run by missionaries were; they said they spoke Russian "out of politeness." When they returned to the village after boarding school and military service, young adults struggled to relearn their native language.

Finally, the Yup'ik distinguished themselves through their sense of place. Sireniki was prehistorically and historically Yup'ik, and the Yup'ik felt connected to this place even though the current population of Sireniki was a combination of Yup'ik peoples from other communities in the region. Because of their Soviet education and the outside control over the village economy and politics, the Yup'ik, except for a few zealots, did not wish to exclude non-Yup'ik from the village; but there was a general feeling that non-Yup'ik were outsiders and by definition the "other."

The Chukchi

> Andrei looked down at the young Chukchi woman, Iuliia, from the top of the *vezdekhod* [all-terrain vehicle] on which we had been traveling for two days across the tundra carrying supplies to the reindeer brigades. The driver had stopped to make tea and give the passengers a much-needed rest from the bone-breaking ride of this tanklike vehicle. Although his consciousness had been numbed by the ordeal, Andrei immediately became fixated on Iuliia's feet in their house slippers. Finally overcome by curiosity, the city-born Russian spoke up: "Why are you wearing house slippers on the tundra? House slippers are to be worn at home." Iuliia retorted, "Why not? Isn't the tundra my home?"
>
> EDITED DIARY ENTRY, 1990

The first extensive ethnography of the Chukchi was *The Chukchee* by Vladimir Bogoraz-Tan (1904–9). Bogoraz's remarkable work gives us unprecedented insight into the material life, economy, social organization, and spiritual beliefs of the Chukchi people at the turn of the twentieth century. Because of the comprehensiveness of Bogoraz's work and that of other noted Russian ethnographers (Antropova and Kuznetsova 1964; Gurvich and Dolgikh 1970; Krushanova 1987; and Vdovin 1965a), I will only briefly outline some of the main features of pre-Soviet Chukchi life.[3]

Bogoraz divided the Chukchi, or Luoravetlan ("real people"), into two social-cultural groups, Maritime Chukchi and Reindeer Chukchi.[4] The two groups spoke the same language, today called Chukotkan, but had very different subsistence strategies. The Maritime Chukchi economy, based on sea mammal hunting, was (and still is) very similar to that of the Yup'ik, while the Reindeer Chukchi economy was based on nomadic reindeer herding. In addition, Bogoraz noted that there were more social, economic, and cultural similarities between the Reindeer Chukchi and the Koriak than between the Reindeer Chukchi and the Maritime Chukchi.

The distinction between the Maritime Chukchi and the Reindeer Chukchi is important in contemporary communities. When I was in Kamchatka in 1992, this point was made very clear to me by a Chukchi man in the village of Achavaiam. As I was explaining to him how I had learned to speak a few words of the Chukotkan language in a coastal village in Chukotka, he became impatient and immediately corrected me: "That's not possible. *Real* Chukchi don't live on the coast." I tried to explain that they were reindeer-herding Chukchi, tundra Chukchi, who had been forced by collectivization to settle on the coast, but he was unmoved. "Real Chukchi don't live on the coast. Those people are different, they aren't real Chukchi."

This differentiation between coastal and tundra people seemed to be somewhat of a contemporary distinction. Other researchers, most notably Bogoraz (1904–9, 1930), I. S. Vdovin (1965a), and A. I. Krushanova (1987), make the point that the two groups had kin ties and on occasion mixed their economies. Some Maritime Chukchi maintained herds of reindeer, for example, and some poorer Reindeer Chukchi left the tundra for the coast to join the crew of a *baidara*, a traditional Yup'ik walrus-skin boat. Thus there is historical evidence supporting the idea that the separation between coastal versus tundra dwellers may have been a manifestation of more recent social processes.

The pre-Soviet territory of the Chukchi stretched from the Arctic Ocean in the north to the Anadyr River in the south, from the Bering Sea and the Sea of Okhotsk in the east to the Kolyma River in the west. After Sovietization, this territory was encompassed by the Chukchi National Okrug (District), created in 1930, an area of approximately 660,000 square kilometers (Dikov 1989). Most likely the inland territory had been occupied by the paleo-Asian ancestors of the Chukchi and their closest neighbors, the Koriak, since 3000 B.P. (Before Present) (Arutiunov 1988; Dikov 1989; Gurvich 1982; Vdovin 1965a). Although there is some debate concerning the genesis of the Chukchi in relation to the Yup'ik, S. A. Arutiunov presents evidence that the two groups are part of a genetically homogeneous population that migrated northward in two waves, possibly as much as two thousand years apart (Ackerman 1984).

The Chukchi expanded their territory from the south (the Kamchatka region) in the fourth and fifth centuries A.D.; from the twelfth to sixteenth centuries the Chukchi engaged the Yup'ik in armed conflict; and by the sixteenth to seventeenth centuries the Chukchi were adapting to a maritime economy and pushing the Yup'ik out of the coastal regions (Ackerman 1984; Gurvich 1975; Krushanova 1987).

The first contact between Russians and Chukchi came in the seventeenth century as Russia continued its eastward expansion in search of new fur resources. A series of expeditions to the Far East resulted in the establishment of a fort (Anadyrsk) in 1649, well within Chukchi territory on the Anadyr River (Dikov 1989; Lantzeff and Pierce 1973; Muller 1967). The Russians made several fairly unsuccessful attempts to extract the *iasak*, the traditional fur tribute to the tsar, from the Chukchi; by 1764 the total amount collected was only 29,000 rubles, whereas it cost 1.38 million rubles to maintain the fort (Antropova and Kuznetsova 1964:803).

The Chukchi were not subjugated by the Russian Empire until the nineteenth century. The size of their population (approximately 12,000) gave them numerical strength, and their northeastern Arctic location isolated them from direct European contact until the seventeenth century (Bogoraz 1904–9:32). Contact between Europeans and Chukchi increased with the advent of trade fairs in the eighteenth century. In 1788 the Russians established a trading center on the Aniui River in the village of Ostrovnoe. This trading fair, and later others in Tuman, Markovo, and Penzhino, created a huge network of trade (primarily tobacco and iron kettles for fox furs) that stretched all the way into Alaska. The increase in trade, in conjunction with some persuasive offerings of knives, tobacco, and kettles, eventually led many Chukchi to pay *iasak* by the mid–nineteenth century (Antropova and Kuznetsova 1964:802–4; Bogoraz 1904–9:53–69).

By the 1850s, American traders and whalers began to visit the Russian coast. They engaged in intensive trade with the coastal populations, both Chukchi and Yup'ik, who in turn traded with the Reindeer Chukchi. Such articles as tobacco, tea, sugar, flour, iron kettles, and knives where traded in coastal communities for furs, skins, and meat. This type of trade continued up until the Soviet period, and the people in Sireniki often mentioned with pride the linguistic skills of their grandparents and parents, who spoke English and had happily traded with the Americans. I was frequently told that the stories of the degradation of local life by the alcohol introduced by the Americans were gross exaggerations invented by Soviet propagandists. Several elderly people expressed great fondness for American tobacco and tea and spoke of their memories of their first American teapot or iron kettle.

In addition, it was pointed out to me that some words in the Yup'ik and Chukchi languages are actually English. This point was driven home when I gave a small gift of soap to a friend's mother on her birthday. She was blind, and she asked her son what it was. He told her in Russian that it was *mylo*, but she didn't understand. Her son thought she didn't hear him, so he repeated the word several decibels more loudly, but still she didn't understand. Then he realized that the difficulty wasn't her hearing but the fact that her Russian was very limited, and he gave her the Chukotkan word—"*So-op!*" Even I understood that.

As the nomads of the Soviet Far Northeast, the Chukchi have been romanticized as fiercely independent and at the same time made the brunt of anecdotes that stereotype them as ignorant and naive.[5] The Chukchi of Sireniki were aware of their long independence from foreign control, of their resistance to the payment of *iasak* and to the Russian Orthodox Christian faith (Antropova and Kuznetsova 1964:824; Bogoraz 1904–9:723–30). Adolescent Chukchi stated with pride that the Russians had never conquered the Chukchi until "*Sovetskaia vlast'*" (Soviet power).

According to V. V. Antropova and V. G. Kuznetsova, the 1926–27 census showed that 70 percent of Chukchi were nomadic. Although the Chukchi were to some extent still a nomadic reindeer-herding people, among the contemporary Chukchi people this pattern had been changed dramatically by collectivization and the introduction of new patterns of herding.

By the turn of the twentieth century, Chukchi mobile encampments consisted of two to ten *yarangi* occupied by several related kin groups who herded their reindeer in common. These groups combined from eight to twelve camps into what Vladimir Bogoraz called a neighborhood and Igor Krupnik calls regional bands (1993:94). In the years after European trade was established, however, these structures began to break down and were replaced by a more flexible system of encampment.

Before Russian contact, the Chukchi encampment had a highly structured organization, with the most senior member's *yaranga* located at the front. According to Bogoraz, this organization approximated a clanlike social structure. Within the encampment, kin groups had mutual social and ceremonial obligations. The Chukchi kin group, or *varat*, was considered "the people of one fire." All the members of one kin group started their fire from a single fire board, which was passed on patrilineally from generation to generation.

Some Chukchi owned huge herds of reindeer; others had few or none. Wealthier herders often took in young men from poorer families to help with the herding. In exchange for his labor the poorer man received meat and skins from the owner's herd, and could leave his own reindeer, if he had any, to multiply untouched. This practice theoretically led to the establishment of a sustainable independent herd for the people in service.

According to Bogoraz, the paternal line dominated Chukchi social organization. Those related patrilineally were considered "of one blood," in reference to the blood painted on the hands and faces of kin during various ceremonies in which reindeer were sacrificed. The most basic familial relationship was formed by those who lived together (ra'yirin, literally "a houseful"). A man could marry only after an extended period of bride service; residency was patrilocal. The marriage ceremony consisted of the painting of the sign of the groom's family on the bride in reindeer blood. Although polygamy was acceptable, as in other societies, only a very wealthy man could afford more than one wife.

Labor was very strongly divided by gender among the Chukchi. Bogoraz found that the general position of women was considerably lower than that of men, and that women did considerably more and more difficult labor than men did. Women were responsible for primary child care, subsistence gathering, skinning and butchering, food preparation, and the processing of skins and sewing of garments, to mention only a few of their tasks.

As we have seen, the Chukchi residents of Sireniki were a fairly recent addition to the village. Before the Soviets started settling nomadic groups in Chukotka villages in the 1950s, the Chukchi of Sireniki were members of a distinctive band referred to in the Soviet records as the Kurupka Chukchi, named after a river that flowed through their territory.[6] The first inventory of the Kurupka band was taken in 1926 as part of the First Polar Census of Russia, which recorded 18 households with 83 people. By 1937 the group was recorded as having its own native council (Kurupkinskii Natsional'ny Sovet) and including 74 people in four camps of 11 families with a total combined herd of 638 reindeer. The next reference to the Kurupka group, in 1939, recorded four camps of 89 people. This record was made for the Nomadic Council secretary, who maintained yearly population figures for the region. In 1943 the group had grown to 101 Chukchi and one Russian, presumably a transient on komandirovka.

On a map of the various Chukchi bands on the Chukotka Peninsula prepared in the 1960s (Gurvich and Dolgikh 1970) the Kurupka Chukchi territory is shown as occupied by 100 people of 20 nomadic families living in three to five camps. It should be noted that the Kurupka group continued to grow at a seemingly unnatural rate; they numbered 120 in 1944 and 225 in 1945. Presumably people were moving into the area from other regions.

In 1951 the Nomadic Council was disbanded, the state policy of settling nomadic people in villages was put into practice, and the collectivization of the Kurupka Chukchi's herd into the state farm was begun. In the 1940s the Kurupka group had been collectivized on paper, but they seem to have continued to live their nomadic life unhindered by the bureaucracy. Then in 1958–59 the group's four camps were formed into three brigades.

The Sireniki people's memories of the events of this period differ from the official version. They recalled the forced relinquishment of family herds, the settling of the nomadic Chukchi in Sireniki, and the mandatory attendance of children in Soviet schools. This last requirement meant that while parents continued an essentially nomadic life as they attended to the collective farm's herds, their children were sent away to boarding schools that did not value Chukchi language or culture.

Nadia, one of the Chukchi women in Sireniki, told me how the collectivization affected her life. When her grandfather refused to give up his herd of 13,000 reindeer to the collective farm, he was taken away and his family never saw him again. A Yup'ik woman told me she had seen Nadia's grandfather in a makeshift detention center in Provideniia several years later; she assumed that he died there.

The government returned 500 of the original 13,000 reindeer taken from Nadia's family, which represented their livelihood, but the following year the government reclaimed 300 as a tax. The family then was so poor that they found it difficult to support themselves. Her relatives decided to separate and settle in different villages along the coast.

I should point out that the numbers of reindeer in Nadia's recollection seem very high, as the environmental carrying capacity for an individual family's herd was about 2,000. The minimum needed for a family to survive was about 200 (Leeds 1965). Krupnik (1993) records community herds of more than 14,000 among the Inchun' Chukchi in 1937, with the largest family herds being in the 1,000-plus range, but that was in a different environment; it is unlikely that the entire Chukotka Peninsula ever supported a combined herd of more than 5,000 reindeer. Krupnik suggests that Nadia's father may have been from an interior region where herds were much larger, or that she may be remembering the total community herd rather than her grandfather's personal holdings.

In 1958 Nadia's father chose to come to Sireniki because his wife's brother was from there. They set up their *yaranga* about a kilometer from the village, and from there the children walked to the village school every morning. It was not until many years later that they moved into village housing provided by the state farm.

Another puzzling aspect of this story was that postwar collectivization did not routinely entail arrests and imprisonment. These actions are more likely to have occurred in the 1930s, when the Party was looking for kulaks and shamans to arrest as enemies of the people. It is likely that these stories—the confiscation of herds, the arrests, and collectivization—have become condensed into one event in the memories of people who were very young during those times.

[27]

In contrast to the Yup'ik, the Chukchi found the village foreign. The tundra provided their sense of place and orientation. Adults over the age of 30 were born on the tundra. As children they spent most of their summers there, and therefore were fluent in the Chukotkan language. During my fieldwork, many Chukchi had jobs that kept them in the village in the summer, but they maintained their connection to the tundra through vacation trips there and tending to their personal reindeer.

Although many were born in the village, the Chukchi had an uneasy relationship with Sireniki. They felt their outsider status not only because of the occasional Yup'ik adolescent's racist remark but because of their own tenuous relationship with the sea and its creatures. For the Chukchi, the tundra was distinct from the village and the sea, which were the domain of the Yup'ik.

The Newcomers

> We're from the *materik* [mainland] and we try to continue
> life here as there. The two lifeways are incompatible, so the
> people are incompatible.
>
> VITIA, A RUSSIAN TEACHER

It is not possible to discuss a unified Newcomer identity because Newcomers were not a single-culture group. Newcomers include people from a variety of cultures, most prominently Ukrainian, Russian, and Belorussian. By virtue of being from the West and educated in Soviet schools, however, most Newcomers shared some cultural assumptions and therefore were part of a loose cultural collectivity.

As I mentioned earlier, Newcomers immigrated to the area in pursuit of economic or ideological goals: to make more money than they could get at home or to bring socialism to the "primitive" North. Many were young university graduates looking for jobs in their specialties that were unavailable in their own regions.

In Sireniki the Newcomers filled niches in the infrastructure—in schools, warehouses, transportation, administration—leaving few of these economically and socially advantageous positions open to native peoples. Native people saw the resulting economically stratified system as discriminatory. Although in theory Soviet ideology did not condone discrimination against native peoples, its Russified forms inherently conferred advantages on Newcomers.

To the Chukchi and Yup'ik, Newcomers were the human embodiment of the Soviet state and the physical implementation of change among them. Newcomers were the contemporary colonizers of Sireniki, a group devoid of cultural or spiritual connection to the village and its surrounding environment. They were the perpetual outsiders. Although some individuals had been born in Sireniki and others married local people and made their homes there, the majority considered themselves transients.

Soviet policy, whether the somewhat culturally sensitive program of the Committee of the North or the more radical approach of the Great Transformation, was essentially paternalistic in its view of indigenous peoples and their cultures. Contemporary policy makers and many academicians recognized the value of cultural diversity but believed that minority peoples should maintain their cultures within the Soviet format of "socialist in content, nationalist in form." More plainly stated, it was acceptable to wear native traditional dress, to perform traditional dances, and even to speak indigenous languages; but if you spoke Yup'ik or Chukotkan, what you talked about should be socialism (Dunn and Dunn 1962,1963; Hughes 1965; Kouljok 1985; Krupnik 1987; Lebedev 1988; Vakhtin 1992; and Vucinich 1960).

By the 1990s the socialist rhetoric had been dropped by all but the staunchest of Party members, but the paternalism it engendered among the Newcomers remained. Newcomers believed that Sireniki would fall into ruin without them; that Yup'ik and Chukchi students were "slower" in school than Newcomer children and less successful in the university, not because the system rewarded adherence to Russian cultural ideals but because of some mental / genetic handicap. Vakhtin and others have recorded this attitude toward native peoples across the northern areas of the Soviet Union. Vakhtin quotes a Yakut informant as saying, "In Cherskom they look at us as people of lower quality." More enlightened Newcomers have respect for the abilities and knowledge of the reindeer herders and sea mammal hunters, but rarely does that respect extend to the cultures as a whole. One of Vakhtin's informants very succinctly stated his feelings about the system's support of the dominant culture: "Our program doesn't teach national specialties; there is one program and it is for Russians, for natives it's not important whether they can learn or not" (Vakhtin 1993b:21).

Some of these Newcomer attitudes were more urban than racist. People from the city generally felt culturally (as in high culture) superior. They pointed to the inaccurate grammar, the manners, and the generally "poor physical appearance" of the local people as indicators of their inferiority. A Russian teacher from Leningrad once told me Siberian people, Russians and non-Russians alike, were *grubye* (rough). When she first came to the North to teach, she never went out in public without being "properly dressed"—including white gloves. She emphasized the white gloves as representing the pinnacle of civility. She said her colleagues often chided her about the way she dressed, but she did not change. "After all, I was from Leningrad. It was unthinkable that I would dress any other way," she told me.

An incident that occurred in Sireniki several weeks before I arrived was recounted to me on numerous occasions as an example of the difference between Far Eastern people and western Russians. It happened that Yevgeny Yevtushenko, the famed Russian poet, visited Sireniki in the summer of 1989. (I assume that he was collecting material for his book *Divided Twins*, published in 1993.) The Russian literature teacher described to me how the visit unfolded. According to her, Yevtushenko didn't try to hide his disdain for the conditions in the village and for its people. She had been eagerly looking forward to his company for what she felt was much-needed intellectually stimulating conversation, she said, but he drank heavily, stayed in his room, and barely ventured into the village to become acquainted.

When the night came for his public recital, she said, the entire village dressed as if they were going to the Bol'shoi Theatre and eagerly awaited the poet's appearance in the concert hall. Yevtushenko stumbled in late, in a disheveled suit and huge rubber boots, which made a loud clopping noise as he walked across the stage. She was embarrassed and ashamed of his "performance." "Who did he think he was? He showed up that way just to let us know that he held us in nothing but contempt. That he thought of us as morons." Clearly Yevtushenko did not distinguish the Newcomers from the natives. In fact, he treated all of the villagers the way many Newcomers treated the native people.

These attitudes were so routinized and expected even by the native people themselves that they conferred definite social advantages on Newcomers. Advantages also accrued from the way the system controlled access to material resources, from job assignments to special goods in the village warehouse and store. In Sireniki, as all over the former Soviet Union, access to material goods carried with it a certain amount of social influence and power.

This is not to say that all interaction between Newcomers and local people was negative. Irina Efimovna, a senior teacher who had lived in the village over twenty years, greatly respected the knowledge of native cultures and their traditions. She assigned her science students to interview their parents and grandparents for ethnobotanical information. Through such assignments she hoped to "instill respect for their own cultural knowledge." She was the only Newcomer who verbalized to me her recognition that Yup'ik and Chukchi cultural values differed from her own and that these differences made them less successful in a Russian-dominated educational system.

Aleksandr Georgievich, also a teacher, spent much of his free time in the company of hunters. Like many Russians, he loved nature and considered hunting an integral part of communing with nature. He had great respect for the skills of Yup'ik hunters and frequently accompanied them on hunting expeditions. Other Newcomers also felt this kind of connection with the Chukotka environment and its people. They married local people, raised their families in Sireniki, and made their homes there. However, these were the exceptions.

Most Newcomers failed to recognize that they were structurally advantaged rather than innately more intelligent than local people. This perception and the structures that supported it led to tension among the Newcomers, the Yup'ik, and the Chukchi, and these tensions reinforced each group's collective identity.

[2]

The Social Context: Relatives, Residence, and Space

> He is my brother, she is my sister, she is my mother's sister,
> she is my father's brother's wife—hell, I'm related to every-
> body in this whole village!
>
> KOLIA, CHUKCHI HERDER

In order to unwrap Sireniki economic and political organization, one must understand village social relations. Relationships between kin and between unrelated people in the village provided meaning and context for Yup'ik, Chukchi, and Newcomer social and cultural reproduction.

Relatives and Kin

In Sireniki, traditional native kinship systems based on principles that structured descent had meaning only among the oldest generation. What G. A. Menovshchikov (1962) and Charles Hughes (1964, 1965) described as patrilineal descent and patriclan organization among the Siberian Yup'ik no longer held meaning for the younger Yup'ik generation. Other traditions such as betrothal in childhood, arranged marriage, and close-kin marriage had been abandoned as well. A similar process had occurred among the Chukchi; their system of bride service and a preference for close-kin marriage had disappeared.

With the Great Transformation and the declaration of many native practices to be "criminal tribalism," coupled with the increased mobility of local populations and the in-migration of nonindigenous peoples, exogamy and personal choice had replaced older patterns of marriage. By the 1940s the Soviet system of officially registering marriages was enforced, even in remote villages, because wherever there was a collective farm there was a Soviet administrator to oversee the new regulations. Therefore, the system of family control over marriage and reproduction changed, and with it indigenous kinship systems.

This is not to say that contemporary families had no say in the marriage choices of their members; they still exerted their influence through the strategies that all families know. By the time of my research, however, marriage by personal choice, "for love," was prevalent in the discourse of the younger generations. A kin group's desire for close-kin marriage partners had shifted to the family's concern over a chosen partner's parenting skills, profession, personality, and use of alcohol.

These changes in the kin group's control over its members were followed by changes in native discourse concerning kin. Just as with the rules of descent, Yup'ik and Chukchi kinship terminology had been transformed among the younger generations of Sireniki. Few young adults could remember native kin terms beyond the most basic relationships—mother, father, sister, brother. For the others, Russian kin terms had supplanted native ones. A Russian kin term, however, did not necessarily indicate a Russian conceptualization of the relationship.

Among the Yup'ik and the Chukchi, kinship terms were lumped by gender and generation. *Sestra* (sister) and *brat* (brother) included not just lineal kin but all kin of ego's generation. People knew the Russian terms for cousin, *dvoiurodnaia sestra* and *dvoiurodnii brat*, but rarely used them. Such terms as *tetia* (aunt) and *diadia* (uncle) designated not only kin of ego's parents' generation but anyone of that generation. This use of *tetia* and *diadia* was not unique to the Yup'ik and Chukchi; Newcomers extended these terms in the same way. Such usage could also denote fictive kin or simply warm respect. A close friend of one's parent might be called "auntie" or "uncle."

The same pattern was used for people of the grandparents' generation. *Babushka* (grandmother) or *dedushka* (grandfather) was applied to any elderly person, even to a complete stranger, as a sign of affection or respect for old age. This was another practice common to all three groups, Chukchi, Yup'ik, and Newcomers, but it seemed to be reserved primarily for village discourse. If one were to address an unfamiliar urban woman as "Babushka," the likely response would be "Kakaia ia tebe babushka? [How is it that I'm your grandmother?]" in an indignant tone.

One woman referred to her nephew (her sister's son) as "brother" and her mother, the boy's grandmother, called him "son." Because he was being raised by the grandmother, in their view he was structurally a brother and son rather

[33]

than a nephew and grandson. These were not necessarily "traditional" (pre-Soviet) concepts; the Yup'ik and Chukchi used such kin terms as a way of conceptualizing social relationships and expressing social responsibilities.

Earlier researchers of the Siberian Yup'ik (Chlenov 1973; Hughes and Hughes 1960; Krupnik 1993; Menovshchikov 1962, 1964; Sergeev 1962) and the Chukchi (Bogoraz 1904–9; Gurvich 1982; Krushanova 1987; Vdovin 1965a) have made detailed linguistic and genealogical investigations, categorizing and labeling the kinship system of each of these people; I will not repeat their descriptions here. After Sovietization, all three groups in Sireniki had bilateral kinship systems; that is, both consanguineal and affinal kin were recognized as being related to ego. More important than recognition of relationships as being "by blood" or "by marriage," however, was people's reliance on these ties for economic, political, and social support.

Families and Households

Because anthropologists debate the applicability of the term "family" to non-western people, it is necessary to justify its use in this context. For the purpose of this analysis, the term "family" is to be understood to include groups of people united by production, reproduction, and consumption and by emotional bonds. This is not to deny that the term "family" has certain Eurocentric semantic associations, as well as anthropological historical usages (Bender 1967; Yanagisako 1979). The concept of family, however, as well as the term itself, *sem'ia*, was used in Sireniki, and it provides the reader with a better understanding of village social organization than its conceptual counterparts, domestic group and household.

A second term that was used locally to describe kin relationships was *rodstvenniki* (relatives). A relative was someone who was believed to be either consanguineally or affinally related to ego, although one might not have known the exact connection. When I questioned people about kin relationships, I often heard, for example, "She's a distant relative through my grandfather. I don't know exactly how, just that we're related."

In Sireniki there was a general consensus that "relatives" were, or should be, important, but no one could give any practical reasons. People answered yes if I asked, "Are relatives important?" but if I asked, "Why are relatives important?" they could only say vaguely, "Relatives help one another." A brawl between relatives, people agreed, was more shameful than a fight between unrelated persons. But again, no one could say why it was more shameful for relatives to fight.

Whenever I asked, "To whom are you related?" it was not uncommon for one of my hosts, after naming the members of his or her immediate family, to say, as Kolia did, "I'm related to everyone in the whole village." As the Yup'ik and Chukchi understood kinship, this perception was probably accurate.

Sometimes "relatives" may be fictive kin created through the reciprocal giving of reindeer and sea mammal products. "We consider them our relatives, because they take care of Mama's reindeer. We give them gifts at birthdays and New Year's as if they were actually related to us. They are like relatives, but not real relatives," explained a young Yup'ik woman when she was telling me about her family's relationship with a Chukchi family.

In contrast to the concept of a "relative" (a person who "should be" important), the concept of "family" (people who are "actually" important) could be articulated. Individuals cited concrete economic, political, and social reasons for why "family" was important: "My sister takes care of my children because we are one family"; "It's shameful for two people of the same family to sleep together—they'll start a fight in the family"; and "We eat together frequently, because we're one family."

The family was at the core of social organization in Sireniki. Not surprisingly, Yup'ik, Chukchi, and Newcomers had decidedly different structures of family organization. For the Chukchi and Yup'ik a "family" was related through blood and marriage and had close social contact and responsibilities. A "family" formed a domestic group, sharing economic and social responsibilities, frequently eating together, and pooling economic resources and labor. A "relative" was more distant. Relatives could be related through blood or marriage or, as we have seen, not related at all.

Some people in the village were known to be half-siblings through their parents' affairs, but these people did not recognize each other as related. A relationship of this kind was considered a "family secret"; everyone knew about the relationship but no one acknowledged it. Blood and marriage were not enough to create a relative or a family; specific social criteria must be fulfilled—public recognition, sharing of resources, mutual emotional aid.

In contrast to the Yup'ik and Chukchi, Newcomers were there either alone or in nuclear family groups, so as long as they were in Sireniki, kinship as a basic principle for social organization was not an option for them. Occasionally Newcomers helped a sibling or extended family member get a job in the village. Such a person might then become part of the Newcomer's domestic group. They helped each other economically, sometimes lived together, but this arrangement was the exception among Newcomers. Class, Party membership, nationality, work, and friendship formed the basic social groupings for Newcomers, not principles of kinship.

In Sireniki, Newcomer households resembled George P. Murdock's (1949) description of the nuclear family: "a married man [and] woman, with their offspring, although in individual cases one or more additional persons may reside with them."[1] This was a function of Soviet structure, however, not the Newcomers' natal cultural model for family organization. They would have preferred a more extended family structure, but because the Soviet government had designated Chukotka a "closed travel zone," owing to its proximity to the United States and the limited Sireniki job market, only nuclear families could make the move.

Many Newcomers were emotionally very close to their parents and other lineal and lateral relatives. They frequently took their vacations, sometimes lasting up to six months, at their parents' homes. Many expressed a desire to move back home so the grandparents could see and participate in raising their grandchildren. In fact, their culturally accepted model was for retired grandparents to take care of the grandchildren during the day while the parents were working. Newcomers, in other words, had a cultural model of a more extended family organization; but the structural, logistical, and legal constraints forced them to leave their extended families behind when they came to Sireniki.

Of 58 Newcomer households in Sireniki, 42 were composed of nuclear family groups. One such family was Valia's. She was a seamstress and her husband worked for the state farm. They were living with their two children in a three-room apartment until the oldest daughter married and moved to Provideniia. Valia and her husband moved to the North as a young couple for the better wages, and looked forward to returning home to Ukraine when they had enough for a good retirement. No other family members were living in Sireniki, and they depended on a network of friends when they needed help.

Friendship was very important to Newcomers. Newcomers created strong bonds of friendship. For Russians in general, friendship was a means of survival. *Druzhba* (friendship) was from the soul and carried with it intense responsibilities and obligations. Francine Markowitz (1991) describes *druzhba* as "encompassing; it is an emotion, an institution, a multi-functional connection between two or more nonrelated people. As a result, friendships in the Soviet Union are intense." The intensity of these bonds was accentuated in Sireniki by the Newcomers' social and physical isolation.

A few Newcomer households were organized into extended families of parents and their children who had grown up and married locally; some were single-parent households; and some were unmarried households. Veronika moved to the North with her husband (later deceased) and was a teacher in the local school. When her son returned to the village after his military service, he married a young Newcomer woman who had also grown up in the village. With no other housing available, the young couple lived with Veronika.

Unmarried individuals who came to Sireniki lived in dormitories or multi-family apartments. Some lived in groups with siblings, co-workers, or other

Newcomer families. These living arrangements often depended on the availability of space, on the government's enticements to professional people, or on personal connections rather than on preference.

Consider the living situation of Pavel, a schoolteacher who arrived in Sireniki in the spring of 1990. Until his wife and two children could join him, he lived in the teachers' "dormitory," a three-room apartment he shared with an unmarried couple and two single women, one of whom was me. He had been promised an apartment by the school director as soon as his family arrived and one became available, but for the present he lived as a single man while his wife and two sons remained with her mother in Ukraine. Pavel was expecting them to join him in the fall. This agreement with the state farm ultimately caused some friction between Pavel and the other teachers sharing the apartment because they had lived in the village much longer (one had been born there) and had not yet been allotted apartments of their own.

Yup'ik and Chukchi domestic organization was decidedly different from that of Newcomers. The Yup'ik and Chukchi, having grown up locally, were not guaranteed separate housing as an inducement to take jobs. Unless an apartment was made available through one of the social or political mechanisms, families stayed where they were, even if they expanded.

Although local officials tried to provide separate housing for married couples with children, apartments were not always available; thus it was not uncommon to find parents, married and unmarried children, and grandchildren living in a one-room or two-room apartment. At one point both of Kawawa's sons and their wives (one pregnant, the other with a two-year-old) were all living with her in her two-room apartment. After much complaining to and cajoling of the village council, one son and daughter-in-law were finally given a makeshift apartment, barely 12 feet by 15 feet, which at one time had been the local book repository.

Yup'ik and Chukchi families were primarily matrifocal: their domestic activities centered on the eldest female member of the group. This arrangement was due in part to the fact that Chukchi and Yup'ik men didn't live nearly as long as women (or as long as male and female Newcomers).[2] Thus the grandparental generation was disproportionately female. Older women were the *glavy* (heads of household) of much of the housing available to local people, so their households became the focal points of family activities.

The married and unmarried children, their spouses, and the grandchildren who lived with a woman were not the only members of her "family." Other married and unmarried children who resided elsewhere still contributed to the parental household, often preparing and sharing meals, sleeping over, and sending their children to their grandmother in order to give themselves a personal break from the daily routine. Grandparents often functioned as primary caretakers, especially before and after school, while parents were at work.

Adult children and grandchildren helped their parents and grandparents with the more arduous physical tasks around the apartment, such as cleaning, maintenance, painting, remodeling, laundry, carrying groceries, and removing garbage. Children who did not actually live there would visit frequently. It was not uncommon for an adult child and spouse to visit their parents three or more times a day: for tea in the morning, during lunch break, for tea or dinner after work, and in the evening to watch television or simply converse about the day's activities. One young Yup'ik man had lunch and dinner at his maternal grandmother's house every day while his wife and children were on vacation.

Both Yup'ik and Chukchi preferred to live close to family members. On several occasions people remarked that should the apartment next door to a parent or sibling be vacated, they would move in. Over the years, a number of families had managed to occupy groups of apartments in the same building.

In the spring of 1990, while Kawawa's two married sons were living with her, two of her daughters and their children had an apartment just down the hall. Her third daughter frequently shared tea and meals with Kawawa and dreamed of moving in next to her mother and sisters. She often said, "If they [the people in the next apartment] moved out, I'd move in—that would be great. It would be so much easier to help Mama if I were living right here." At that time she was living in a small house only a two-minute walk from Kawawa's apartment.

Other families shared residences seasonally. Many houses and apartments were of substandard construction and were impossible to keep warm in the winter. Because of their undesirability, they were frequently the first apartments for newlyweds and young couples with small children. When the winter winds started, these families moved in with their parents or grandparents for the coldest months.

The seasonal change in the composition of a household occurred not only because the housing was uncomfortable but also because of the local disease ideology. People believed one caught a cold or the flu by getting physically cold—especially children. If one sat in a draft, whether cold or just cool, one could be assured of getting a cold. Further, it was very inconvenient to stoke a wood stove all day while taking care of infants. All of these factors led many families to cohabit during the winter months.

Although the Yup'ik and Chukchi shared the basic pattern of household organization, they differed in that many of the Chukchi men were reindeer herders and worked away from the village for a large part of the year. In the winter the herders spent one month on the tundra and one month in the village. As a result, the domestic unit expanded and contracted with the work schedules of husbands, sons, and siblings.

In the summer some Chukchi women went to the tundra to cook for the brigades, operate the base camp radios, and work skins for the herders' clothing. These were primarily elderly women, but on occasion younger women took vacation time to live on the tundra with their mothers and husbands. Chukchi residences in the village were often almost empty in the summer, occupied only by teenagers who preferred to go to the school's day camp; relatives in the village kept close watch on them.

Etau was a Chukchi *brigadir* (chief herdsman) who worked with his stepson on the tundra. In the summer months Etau's wife erected their *yaranga* on the tundra near the base camp of his brigade. There she worked skins, dried meat, and gathered greens and berries to store for the winter. His daughter, who had a young son, held a permanent job in the village and lived at her parents' house year round. In the winter Etau's son rotated between the village and the tundra on a schedule set by the state farm: one month on the tundra, one month in the village. Etau's responsibilities as *brigadir* kept him with the herds on the tundra most of the time; he was seldom seen in the village.

In another Chukchi family, Lena and her husband, Serezha, worked full-time in the village, he in the village garage. Lena's elderly mother, who lived with them, continued to go to the tundra every summer. She set up her *yaranga* near the base camp where her son, nephews, and grandsons worked. On occasion Lena took her vacation time and, accompanied by her youngest son, joined her mother on the tundra. Lena dreamed of Serezha's getting a job as a *vezdekhod* driver for the third brigade so they could all spend their summers on the tundra together. As it was, her husband stayed in the village and her oldest son chose to stay with him rather than accompany his mother to the tundra.

Very few of the younger women were able to help their mothers in tundra camps, even if they wanted to. In the summer of 1990, eight *yarangi* were erected near the three reindeer brigades. Seven elderly women spent the entire summer in these *yarangi*; four younger women spent a few weeks there. One woman of late middle age expressed great sympathy for the elderly women whose daughters never came to help them. It didn't seem to matter to her that the daughters had jobs that they could not abandon. The important thing was that they were not fulfilling their (cultural and collective) duties to their mothers.

Native families not only provided economic and physical support but depended on each other for social and emotional support as well. People conferred with parents and siblings before making important life decisions. Children consulted their parents about marriage plans, career decisions, and even apartment choices. Among the Chukchi and Yup'ik the ideal was for same-gender siblings to be very close and confide to each other the most intimate details of their lives.

On summer weekends Yup'ik and Chukchi organized tundra picnics or fishing trips with siblings and cousins. Although people had friends outside of their kin group, best friends were often kin of the same gender and generation. A close friend who was not a relative was usually an *odnoklassnik* (classmate). On occasion, two people who worked together would become friends. Among the Chukchi and Yup'ik, however, nonrelated friends who helped each other financially, with child care, or with work were rare. In contrast, these were the primary types of friendships among Newcomers.

Families not only supported their members but also exerted control. One young Yup'ik woman had been offered a very good job as a reporter for the native-language radio station in Anadyr. She was very excited about the offer, with its possibility of bettering her economic circumstances and providing her daughter with more advanced educational opportunities. When she told her mother, however, the mother became very upset. "What will I do here without you? . . . What if I die while you're in Anadyr? We may never see each other again. . . . Two of my daughters already live away from me. If you go, I'll have only one." Eventually she prevailed, and the daughter turned down the job; she couldn't bring herself to say no to her mother. Later she rationalized her decision by telling herself that if she had left and things hadn't worked out, she would have lost her apartment; it would have been difficult for her daughter in a new school; perhaps it would have been "dangerous for us alone in a big city."

Another young woman, widowed with two children, was persuaded by her mother to accept an offer of marriage against her own judgment. Her mother's main concern was that the household was without the physical and economic support of a man. In her mother's view, this was an insecure and therefore untenable situation. She viewed marriage as her daughter's only chance to provide for their joint household. When it came to choosing marriage partners, the Chukchi and Yup'ik were not always free to do what they liked.

Female, Male, and Marriage

Gender separation and gender identity were sharply marked among all three groups in the village. Small children divided themselves in their play activities. Chukchi boys as young as 2 could be seen practicing with their lassos at the reindeer slaughter. Small Yup'ik boys practiced harpooning their first walrus, using sticks for weapons and unsuspecting dogs for targets. Girls had dolls and were encouraged to play the role of mother. When I asked, "What do you want to be when you grow up?" boys answered "A hunter," "A herder," or "A *vezdekhod* driver"; girls wanted to be nurses, seamstresses, and mothers. These early choices carried over into adulthood.

The perception of women as mothers was cross-cultural. Chukchi, Yup'ik, and Newcomer women alike unquestioningly took it for granted that their primary role was that of mother. Adolescents started flirting in their early teens, and by their last year of high school they were actively seeking sex partners. Girls' sexual activity generally started around this time, but not with peers. Most of their male partners were a few years older than they, often one of the young men in military service stationed in the village. These relationships rarely led to marriage; marriage partners were most often chosen from one's own group (73 percent of all marriages were endogamous).

In Sireniki, getting married was not as important for women as having children. Although marriage was preferred for women, a woman who was still single in her late 20s was often counseled by family and friends to conceive a child without a husband. The Yup'ik and Chukchi had no strong concept of illegitimacy, but Newcomers did, and they followed the same practice. Such high value was placed on having children that Newcomer women preferred the stigma of unwed motherhood to the humiliation of being childless.

Births to single women were common in all the northern areas (Bogojavlensky 1993). If a woman's first child was born while she was single, she continued to live at home with her parents or siblings. Many children born to married couples had been conceived before the marriage. Of twenty-three Yup'ik and Chukchi children born in 1989–90, eight (or 35 percent) were fathered out of wedlock by Newcomers, reportedly soldiers.[3] None of the eight unions led to either marriage or a stable relationship. When the soldier left the village, the woman usually married someone local and had more children with her husband. Her first child was fully accepted by her own family and by her husband and his family.

Many couples chose not to marry formally and register with the village council; by living together they signified to the community that they were "married." Such couples referred to each other as husband and wife, and everyone in the village considered them married. Eventually such couples showed up in the official village registry as "married," even though no official registration ever took place. This practice was especially common among older couples whose unions antedated the state farm. In this way the state government recognized native practices.

Such informal unions were not marked by a public ceremony. In describing the lack of ceremony among the Siberian Yup'ik, Charles and Jane Hughes (1960) state that after the couple had consummated a marriage, the bride moved in with her husband's family, bringing gifts. Among the Chukchi, who practiced bride service, after the prospective husband had worked for the woman's family, she accompanied him to his family's encampment in her new social status as wife (Bogoraz 1904–9).

One evening two sisters regaled me with tales of their oldest sister's suitors, several young men who had been in bride service to their family. The suitors had worked very hard, each in his turn, in service to the family in hopes of gaining the oldest daughter as his wife. The younger sisters theorized that their father kept refusing the unions not only to delay their sister's departure but to get extra help with his herd.

When a marriage was to be registered, the bride's family held a large public ceremony if they could afford it. The usual Soviet practice in a small town was for a couple to register at the town hall and then make the rounds of the town having their picture taken with all the local statues. Sireniki, where the streets are often clogged with snow, had only one statue (the obligatory bust of Lenin), and in winter the Arctic night has begun to fall by 2:00 P.M., so couples dispensed with that tradition. In all other ways the wedding ceremony was very similar to weddings performed throughout the Soviet Union. The vows were secular Soviet, the bride wore a white wedding gown, the groom wore a suit and tie, and after the ceremony there was a large banquet with eating, drinking, gift giving, and dancing until early morning.

Because there was little variation in the observable events, one wedding I attended in Sireniki can stand for all the wedding ceremonies that took place during my stay there. The groom was a young Yup'ik from Sireniki; the bride, also Yup'ik, was from the village of Novoe Chaplino. The couple had met in Sireniki when the young woman was visiting her sister, who had married a Sireniki man.

The ceremony and wedding feast were held in the village cafeteria. Invitation cards were purchased at the local store, filled in by hand, and hand-delivered throughout the village by the groom's sisters. When the ceremony began, the guests stood in the hall, women on one side and men on the other, as the bride and groom walked in together. After the president of the village council read a brief statement about the couple's responsibility to each other and to the state, they and their witnesses signed a registry. The legal formalities over, the fifty-odd guests took seats at long dining tables arranged in a horseshoe shape. Bottles of vodka and champagne were set out and the tables were covered with plates of sausage, caviar, cucumbers, and reindeer tongue.

The wedding feast began with a toast made by the groom's father. In Russian style, everyone drank to the bottom of the glass. As the couple kissed, the crowd shouted out *"Gor'ko! Gor'ko! Gor'ko!"* (bitter). At various intervals throughout the banquet the crowd spontaneously broke into the chant again: *"Gor'ko! Gor'ko!"* That was the cue for the couple to kiss again, until eventually the crowd decided it was *"Sladko!"* (sweet).

The opening toast was followed by more toasting from well-wishers. Then came the main course, chicken and potatoes, which female relatives had spent

[42]

all day preparing. (Having the family help cook was a cost-cutting measure; the rest of the meal was prepared by the head cook of the state farm cafeteria.) The finale was the wedding cake.

Once everyone was temporarily sated with food and drink, the presentation of gifts began. Each gift was accompanied by a short speech by the presenter. The main gifts were from family members—Oriental rugs, linens, furniture, china. Other guests gave cash and smaller household items. After all the gifts had been presented, the feasting continued; later a small local band started to play contemporary music and people started dancing. At one point during the evening the local traditional dance group performed native songs accompanied by drummers playing drums made of wood and stretched walrus stomachs. Someone commented that this was the "first time in memory anyone had requested native drumming at a wedding." No one was really surprised, though, because the groom's family was considered one of the more "traditional" ones in the village.

Aside from the drumming, there was nothing to distinguish this ceremony among the Yup'ik from a contemporary Chukchi or Newcomer ceremony. The format was basically European, not unlike civil weddings performed in the United States. For those who could afford it, this type of ceremony replaced Yup'ik and Chukchi "traditional" marriage practices, which were notable for their lack of ceremony.[4]

Another form of traditional marriage was "bride stealing." In the past, according to oral accounts, Yup'ik brides were "abducted." (Bogoraz [1904–9] records this practice among the Chukchi as well). One Sireniki marriage in 1990 was locally interpreted in this way. A young Russian who had been acquainted with a young Yup'ik woman for several years "stole" her from her home. What had happened was that one evening the young man got in the middle of a family quarrel, which turned violent under the influence of alcohol. In order to protect the young woman from the possibility of abuse, he persuaded her to leave Sireniki with him that night. Later, when she related the story to friends, she said that her husband had "stolen" her from her family. Although she was speaking half in jest, there was a reference to a traditional practice in the comment. Her family would have preferred her to have a ceremony, but because she was in her late 20s and childless, they were willing to recognize the "abduction" as a marriage because it might be "her only chance" to marry.

In Sireniki all people of middle age had chosen their spouses themselves. Older people felt that this was generally a good idea. Older women spoke about their experiences of having had a husband chosen for them and felt that this new pattern was a "good thing," that their own children could marry "for love." One woman told me of being betrothed in childhood without her knowledge. She found out when the young man came to her to ask to be released from the betrothal so that he might marry another woman.

Another Yup'ik woman, watching her son and his fiancée's public display of affection, said that "young people talk and look at each other, this is a good thing." She was referring to something she had told me earlier, that when she was young couples didn't look at each other. They were supposed to act very shy; even older married couples talked very little and avoided eye contact. The woman's older sister, who under the Soviets had gone to school and become the first Yup'ik schoolteacher in Chukotka, had married a "very kind man of her own choice." The woman said she had envied her sister for having had that freedom.

On several occasions the same woman reminisced about the time in her youth when she had been close to a young man who was an accountant for the collective farm. They had grown up together and both had a passion for reading. She told of their adolescent courtship; of his reading to her in the *yaranga* by a seal-oil lamp while she sewed her family's garments. They had wanted to marry, but her father forced her to marry another man because he was a good hunter and she would "never be hungry." She felt that, as a result of this arranged marriage, her life had been very difficult.

Her husband, too, had loved someone else, but their families had decided they should marry, and so they did; to her it was inconceivable not to do as her father wished. After their marriage, her husband continued an affair with his original love, and even fathered a child with her. The younger women in the village exhibit extreme jealously over their husbands' indiscretions, but this woman was friendly with her husband's lover. For her the tragedy was not the affair but the forced marriage that had kept her and her husband from their true loves.

Infidelity, especially male infidelity, was a frequent topic of discussion and gossip. Although it was not considered acceptable behavior, it occurred so frequently that it was all but taken for granted, though it was the cause of many quarrels. Because the village was so small, infidelity was very hard to conceal. A frequent topic of conversation among women was their husbands' affairs. More often than not, the wife knew the identity of the other women, and there were occasional public confrontations. While men's affairs were excused as healthy or "natural," women's extramarital affairs were socially condemned. A man who discovered that his wife was having an affair might resort to violence against her or her lover.[5]

Although the contemporary model was marriage for love, not all marriages were formed under these "ideal" conditions. Many women said they married because of the difficulty of living alone, financially as well as socially and personally. The village doctor, Tania, a highly educated and "modern" Chukchi woman, was married to a young Newcomer who had also been raised in the village. Although Tania confessed on many occasions how desperately she loved Iurii, she also expressed the view that the union wasn't perfect, as he was less educated and several years younger than she. She wanted to be married in order to have children, however, and she was already 25; in her estimation, her prime childbearing years were passing. Although Iurii did not share her commitment to the marriage, she rationalized her decision to marry: "Who better will I find here?"

Tania's marriage prospects were limited by the Soviet restrictions on jobs and travel. Although she could apply for openings in other areas, she knew that a Chukchi woman's chances of obtaining a position outside Chukotka were very slim. She had carefully considered all of these factors before making her decision to marry Iurii. Love was not the only, and perhaps not the prime, factor in her decision to marry.

Because I am a woman, my access to information from the young male population was fairly limited, especially when I was trying to gather data on personal subjects such as choosing a marriage partner. Most of the young men with whom I spoke on this subject (the brothers of close female friends) chose their partners for love. If the woman was from outside the village, they had met while studying at an institute or while one of them was visiting relatives in the other's village. Most young men didn't marry until after they had completed their mandatory military service, at approximately age 20. Because their female classmates preferred the older servicemen in the village as partners, adolescent males had few opportunities for intimate relationships with their peers.

When Chukchi and Yup'ik men returned to the village after service or university and institute studies, their options for marriage were also limited. Young Chukchi men who went to work on the tundra were at a particular disadvantage, because their schedule kept them away from the village for months at a time. This problem was institutionalized among herding people who practice *proizvodstvennoe kochevanie* (production nomadism). Among herders in the Magadan District (including Chukotka), 41.8 percent were bachelors (Donskoi 1987:85). Some of them may have married later in life, particularly because so many widows were available. Because of the high mortality rates among Chukchi men, however, it was likely that many would die bachelors in their 40s and early 50s.

The 25-or-older bachelor herder was a frequent subject of conversation among his female kinswomen. "He needs to find a nice young girl and have some children," they would say, or "I don't understand why he can't find someone. He should go to another village and look," or "He needs to drink less and get married." One young herder in his early 30s admitted that he wanted nothing more than to get married and have children, but "It's too late for me." He

[45]

saw his work schedule, his drinking habits, and his "morose" character as obstacles. He was probably correct in believing that if a man was still unmarried by the age of 30, his chances of finding a partner were slight.

Young Yup'ik men, who didn't live in such isolation, had more opportunities to meet young women from Sireniki and the surrounding villages. Of Yup'ik men between the ages of 20 and 30 who hunted, 46 percent were married, in comparison with 10 percent among the Chukchi herders. Of the men over 30, 81 percent of the Yup'ik hunters and 72 percent of the Chukchi herders were married (these figures include widowers but not divorcees, unless they had remarried). Since the 1960s the structure of herding had changed in such a way as to make it easier financially to support a family but more difficult to find a wife.

Another reason for the discrepancy in the marriage rates of herders and hunters may have been the local perception that Yup'ik men were more Russified and therefore more desirable marriage partners; but research is needed to confirm this impression.

The marriage ceremony in Sireniki contained very little cultural content from the Yup'ik, the Chukchi, or any of the cultural groups that made up the Newcomers. Marriage for love among young adults and marriage for economic and social reasons among the middle-aged had replaced the ancient forms of bride service, child betrothal, and arranged marriages, both in practice and in native discourse. Unregistered marriages looked more like the ancient custom, when two people unceremoniously cohabited, than did registered marriages with their Soviet wedding ceremonies.

People's reasons for choosing to live together rather than marry were very similar to those in Western industrialized countries. Adolescents wanted to escape their parents, or were afraid of commitment, or had no interest in having children yet; one partner might have an apartment and it was more expedient to live together than to live separately; or a Newcomer who did not intend to stay in the village permanently might want a *vremennaia zhena* (temporary wife) but no permanent bond.

All of these factors contributed to a new form of marriage in Sireniki that bore little resemblance to the marriages of their parents and grandparents. Even though marriages looked contemporary, however, prior cultural forms and meanings were contributing factors in these unions. As I mentioned earlier, 73 percent of marriages were endogamous. Whereas the Soviet model predicted cultural homogeneity and group exogamy, the Yup'ik, Chukchi, and Newcomers chose their marriage partners primarily from within their own cultural groups.

Out of 163 registered marriages, 119 were ethnically endogamous. The highest rate of endogamy, 61 percent, was among Newcomers; the rate among the Yup'ik was 48 percent.[6] More than half (52 percent) of the exogamous unions were between Yup'ik and Newcomers; 42 percent were between Chukchi and Yup'ik; only 6 percent were between Chukchi and Newcomers. In 22 Chukchi exogamous marriages, 18 of the spouses were Yup'ik (14 husbands, 4 wives); in 44 Yup'ik exogamous marriages, 23 of the spouses were Newcomers (19 husbands, 4 wives). There were only three registered marriages between Newcomers (Russian husbands) and Chukchi (wives). Three Newcomers married partners of other groups (Evenk, Dolgan, and Tatar).[7]

The highest rate of exogamous marriage was between Yup'ik women and Newcomer men, for several cultural and structural reasons. The people themselves attributed the high rate of Yup'ik exogamy to the fact that the Yup'ik were a settled people and had more time to "get used to" the Newcomers, who had been living in the village since the 1930s. As we have seen, some of the exogamous unions were between the young soldiers who served in the village and young native women.

Marriage created a broad spectrum of social ties across group boundaries. An exogamous union created relationships beyond the conjugal couple. It was a tie between social groups and provided each group access to the other. Consider the case of Sveta and Iurii.

Sveta (a Yup'ik), who before her first child was born worked as a cashier, was married to Iurii (a Newcomer), a laborer in the state farm. In 1990 they had been married for several years and had two daughters. Through Sveta, Iurii came to enjoy Yup'ik foods and had integrated himself into the Yup'ik community. Iurii helped Sveta's widowed father, Ivan, with mechanical work and general home repairs; and because of the inadequacy of their own cabin, during the winter months Sveta, Iurii, and their daughters moved in with Ivan. Iurii also enjoyed hunting and was quite skilled. When one of the hunting brigades became a cooperative venture, one of Sveta's relatives asked Iurii to join the brigade, and he did.

Iuliia and Aleksei were also an exogamous couple. Although Iuliia (a Yup'ik) and Aleksei (a Newcomer) worked for the state farm in capacities unrelated to traditional economic activities, Aleksei was integrated into Iuliia's Yup'ik family. On weekends and whenever her father (a *brigadir*) needed an extra hand, Aleksei went hunting with him. Aleksei and Iuliia had many friends among both the Newcomer and Yup'ik communities. Holidays and birthdays were celebrated with both family and friends. The couple were able to meet their obligations to Iuliia's family and keep their associations with the Newcomer community.

Other marriages were not so well integrated. Several native women complained that their Newcomer husbands wouldn't eat sea mammal or reindeer meat, and no other meat was available at the store. They worried about their

[47]

ability to provide properly for their husbands on such limited resources. Still other women were berated by their husbands for their "primitiveness" and "backward" ideas. Not all the exogamous marriages created a bridge between groups.

In Newcomer discourse, the Yup'ik were more Russified than the Chukchi, and therefore made better partners. Newcomers also liked to think that because Newcomer men were less public about their drinking than Yup'ik and Chukchi men, they drank less and so were preferred choices for the local women. One Russian woman explained: "Educated native women want Russian husbands because they're better educated and don't drink like native men do."

Yup'ik and Chukchi women agreed that Newcomers made good partners, but not because of their alleged sobriety. Many native women believed that children of mixed parentage were "healthier." One Chukchi woman confided that she was in love with a Chukchi man but preferred to have her children with a Russian, because "Russian children are stronger." She got her wish: she had children by a Russian and then married her Chukchi. Both Chukchi and Yup'ik women liked to claim that their half-Russian children were larger and healthier than children of pure (so to speak) Chukchi or Yup'ik parentage. This "strength" was reason enough for some women to seek partners among Newcomer men.

Undoubtedly another aspect of the rate of exogamy between Yup'ik and Newcomers was the Europeanized concept of beauty. People praised the light complexions of some babies and made teasing comments about the ones with dark complexions. People also pointed to "narrow-eyed-ness" (*uzkoglazie*), or epicanthic folds, as an undesirable characteristic; even children used the term as an epithet to taunt each other. The lighter skin and rounder eyes of children of mixed parentage were considered more attractive than dark skin and epicanthic folds. Unfortunately, I was unable to collect more than anecdotal evidence of the degree to which this preference affected mate selection.

There were also structural advantages to exogamy. Newcomers were in structurally advantaged positions and received higher wages. They also had contacts in other areas of the Soviet Union and therefore access to goods, residency, and family support outside of Sireniki. Although these things were perceived as advantages, however, no one ever discussed them as reasons for choosing a marriage partner.

Even though the form of marriage had been Sovietized and people chose their partners on the basis of very contemporary criteria, most were still choosing to marry primarily within their own groups. There was still a general belief that it was better to be in the company of one's own group. This was one of the ways in which the Chukchi, Yup'ik, and Newcomers maintained the integrity of their own collective group identity.

Relations of Production

Kinship was vital to Yup'ik and Chukchi economic organization, as it is among all nonindustrialized peoples. Kin relationships provided membership in hunting crews and herding brigades. The Yup'ik had no formally structured kinship relationship, such as the avunculate, that designated the composition of a hunting brigade, but in five out of six brigades a genealogical kin relationship connected the primary crew. People hunted primarily with relatives: siblings, father's sibling's sons, mother's sibling's sons, father's father, mother's father, and so on.

These types of kin-based working groups were also prevalent among the Chukchi. Reindeer-herding brigades were largely kin-based. Although a brigade's composition was designated by the state farm, the *zootekhnik* (a veterinarian with training in economics who acted as the top administrator of the reindeer brigades) confessed that he gave the most weight to a herder's personal choice of brigade, and herders chose primarily to be with relatives. When I asked why they chose a particular brigade, herders would say that their fathers, uncles, or older siblings worked on that brigade. However, among the youngest herders, 16-year-olds who had dropped out of school but did not yet qualify for military service, friendship was an important factor in brigade choice.

Chukchi women, too, worked with their kin when they could. Those who worked on the tundra worked exclusively on the brigades of their fathers, husbands, and sons. One younger woman was a cook on the brigade where her father was the *brigadir* and her husband was a herder. Another woman was married to a herder and chose to work on the brigade with him even in winter.

Yup'ik women also chose to work with relatives. During the summer months female relatives (mothers, daughters, siblings) gathered greens together. Throughout the year female kin work groups processed sea mammal and reindeer meat. Both Yup'ik and Chukchi women shared such activities as sewing, housework, and baby-sitting with their female kin.

The Chukchi slaughtered their privately owned reindeer and processed the carcasses only in kin groups. This was made very clear to me when I participated in my first reindeer slaughter. People refused my help when they were butchering their own reindeer, but happily accepted my assistance when they started processing the state farm's reindeer.

Sometimes the key relationship in a production group was friendship rather than kinship, although often friend and kin were one and the same. Men and women organized their work for the state farm during the reindeer slaughter on the basis of friendship. These friendships were sometimes formed on the basis of a work association, such as belonging to the same *kollektiv*, but more often the friends had been classmates.

Although reindeer herding was almost exclusively a Chukchi activity, Sergei, a young Yup'ik man, spent one fall with the brigades. When I asked how he had chosen a brigade, he answered that his *odnoklassniki* had invited him to work with them. Because Sergei was a hunter and had no previous experience with herding, the invitation was a big responsibility for his old classmates; but *odnoklassniki* had a very special relationship and his Chukchi friends willingly took on the obligation for his training.

The relationship between *odnoklassniki* was an interesting one, especially in Sireniki, which had such a small population. A class that graduated from the eleventh grade generally consisted of about ten people. These people had truly grown up together. They went through all of their school years together, and during adolescence they spent their free time together on picnics or day hikes. Photo albums were filled with pictures of these outings, showing groups of young men and women sitting by a fire, singing to someone's guitar, and sharing the food each contributed. Such photos prompted fond memories of the times spent with one's *odnoklassniki*. Not surprisingly, these relationships continued into adult life.

As adults, people would ask their *odnoklassniki* for help with various subsistence pursuits—fishing, gathering eggs, hunting for fur animals—or with housework and baby-sitting. These relationships might be cross-gender. On several occasions people mentioned to me that someone had become jealous of his or her partner's opposite-gender friend. One young man declared, "I told her that was ridiculous. Zhanna was my *odnaklassnitsa*, we're supposed to be close." Friendships between men and women in Sireniki were very rare and tended to arouse jealousy, but there was social tolerance of such relationships among classmates.

Often *odnoklassniki* were also kin, and it was difficult to sort out which relationship was felt more strongly. One pair of young women who were always in each other's company were pointed out to me as *odnoklassnitsy*, and only much later did I learn that they were also "sisters" (cousins).

Whether there was a kin connection between *odnoklassniki* or not, many of the sentiments, responsibilities, and obligations were kinlike. People felt that a request from an *odnoklassnik* was much like a request from a relative and should not be refused.

Although kinship could determine working groups and even friendships, it was not the exclusive factor in social organization. One *baidara* had a crew of primarily unrelated individuals, and many men on the herding brigades were not related. Yet people felt kin relationships were extremely important: kin shared labor, social responsibilities, and financial obligations. Most nonworking hours were spent in the company of kin.

A Gendered Division of Labor

In Sireniki the division of labor by gender was marked in both the public and domestic spheres. Women did the primary housework, such as cooking, cleaning, laundry, and child care. Men were responsible for making repairs to the apartment's structure, hauling bulky items, driving, and subsistence hunting. The domestic division of labor in Sireniki was not dissimilar to the division of labor in any Russian working-class town. People had a definite sense of what was "men's work" and what was "women's work."

Not everyone unquestioningly accepted the parameters of this division. Women, especially those in their 30s and younger, complained about having to work a full day on the job and then working again at home. A few men sympathized and were willing to help with the housework. Men without mothers, wives, or sisters were forced to do their own housework, but the Yup'ik, Chukchi, and Newcomers all perceived housework as "women's duties." This division of labor was so pervasive that when I was sharing a three-room apartment with a couple, another single woman, and Pavel the schoolteacher, the two men expected us women to cook and clean for them.

At the state farm the roles of men and women were less sharply defined. Women and men filled administrative positions, and women were doctors,[8] teachers, builders, and painters. In other villages they were the directors of state farms. Although there were some exclusively male and female professions, on the state farm men and women interacted more frequently than they did in traditional economic activities. But even the nontraditional jobs on the state farm were divided by gender.

The ideology supporting these gender divisions on the state farm came from the Newcomers' cultural ideals. Men worked as machinists, electricians, tractor operators, *vezdekhod* drivers, and heavy laborers. Women worked as nannies, nurses, sales clerks, cleaners, seamstresses, accountants, and bakers.

Among the Chukchi and Yup'ik, such activities as slaughtering reindeer, skinning walruses, drying fish, and working skins were sharply gender-divided, even when the activity was regulated by the state farm. Jobs that existed before Sovietization, such as sewing, skin working, hunting, and herding, were gender-specific, even if they had been incorporated into the state farm system.

Women who worked in the skinning and sewing *kollektiv* did the tasks their mothers had done before Soviet intervention. They removed the fat and scraped the sea mammal hides brought in by the hunters; they tanned, softened, and sewed sea mammal and reindeer skins into clothing for the state farm; and they sewed the walrus skins onto the *baidary*. Men worked as their ancestors did, as hunters and herders.

When I inquired into the justification for dividing work by gender, the answer was inevitably "It's our tradition. Women have their work and men have theirs." As for the domestic division of labor, "Women give birth and therefore feel more responsibility to the children than men. So women feel a stronger responsibility to take care of the work in the house." This perception did not vary among the three groups. With the exception of the intelligentsia, who were familiar with the Western concept of feminism and often pointed to the hypocrisy of a revolution that liberated men and not women, Newcomer women gave the same justifications as Yup'ik and Chukchi women for the gender division of labor in the village.

It was not unknown for hunters to accept female help. In native tradition, when a family didn't have enough male members to supply a full *baidara* crew, prepubescent girls were allowed to help by paddling the *baidara*. Adult women, however, were never allowed on a hunt; the more traditional Yup'ik still considered women, particularly menstruating women, offensive to sea mammals.

As with many things under the Soviet regime, cultural sensibilities could be sacrificed for economic expediency. During World War II, when a large number of men were absent from the village for military service, it was necessary for women to take the place of men in the hunting crews. The Yup'ik dealt with this challenge to a fundamental spiritual-gender boundary by allowing the women only to run the motors (as, in tradition, a prepubescent girl could only paddle the *baidara*) and not to actually kill the sea mammals. After the war, when the men returned to the village and it was no longer economically necessary for women to join hunting crews, women returned to their own gender-specific labor.

The women who participated in those hunting expeditions while I was there were very shy about discussing their activities. The most they would say was that they indeed had tended to the motors and that they were very nervous about going hunting.

When I said I wanted to travel with a hunting crew, I met more resistance from women than from men. After I returned from a hunt, the women blamed me for bad weather and generally teased me for having participated in a male activity. It was the gender boundary that was of most concern to these women, not the spiritual boundary. Because the gender boundary was reinforced daily by the Soviet labor structure, as well as by their own cultures, it had more relevance to these people and was more significant than the spiritual boundary (which I had also breached by participating in the hunt).

Although Soviet ideology did not recognize a gender division of labor in the public domain, in reality the public domain mirrored the private domain. Despite the professed equality of women, the gendered division of labor persisted. It was the cultural construction of the Newcomers, Yup'ik, and Chukchi alike.

The Structure of Social Space

> Drinking tea in an old apartment.
> Waiting for summer in an old apartment.
> An old apartment where there was light, gas, telephone,
>   hot water, radio, little daughter.
> A tolerable, individual home. One family, two families,
>   three families.
>
> VIKTOR TSOI, 1986

Before we can fully understand the social context in Sireniki, we have to understand household organization and how Soviet architecture impinged on local residential groups. The Soviet architecture in Sireniki, a style typical of most northern cities in the former Soviet Union, not only framed the landscape but designed the physical space of its households, and in doing so it physically structured kin groups.

The living space of the village consisted of eleven two-story apartment buildings with eight to eighteen apartments per building. Other large domestic buildings were the military officers' apartment house, a dormitory for border guards, and a large civilian dormitory. The remaining living spaces were small individual houses or cabins that had been divided into one-room apartments, two or more per house.[9]

The apartment buildings were divided into *odnokomnatnye kvartiry* (one-room apartments), similar to efficiencies with a separate kitchen (a kitchen is not counted as a "room" in Russia); *dvukhkomnatnye kvartiry* (two-room apartments), with a separate bedroom; and *triekhkomnatnye kvartiry* (three-room apartments), with two bedrooms. For the most part these apartments were occupied by related individuals. Because housing was scarce in the village, however, several three-room apartments were occupied by unrelated individuals or families who shared the kitchen and bathroom.

[53]

The civilian dormitory was a long Quonset hut–like building with single rooms on either side of the corridor. The single rooms were occupied by single individuals and families. As the dormitory was without plumbing, the residents considered this living situation very substandard. The unattached houses, although also divided into one-room apartments and without indoor plumbing, represented a slightly higher standard of living. The state farm delivered potable water to these houses. A metal pail covered with a lid served as a toilet. It sat in the corridor in the summer and in the kitchen in the winter. One lost all sense of modesty when forced to use a honey bucket in a kitchen crowded with both women and men. The bucket's contents were disposed of in the garbage bins.

Living space was controlled by the state farm and the village council. The housing code gave preference to those who had resided in the village the longest, and they were given their choice of apartments on a first-come, first-served basis. Under this plan, one would have expected local people to control the choicest apartments, but enough exceptions preempted this provision to enable Newcomers to occupy the most modern and convenient apartments.

The main exception was a government-sanctioned policy aimed at attracting "qualified specialists" to the northern regions. The government not only guaranteed high wages but also promised young couples their own apartments. For young families from large cities, where the endemic housing shortage forced them to live with in-laws, this was a powerful enticement. So the Newcomers received the more spacious and convenient apartments and local people who had lived in the village much longer were forced to accept less desirable living quarters.

Though the apartments, unlike the cabins, had running water, it was not always potable. Some buildings had such poor insulation that people had to move in with other family members during the winter months. Apartments that faced north were colder and less desirable than those with a southern exposure. The less desirable apartments were most often occupied by local people.

Olia and Sasha provide a good example of the motivations for accepting the living conditions in Sireniki. They moved to Sireniki from Ukraine, where they had lived with Sasha's mother. Olia told me how difficult it had been, all three of them in a small apartment; she and Sasha's mother had such different temperaments that they argued frequently, and the conflicts strained her relationship with Sasha. She had encouraged Sasha to come to the North so they could have their own home and build a life together.

Sasha, as an electrical specialist, had gotten a job in Sireniki with the guarantee of an apartment for his family. They lived in a one-room apartment in one of the houses. Although they complained about the lack of plumbing, they had remodeled the room to their liking and were very content with the arrangement, especially when they remembered how they had lived in Ukraine.

Olia and Sasha had one child, whom they sent to live with Sasha's mother for a year when she reached school age. Because Chukotka, so close to U.S. territory, was a closed travel zone, the grandmother would have had to cope with a lot of paperwork to come and live with them, so it was easier to send the child to her. This was not an uncommon practice among Newcomers. Such an arrangement was felt to be emotionally beneficial to grandparent and grandchild. In addition, sending the child to a grandparent was believed to improve the child's diet during the critical growing years. In Ukraine, Sasha explained, his daughter had access to fresh fruits and vegetables, unavailable in Chukotka. This attitude was shared by most Newcomers.

The government's enticements were not the only limitations on access to housing. Some people were convinced that they had been denied access to better apartments because they were too vocal in their complaints to the state farm administration or the village council. Others said they were kept out of the better apartments because the Newcomers in the building didn't like the way native foods or drying skin clothing smelled in the corridors. One Newcomer confided that a young professional Chukchi woman who was recently engaged and pregnant wouldn't receive the apartment she had been promised "because the neighbors complained that they didn't want to live next to *mestnye* [locals]."

Although this was the housing pattern as the local people perceived it, in fact some Newcomers were forced to live in dormitories, especially if they were single; to share apartments with unrelated families; or to live in the unplumbed cabins, because nothing else was available when they arrived. And some local people, through the correct application of the residency rule, through length of service to the state farm, through inheritance, or through social connections, managed to occupy the "modern" and more "convenient" apartments. It was not uncommon for someone to wait ten years or more for a "proper" apartment. Even if one were not bumped from the list to accommodate a Newcomer or to punish politically unpopular ideas, a single person might still be jumped over in favor of a couple expecting a baby.

The entire business of obtaining an apartment and the convenience or inconvenience of its floor plan and location were frequent topics of conversation in Sireniki. As Viktor Tsoi's song suggests, discussing apartments was a national pastime, an institutionalized conversation for most of the Soviet population.

When two people met for the first time, the question most frequently asked was "How many rooms does your apartment have?" If a single-family household had more than two rooms, it could be inferred that someone in the household had social position, wealth, or connections.

The limited living space restricted social options. Families that wanted to live together were forced apart and families that wanted to live separately were forced together. Living quarters in Sireniki, as all over the Soviet Union, were structured on principles developed in Moscow. The state's urban-based space allotments, absurd when applied uniformly across a territory covering over 8.6 million square miles and eleven time zones, required everyone but the Party elite to adjust to the bureaucracy's dictates.

The cultural concessions made by local people were most obvious among the Chukchi. Because several Chukchi families chose to spend their summers on the tundra, it was possible to compare the use of space in the Soviet-constructed apartment buildings with that in the Chukchi *yarangi*. As we have seen, village family groups were forced by space limitations to live in separate apartments. Although they had various strategies to compensate for these arrangements, such as shared meals, frequent visiting, and obtaining apartments in the same locale, they still lived in separate spaces. When they went to the tundra, in contrast, they lived together. The elderly erected their *yarangi* in the same way Bogoraz described almost a century before, and archaeological evidence indicates that tundra housing was constructed in much the same way for a millennium (Ackerman 1984).

The *yaranga* was a circular structure of wooden poles and reindeer skin, although now canvas might replace worn skins. It was entered through a skin-flap door on the southeast side. The front area contained the hearth, a small fire pit surrounded by stones, with a work area on either side. In the back of the *yaranga* was the *polog*, or sleeping bench, a square tentlike structure of four walls and a ceiling (sewn from several reindeer skins) atop a thick mat of branches covered by walrus skins. All of the reindeer skin coverings were turned hair side in, revealing the richly stained red hide to the open entry room.

The *polog* was shared by everyone in the family, with men at stage right and women to the left. The oldest lay on the edges, while toward the center lay progressively younger children and mothers with babies. In the center might lie a couple. Everyone who came to the tundra, as well as herders when the herd was close to the base camp, stayed in the family *yaranga*. They ate, worked, played, and slept there. When the Chukchi were first moved into apartments in Sireniki, they erected their *pologi* inside the apartments. Yup'ik who had lived in *yarangi* before collectivization had done the same thing fifty years earlier.

These very different styles of space use were symbolic of the basic dichotomy between native culture and Sovietized culture. The Soviet system demanded conformity to a particular design, be it physical or ideological. The Soviet conception of the world was not necessarily diametrically opposed to native conceptions, but native peoples, whether consciously or unconsciously,

[56]

were forced to prioritize core cultural values in their adaptation to the changes brought about by their interaction with the Soviet system.

The Newcomers, Chukchi, and Yup'ik all had unique social organizations, which they reworked, both structurally and culturally, within the Soviet system in order to give meaning to their new social context. Among the Yup'ik and Chukchi of Sireniki, family and the domestic group were the key elements of social organization. Family was important to the Newcomers too, but the structure of their lives in Sireniki made friendship a major component of their daily social organization.

Kin relationships among the Yup'ik and Chukchi organized labor, economic and political support, and friendships. Newcomers, by virtue of coming to the North without their kin, were forced to depend on friendships, work relationships, Party affiliation, and structural connections for such support. Through political and economic policy, the control of physical space, and ideological goals, the Soviet system dictated many aspects of village social organization. The Chukchi and Yup'ik worked on Soviet hunting, herding, and labor brigades for the state farm, rather than for the benefit of their households. Similarly, the domestic group was forced to adjust to Soviet-constructed apartment houses. All the same, native people continued to base their social relationships on Chukchi and Yup'ik models. People chose to work with kin both within and outside of the state farm context; therefore, kinship was still one of the main organizing principles of the relations of production for these groups.

As in other aspects of Sireniki life, people had adapted within the constraints of the larger state structure. They manipulated Russian kin terms to fit their own concepts of social relationships; kin lived in separate apartments but they shared meals, child care, and household responsibilities; men chose to hunt and herd on brigades to which they were connected through kinship; and women chose kin as working partners. Although Soviet policies had affected and continued to affect indigenous social organization through relocations, inmigrations, control of space, and economic reorganization, the Chukchi and Yup'ik of Sireniki continued to structure and restructure their lives as well as interpret their physical and cultural landscape in their own ways.

[3]

Life Cycle and Ceremony

One of the fundamental elements of life in Sireniki was the natural cycle and rhythm of the environment to which the human life cycle was intimately tied. The Soviet five-year plans and six-day workweeks were forced to bow to the seasonality of life in the Arctic. Because the people of Sireniki were dependent on the sea and the tundra for basic sustenance, it was impossible for the Soviet economic imperatives to exert complete hegemony over the natural, and thus cultural, cycle of life in the village.

Life in Sireniki followed the seasons. Herders marked their work by the spring birthing of reindeer calves and the fall molting of antlers; hunters watched for spring walrus and winter ice; and women on the fox farm matched their schedules to the foxes' own cycles of breeding and birthing. The natural cycle of the seasons, once symbolized by the life cycles of the animals the villagers hunted and herded and the plants they collected, still structured much of their lives. The Yup'ik marked the calendar year by the various subsistence activities of the seasons. December to January was the "month of ceremonies"; January–February was "a lot of frost in the corridor"; March and April were "the birth of seals"; May was the "rivers open"; June was "summer woman" or "when the light starts to shine"; July was "begin to collect eggs"; and August was "when the reindeer begin to cry [or rut]" and "green shines golden"; and September through November were "when small birds begin to jump in the water." Just as the seasonal cycle escaped the Soviet grip, so did the life cycle of the people.

Contemporary life cycle events and their associated rituals were negotiated space between the demands of the Soviet government and the imperatives of the Yup'ik and Chukchi cultures. Women went to a Soviet hospital to give birth and submitted to the rigidity of Soviet medical procedures, but they were sustained by the cultural beliefs in the spiritual power of pregnancy and the reincarnation of souls in the newborn. Marriages were registered by the local council, but many couples who chose not to register still carried the social / cultural obligations of married men and women in their own groups. Finally, red stars rose above the graves, but funeral pyres were still ignited; and after a funeral, all participants were swept clean of the spirits of the dead before they reentered the village. Although the Soviet government had succeeded in dominating many aspects of the villagers' lives, life cycle events were still marked by their own rituals, steeped in their own cultural meaning.

Parents and Children

Children were highly valued by all the groups in Sireniki. As we have seen, childlessness was a humiliation; no woman would choose not to have children. Because these people lacked both contraceptives and a concept of illegitimacy, there were few barriers to pregnancy, medical or cultural, and most Chukchi and Yup'ik women had their first child in their late teens or early 20s.

The pill was unavailable; many women complained about IUD's; and if one managed to get a diaphragm, it was impossible to buy the spermicide. Therefore, the primary method of birth control was abortion. I found no philosophical or ideological barriers to pregnancy terminations, but many young women were afraid of the medical risks associated with abortion, especially sterility, and chose to give birth instead. After a woman had several children, abortion became her method of birth control; and it was not uncommon for a woman in her late 30s to have had ten or more abortions (Pika 1996).

During her pregnancy a woman was monitored and counseled by the doctors in the village on such topics as nutrition, smoking, drinking, and infant care. Women continued to work up until the day they gave birth. Among the Chukchi and Yup'ik, contemporary Soviet medicine was supplemented by local beliefs entailing a system of behavioral rules that were said to ensure the health of the infant. Young women's behavior was monitored by older female family members for proper observance of cultural traditions.

For example, pregnant women were admonished for chewing gum while they were pregnant, as it might result in a baby that constantly drooled; they were told not to stand in doorways because that could cause a difficult delivery; and they were not supposed to wake up too late or the child would be lazy. One Yup'ik woman refused to accept any gifts for her child or to buy any clothing before the birth because her mother had told her doing so could bring harm to her unborn child. A young Chukchi woman was afraid of an older, childless hospital attendant. Other women had warned her not to let the attendant stare at her, specifically at her stomach, as it could cause harm to her child.

"Harm" was always an amorphous threat. Some women described "harm" as birth defects, while to others it was stillbirth. Harm was inflicted by bad spirits—not metaphysical beings, but a bad essence that could cause bad things to happen. As we shall see, the idea of bad essence was carried over into many aspects of life. People didn't whistle in their houses or on the tundra for fear of drawing bad spirits; talk about future possible bad events was always followed by spitting, to spit out the bad words for fear they would come true. Children were especially susceptible to a sort of "evil eye." By staring, and thus coveting, a particularly attractive baby, one could make the child ill. Many of these ideas were not exclusive to the Chukchi and Yup'ik; Newcomers believed them too.

Like many of the "old ways," the rules for behavior during pregnancy were not taken too seriously by young women, but were not completely ignored either. It was difficult for the younger generation to know what they should do. They were not sure what practices they could attribute to ancient superstition and what were dangerous to ignore.

Because the hospital facilities in Sireniki were inadequate, local doctors sent women to Provideniia to give birth. Several weeks before the calculated delivery date, the pregnant woman was put on a medical helicopter and taken to the Provideniia Regional Hospital for admission to the maternity ward. This arrangement was far from ideal; most native women would have preferred to give birth in the village, close to their families.

The maternity ward at the Provideniia Hospital was a dormitory-style arrangement, with all of the pregnant mothers in one room. Only patients were admitted to the ward. When families visited, as they frequently did, to bring fruit and other things to supplement the very poor hospital food, they had to meet the patient in the hallway, after she had obtained permission from the staff to leave the ward.

Neither were family members allowed into the delivery room. When I told people that in the United States husbands generally wanted to be in the delivery room to help their wives and to experience the birth of their child, women and men alike grimaced at the thought. A friend suggested that perhaps American men "agree" to be at the birth, rather than "want" to be there. Women couldn't imagine what the men would do there, and men couldn't imagine witnessing the "mess" of blood, the screams, the exposure of their wives' bodies.

During birth, stoic behavior by the mother was considered commendable. Women talked about how they did not scream during childbirth and pointed out "weaker" women who did. I always suspected that this was an expectation set up by the hospital staff for their convenience. When I was in the hospital, I heard nurses on several occasions gossiping about patients who cried, both maternity and general medical patients. It was clear they were disdainful of such behavior, and they expressed the opinion that patients who complained of pain were weak. Long before Lenin, however, Bogoraz noted that Chukchi women were "forbidden" to groan during childbirth or to receive help.

If a young woman was ill after the birth, she was moved from the maternity ward to the general ward. Here she would again be in one room with all the other hospitalized women who were ill (but not contagious). Several native women expressed discomfort at this arrangement because they were very "shy," particularly about their bodies, in front of strangers. One young woman found it humiliating to have to pump her breast milk in front of a roomful of strangers.

This "modern" way of giving birth, a decidedly different form from that described by the older women—they had been attended by village midwives or had given birth alone—had been introduced by the Soviets in their efforts to "improve" medical care in the northern regions. Women of all three groups were less than pleased to give birth in Provideniia because of its distance from the village and because of the general dislike of hospitals, with their poor food and inconvenient patient quarters. Because the Soviet government, intent on "improving the conditions and health of northern peoples," controlled where and how women gave birth, there were no alternatives, and everyone was forced to submit to the process.

A few days after the birth, if all went well, the mother and child returned home, the child swaddled in a shining new satin quilt tied with a large ribbon, a gift of the grandparents or other relatives. Upon their return, family and friends came to visit and bring gifts. Visitors never gave great compliments to the newborn so as not to attract evil spirits, which could produce illness or perhaps the exact opposite of the compliment. If someone said the child had a very sweet disposition, for example, the child might become ill-tempered. Although these beliefs were recognized as "ancient ways," many young people heeded them. Anyone who paid too many compliments to a newborn was chastised. A suitable comment was "You are so ugly!" or "You are a very bad boy!" delivered in that high squeaky voice that adults everywhere reserve for talking to babies. Some Newcomer women and men agreed about the power of a look.

Much of what was labeled "ancient ways" was shared by all the groups in Sireniki. It was a mistake to assume that because the Newcomers were European in appearance and acculturated as good Soviet atheists, they did not have their share of superstitions. The Russians and Ukrainians in Sireniki shared a lively belief in the supernatural and the spiritual world.

After an infant's birth, the mother was entitled by law to stay home for three years to take care of the child before returning to work. During those three years the mother received a pension of approximately 50 rubles a month. Not all women chose to stay home the full three years, and many who had no husband or parents to support them couldn't afford to stay home at all.

Several weeks after the child was born, a date was set for its registration with the village council. The parents chose *svideteli* (godparents; literally, witnesses) for the child, who would be present at the registration ceremony. On the scheduled date, the parents and *svideteli* went to the village council building, where the council president read an oath. The *svideteli* swore to the oath and then signed the registration. The ceremony was the Soviet variation of a Christian baptism; here the *svideteli* swore to uphold the rules of the Soviet state and, in the event of the death of the parents, to be responsible for raising the child under the teachings of socialism. Then the child's name was officially placed in the village registry and the parents received a document of registration and a medal for the child.

Most Chukchi and Yup'ik had several names: their Russian name (the name with which they were registered at the village council), their native name (the name in their own language chosen by a close relative), and several nicknames (the names given by classmates and family members in childhood). The Yup'ik believed in reincarnation, and a child was often given the name of a recently deceased relative. It was believed that the child took on many of the personality characteristics of that person, substantiating the rebirth. Sometimes names came to people in dreams. One woman chose her eldest son's name after she dreamed that his father had called to her in the hospital and used that name when he spoke about his son.

The brother of a close friend and his wife asked me to be the *svidetel'nitsa* and to choose a name for their new baby. I chose my grandfather's middle name, Alexander (Sasha). As the child grew, the family quizzed me about my grandfather's personality and nature, looking for clues to little Sasha's behavior.

After their return from the hospital, young mothers would often be seen wheeling carriages around the village, no easy feat on the unpaved and hilly streets. These walks were a major form of socializing for new mothers, who were otherwise confined to their small apartments. They frequently met other mothers with carriages and shared information, such as what was being sold in the store, or just gossiped. It was not uncommon for a mother to leave her baby outside in its carriage to sleep on the street unattended. If the child started to cry, any passerby would rock the carriage until the child fell back to sleep. Sleeping on the street in the fresh air was considered good for the child's health.

Although powdered milk was not always available in the store, many children were weaned by six months and put on a bottle with a powdered milk formula. Solid food, either prechewed by the mother or purchased in jars, was also begun at this age. Potty training started almost immediately. When an infant awoke from a nap or was about to be put to sleep, someone would hold her on a child's commode, and a chorus of hissing sounds would erupt from others in the room as encouragement. These efforts did not preclude the use of diapers, which were made of cotton cloth and worn until the child was fully trained, around the age of 3.

Many children were dressed in a *kirkir*, a one-piece garment of Chukotkan design with a flap that could be opened in the rear. *Kirkiry* were made out of unborn reindeer skins, and the reindeer head and ears were often incorporated into the hood of the garment. Some ingenious mothers, in an attempt to save laundry, took this convenient flap design and added it to their infants' cloth trousers.

Other than the mother, the appropriate caretaker was the maternal or paternal grandmother. Young children were often left in the care of grandparents. If the grandmother was not too elderly, she was the preferred caretaker when a young woman returned to work, rather than the *detskii sad* (kindergarten, more frequently called *sadik*). Another option was for the grandparent to pick the child up at the *sadik* early in the afternoon and keep him until the parents came home.

The grandparent/grandchild relationship was considered very special and loving. Some infants were left with their grandparents full-time while the mother attended an institute or university away from the village. It was not uncommon for young children to be sent away from the village to the grandparents in another republic for a year or more. Some mothers complained that the grandparents were always pressuring them to send the child for a visit. For native people and Newcomers alike, the bond of grandparents and grandchildren was very strong and viewed as a natural part of social life.

If the grandparents were unable to care for the child when the mother chose to return to work, the infant was taken to the *sadik*. This facility was run by the state farm, which charged the family a minimal fee for each attending child. Children were taken there in the morning before the parents went to work. They received breakfast, lunch, and a snack; participated in various learning and play activities; and took naps. They were picked up most often by the parent or an elder sibling around 5:30 P.M. and taken home.

The *sadik* was a very large building with many windows, set at the top of the village. The walls were brightly painted with familiar storybook characters, cartoons, and flowers. Each child had a locker where outdoor clothing was hung. In winter this was no small detail, as children wore many layers of clothing against the cold.

Children might be so tightly bundled in so many layers that it became impossible to walk; if they were able to walk but fell down, it was impossible for them to get up. It was not uncommon to come across a crying child lying on his back in the snow like a turtle on its shell, abandoned by a mischievous sibling and unable to right himself.

The *sadik* had a well-trained staff of nannies. These young women had completed two years of training as day-care workers, most of them in an institute located in Anadyr. The day's activities consisted of both play and schoolwork, such as learning numbers and letters. On occasion the children would have a dance class and be taught traditional dances and songs from all of the Soviet republics, including the Chukotkan district.

It was commonly believed that the meals served at the *sadik* were more nutritionally complete than what the children got at home, because the *sadik* was the first place to receive available milk and fruits. Some people put their children in the *sadik* just to supplement their diets with the extras that were rarely available in the store.

All children entered preschool at the age of 5. Preschool was structured very much like grade school, with classrooms, desks, and formal instruction. Here children started to read and write Russian, and some received basic instruction in their native languages. This was the age at which the government required children to leave the full-time care of their families and enter the public, Sovietized domain.

Childhood and Adolescence

Once children started to school, they were encouraged to be independent. Because the village was small and the hazards were few (from the local perspective), children of all ages walked and played at will throughout Sireniki with little supervision. Child rearing was very permissive by U.S. standards. The Hugheses note this method of child rearing among Yup'ik: "Very permissive socialization techniques, much display of affection and indulgence, general lack of punishment, and widespread adoptive patterns all illustrate the 'social encouragements of fertility' and love of children found in this culture" (1960:64). The same could be said of Sireniki in general. One could hear a stressed mother or father shout at a child occasionally, but especially among the Chukchi and Yup'ik, who valued teaching through example and practice rather than through lectures, verbal admonishments were kept to a minimum.

By the age of 7, children were fairly self-sufficient. They walked to school alone in all but the worst winter storms; returned home or went to a relative's house after school alone; and helped with household chores. No one considered it traumatic for children to be left with relatives while their parents were away from the village, even for weeks at a time.

Children who had been tutored by a grandparent in their native language, dances, and stories frequently lost interest in those things once they started school. In school their focus became the Russian language, Soviet learning, and Soviet values. School-age children preferred Western dress to traditional clothing; only if it was very cold and they were engaged in some outside activity such as ice fishing would they agree to wearing a *kuklanka* and *tarbaza* (reindeer parka and skin boots). Even then, they preferred to wear the more "stylish" and "modern" Soviet-manufactured fur or cotton coats and leather boots. This was a time of great transition for children, and although they were not forced to leave the village and study in the *internaty*, as their parents had been, Soviet-style education had great influence on them and undoubtedly contributed to the devaluation of their own cultures.

It was not only the school's Russian emphasis that created a generational break in cultural concepts, but several structural issues as well. One was a law that forbade children under the age of 14 to participate in the hunting brigades, "for the safety of the children." Sea mammal hunting was correctly viewed as a very dangerous activity, but in typical paternal Soviet fashion no one considered that the Yup'ik had been doing it for thousands of years or gave a thought to the effect the prohibition would have on the Yup'ik culture. Various native advocate associations were working to change the law, and by 1991 it was largely ignored, as the border guards rarely came to the beach to check passports before the hunters went out.

Still, the hunters pointed to this law as one of the main reasons so few of Sireniki's young men became hunters. "If you don't learn it when you're young, if the ocean doesn't get into your soul," by the time they returned from military service they didn't want to go to sea. "Hunting is hard work, and if it isn't in your soul, you won't want to do it," explained one of the *brigadiry*. Some young men did return from the military to become hunters. Two in particular were said to have been smuggled on board the *baidara* in sacks by their uncles, so they could gain the skills of the hunt and the love of the ocean from a very early age. One of the two was recognized as particularly skilled with a *baidara* and in hunting, and as a result he was the *brigadir* of the cooperative hunting brigade. In his case, his uncle was able to overcome the Soviet system and inculcate Yup'ik values in him.

After school, various organized activities were available to children, including sports, photography, sewing, knitting, and some native crafts. In the summer, children participated in Pionerskii Lager' (Pioneer Camp). Although the camp was supposed to be set up exclusively for the Young Pioneers, the Communist youth club, in Sireniki all students who wanted to attend the camp did so. The activities were the sort one might expect in a Scout camp. There were camping trips, military preparedness drills, and picnics. These activities were so popular that many children chose to forgo trips with their families to the tundra in order to stay in the village and attend Pioneer Camp. Most parents did not object because Pioneer Camp was not just for fun, it was a "Soviet socialist duty." By staying in the village while their parents went to the tundra, however, the children limited their opportunities to be exposed to the Chukchi way of life.

As children got older, they had opportunities to join in the activities of the state farm. On holidays such as Den' Sel'skogo Khoziaistva (Agricultural Production Day), children were publicly honored for their work in the reindeer slaughter and for assisting their parents at their jobs, participating in the dance ensemble, helping in the yearly school repairs, and doing well in their studies. These awards often carried financial compensation and were coveted.

One of the main social activities for older children in the village was the weekly dance at the Dom Kul'tury (House of Culture), popularly known as the *klub*. At the dance, a disk jockey played tapes of popular music in the main hall. A minimal fee was charged and children of all ages were admitted. Parents voiced some disapproval of the dances because as the evening wore on adults joined in, especially on a holiday weekend. Some of them were sure to be drunk. Most people would have preferred that their children not be exposed to drunken fighting, foul language, and sexual advances, but this type of behavior was so common that it was impossible to avoid, so parents usually gave in to their children's pleas for permission to attend.

The *klub* also provided video shows. Starting in 1990, a wide range of videos (primarily U.S., some German) had been made available in the Soviet Union. Action films were very popular; the films of Bruce Lee, Arnold Schwarzenegger, and Bruce Willis were shown regularly. These films taught children a whole new vocabulary of U.S. obscenities, which they shouted at one another on the street. People frequently asked me to translate some U.S. phrases. Russian, which is a very rich language, has many possibilities for the few U.S. standards, such as "shit," "fuck," and "dammit." Extensive conversations ensued over how to translate these words more exactly. I always took great care to explain the prevalence of their usage in the United States and thus their lack of impact. Their Russian counterparts carried considerably more weight.

One film in particular aroused a lot of interest in Sireniki—the X-rated *Emmanuelle*. Children and teenagers trooped in along with the adults. Although children's attendance was frowned upon, no one did anything to keep them out.

The attitude of parents toward their children's reading "pornographic" magazines and viewing explicit films ranged widely. Some felt that such material was obscene and shouldn't be available to anyone, certainly not to children. Others felt that for adults such material was perfectly natural, but children shouldn't be exposed to it. Still others thought it was acceptable for adolescents because it was something they were going to be exposed to anyway, so why hide it? One mother said emphatically, "I don't want my son to be like I was, knowing nothing. He should be exposed, then he'll know how to do things before he actually experiences sex."

Adults in Sireniki had a naive, almost schoolgirlish reaction when we discussed sexually explicit videos and books. Because of tight Soviet controls over the distribution of sexually explicit materials, they had had very little exposure to pornography, but they were interested in discussing the sexually explicit videos and films they saw at the *klub*. Interestingly, they switched from dissecting every sexual movement to blushing and giggling in embarrassment. Newcomers were more familiar with pornography, as its distribution through various underground networks was much wider in the cities they came from than in villages. Their reactions ranged from puritanical to interested, but they were not naive.

In the summer of 1990 a very dog-eared copy of the Kama Sutra started to circulate in the village. People read it with great interest. They intensely discussed the content with others who had read it and engaged in long recitations of what they thought of the various positions described. These conversations among middle-aged adults were reminiscent of U.S. adolescents discussing their first *Playboy*. One such conversation took place over tea around the kitchen table in my apartment. A male friend showed up with a chart of figures in various sexual positions. The men and women in the apartment looked at the chart with some interest, but also with some embarrassment. Then the chart owner asked, "Which position is your favorite?" Everyone examined the various positions, making remarks and laughing hysterically. Finally one woman, who was from Odessa and considered herself sophisticated, became fed up with the others' antics. She pointed to the figure of a woman performing fellatio and said sarcastically, "That's every woman's favorite position." That was the end of the conversation.

The wide range of opinions about sexually explicit materials was in part due to the fact that the Soviet structure had disintegrated so quickly and the availability of previously banned books and films was so sudden that people had yet to form a consensus about what types of materials were acceptable. I also believe, however, that people were reluctant to censor anything; after the tight censorship of the Soviet era, they wanted to do nothing to discourage the new openness.

In 1990 Aleksandr Solzhenitsyn's *Gulag Archipelago* had been published for the first time in the Soviet Union, and people who read it were appalled by the abuses of the past and by their ignorance of them. This was the reaction of the average person in the village. Academics and other people with access to information in the urban areas and through universities were aware of what had been done under the Stalin regime, but the information contained in *The Gulag Archipelago* was a very disturbing revelation to many in Sireniki. Interestingly, the Chukchi and Yup'ik were not so surprised because they had access to stories of the labor camps through their grandparents' oral history. One Russian woman told me how shocked she was by the book; she didn't believe a word of it. In talking with a Yup'ik friend, the Russian woman was surprised to learn that the friend unquestioningly believed the book's revelations. The Russian exclaimed, "You're a Komsomol member! How can you believe such tales so easily?" The Yup'ik woman replied, "My grandmother told me about this years ago." Because they were marginal to the Soviet system and thus less easily indoctrinated, Chukchi and Yup'ik people were less afraid to repeat the stories of their oppression under collectivization. Stories that Newcomers hid from their families out of shame and fear were common currency in native homes.

Perhaps for this reason and undoubtedly others, censorship in any form came to be equated with Soviet control and deception. As a result, local people eagerly accepted the new openness and the variety of materials that came with it, including sexually explicit books, magazines, and videos. The abuses of the past made censorship seem a worse evil than pornography, so many people hesitated to make this material unavailable even to their children.

After graduation from middle school, young men registered for military service. Every able-bodied male was required to serve a minimum of two years in the army. Men in the village who had served expressed intense disapproval of this state requirement. They recognized that it came at a point in their lives when they could be learning vital hunting or herding skills, or working and building a family of their own. Many lost their childhood sweethearts to local servicemen while they were away. Many resented the fact that they were the lone Chukchi or Yup'ik among hundreds of men from the Caucusus and the Central Asian republics. One young Chukchi complained that everyone kept asking him if he was a Mongolian. The great distance from their families, the social isolation, and the feeling of useless activity led most young men to conclude that their military service was a waste of time.

A few young men and women, after middle school and military service, went on to study at institutes or universities. In Sireniki seven people between the ages of 20 and 40 had completed college studies and eleven had completed technical school. In 1991 nine students were studying at the university and technical schools. The life of a student was not easy, especially one from a small minority group. There were colleges in Anadyr, Magadan, and Khabarovsk that catered to northern native students, but only 20 percent of all students in Chukotka went there and far fewer earned degrees (Novozhilova 1987). A very few students—in 1990 there were two from Sireniki—entered the state university in Moscow or Leningrad (today St. Petersburg). Most students chose to stay in the village and entered the state farm workforce. Because they were untrained, most had to accept low-status manual jobs or work in traditional occupations. Roughly 87 percent of northern indigenous peoples were employed in the traditional occupations of herding, hunting, and fishing, and one-third of these were under the age of 30 (Donskoi 1987).

Adulthood

The point at which an individual attained adult status was unmarked by ceremony. The main public markers of such status were the birth of a child or a marriage ceremony. In the past the stages to adulthood were more obviously recognized. When a Yup'ik or Chukchi girl began her menses, she was secluded from the group for several days; when she emerged, she was a marriageable woman. Charles and Jane Hughes (1960:64) describe a puberty ceremony among the Yup'ik of St. Lawrence Island in which adult women stroked a girl's body in order to ensure "beauty." (Bogoraz doesn't describe menstrual seclusion but notes a taboo against male contact with a menstruating woman among both the Reindeer and Maritime Chukchi and the Yup'ik, the taboo being stronger among the latter [Bogoraz 1904–9:492]). A first-kill ceremony marked the path to adulthood for a young Yup'ik; every animal taken in the hunt that was the first of its species to be caught by him was joyously shared with the entire village (Hughes and Hughes 1960; Bogoraz 1904–9).

One woman recalled how her brother had killed his first fox. In keeping with Yup'ik cultural practices, her father made the boy sell it to the state farm and with the money buy tea to give to the elderly in the village. She said her bother was very unhappy, not understanding why he couldn't keep the fox, until he saw how happy people were to receive his gift of tea. In Sireniki, practices such as this ceased to maintain their meaning among the younger generation, and the contemporary passage to adulthood was marked in the way of most Western industrialized cultures, through marriage, childbirth, and employment.

The Soviet system provided military service as a means of marking a young man's passage to adulthood. When men returned from service, they were considered marriageable and were recognized as adults. For women, rather than the onset of menses as in many cultures, it was marriage or the birth of her first child that marked the passage to adulthood. For women and men who delayed these rites of passage until they were older, completing a degree of higher education or taking a full-time job served to change one's status from adolescent to adult.

The social expectations of adults revolved around their responsibilities to their families and their jobs. Getting married and having children was a social and cultural given. Women and men who did not marry or did not have children were considered marginal. This was a particular problem for Chukchi men who worked on the reindeer herds; it was not so easy for them to find marriage partners. Because the major part of this book focuses on adult behavior, I will not elaborate further here; more detail on adulthood is given throughout the text.

The *Bania*

One of the constants of life in Sireniki was the biweekly trip to the *bania*, which was run by the state farm and was located on the northern side of the village. Women were scheduled for bathing on Tuesdays and Fridays and men on Wednesdays and Saturdays. Because there were few private baths, *bania* night was the only opportunity for most people to bathe, and women started taking their children to the *bania* to be bathed when they were just a few months old. There was always much talk and anticipation about arrangements for the *bania*.

Being of Finnish ancestry, I grew up with the Finnish variation, the sauna, so the almost ritual aspect of bathing with steam was very familiar to me. The *bania* was not just a place to clean the body but a social event and, for some, a spiritual event as well. Since bathing took place in a public arena, it was accompanied by conversations about the week's events, punctuated with gossip. Adolescents and children bathed earlier in the day; the evenings were reserved for adults.

The *bania* building consisted of four rooms: the corridor with the cashier's counter where one paid the 60 kopeks and received a towel; the dressing room, which had benches and open wooden lockers in which to hang clothing; the bathing room, which was lined with benches and where one washed; and the *parilka* (steam room). On women's night the bathers undressed in the dressing room and then entered the bathing area. After choosing a metal wash basin from a stack near the door, women walked to one of the two spigots from which flowed hot and cold water, filled the basin, carried it to a bench, and began to wash. Once they were clean, they entered the *parilka*.

The *parilka* was lined with a high and a low bench. To the left of the door was the brick oven that heated the room and into which the bathers threw water to create steam. When one lay face down on a towel across the top bench, the hot steam rolled across the body. Not everyone liked the hottest spot, and many stood or sat on the lower benches. The heat was controlled by the amount of steam created. A number of women were known for their love of a really hot *parilka*, and when they entered, others exited in anticipation of overheating.

Although for obvious reasons I never witnessed a men's *bania*, I got the sense that it was much more festive than the women's. Especially on a Saturday night, men often took beer to the *bania* and later regaled us with stories of various competitions that had taken place to determine who could last the longest in the hottest steam, a Sireniki version of machismo.

When the room became filled with steam, the women took out their *veniki* (birch branches soaked in warm water) and began to beat themselves or a partner to increase the heat of the body and purportedly improve the circulation. The *parilka* was believed to have many curative properties, especially for colds, congestion, flu, and aching muscles. Bathers mixed pine and eucalyptus oils with the water they threw on the oven, to increase the medicinal qualities of the steam.

After a good steam, women went back to the dressing room and lay covered in their towels on the benches until they were cool enough to enjoy the steam again. Usually one steamed two or three times. After the entire process, women replenished the bodily fluids they had lost through perspiration with juice or tea bought from the cashier and brought to the dressing room. This was the best time for conversation. Everyone generally was in a good mood, and much joking about having gained or lost weight ensued.

A lot of gossip had its origin in the bath, and for this reason some women refused to bathe in such a public forum. Discussions concerning the locations of various bruises and scratches invariably led to gossip about an individual's sexual activities, especially if the woman was single. Other remarks would be made about the cleanliness of one's underwear, the size of one's breasts, or the unsightly skin rashes one may endure. Although these topics seemed trivial, the *bania* was a very important part of one's social indoctrination. Unless one were very old or disabled, anyone who chose not to participate was considered something of an outsider.

The *bania* was the one place I saw Yup'ik, Chukchi, and Newcomer women interacting apparently with no inhibitions, probably because standing naked together gives people a sense of equality. This sense of likeness was important in creating community relationships.

Old Age and Death

> Kawawa told me about a dream she had last night. She
> dreamed that when she died I would take a rock from her
> grave and place it in Alaska. After a year I would remember
> her there and she would be in Alaska. I was disturbed by
> the dream but her daughter reassured me that it was a good
> dream.
>
> DIARY ENTRY, FEBRUARY 1990

The final phase of one's life in Sireniki came at the time of retirement. Although men were of retirement age at 55 and women at 50, people continued to work past this age, often part-time, for a small stipend to supplement their state pensions. The Yup'ik and Chukchi went on hunting and herding well beyond retirement age.

In the summer, retired Chukchi men and women continued to go to the tundra to work with the herds and to keep their *yarangi* there. Yup'ik men advised the younger hunters on *baidara* construction and participated in the occasional hunt. Yup'ik women continued to work for the state farm sewing *baidara* covers and for their families by processing food and sewing garments from reindeer and seal skins. During the fall, pensioners eagerly participated in the slaughter not only of their own reindeer but of the state farm's deer as well. Although their work continued, most looked forward to retirement as a time of decreased work, when they could take long summer vacations at fishing camps and could spend more time with their grandchildren.

Aside from the few Newcomers who had married local people, there were no elderly Newcomers in the village. At the age of retirement, the Newcomers returned home to their natal republics to enjoy their pensions in more hospitable surroundings. Having come to the North to improve their income, they also improved their pensions and their standard of living when they retired back to the *materik*—the mainland, as they called the western USSR. Newcomers planed for this time by buying apartments in their home cities or building dachas nearby and supplying them with all the modern conveniences they were able to collect over their years of service in Sireniki.

Life expectancy in Chukotka, especially among the indigenous populations, was low by the standards of industrial nations. The out-migration of Newcomers and the alcoholism, accidents, and military service that disproportionately affected men produced a feminization of the older generation. Elderly women were the keepers of the culture. More than one young man sought the advice of his mother on traditionally male activities, such as basic hunting skills. One Yup'ik woman told me of her great distress when her son asked her advice on how to tie the seal buoy to the harpoon. She knew the answer, but could explain it only in Yup'ik because she had learned this skill from her father when she was very young. She didn't know the proper Russian words and her son didn't understand Yup'ik—a source of great distress to her.

Older women took part in the local dance group, teaching the dance as well as participating in events as drummers and singers, and some taught Chukotkan dances and songs to kindergartners in the *detskii sad*. These women were viewed by the community as a cultural resource, and although adolescents could be skeptical of the value of their grandparents' knowledge, they too sought advice on matters of fishing, dogsledding, hunting, and native foods. Frequently, as a grandmother started to tell the history of her past life, a grandchild watching television would turn around to listen to her tales.

Although the Soviet system officially respected the wisdom of age, it had no structural outlet for traditional knowledge. A concern that was frequently brought up at school and state farm meetings was that *babushki* and *dedushki* should have official positions for passing on their knowledge. The Yup'ik and Chukchi thought the school was doing a poor job of teaching native languages because the young teachers themselves spoke the languages poorly. They wanted older women to have an official position in the *sadik* to tell stories and teach dances, sewing, and proper Yup'ik and Chukotkan to the children. In addition, people thought that general advice to hunters and herders should be compensated with wages. Public officials listened to these ideas, but in the usual Soviet fashion nothing was ever done. The only time older people were compensated for their traditional knowledge was when they performed recognized jobs such as sewing a *baidara* cover, skinning a reindeer, or participating in the fox slaughter. Pensioners were asked to help when extra labor was needed, and for this work they were compensated as any worker would be.

More than any other aspect of the life cycle, death and its surrounding rituals were infused with indigenous cultural knowledge and performance; yet Chukchi and Yup'ik mortuary ritual and practice were not unchanged. The forty-day mourning period, the yearly return to the grave to remember the dead, burial rather than cremation, the picture of the deceased embossed on the headstone, and the fencing of the grave site—all these practices were Russian Orthodox.

The Russian Orthodox tradition was to return to the grave forty-nine days after the burial. The Chukchi returned forty-three days after the burial, while the Yup'ik returned after forty-nine days. The forty-day *pominki* (memorial meal) was undoubtedly not a coincidence but related to the influence, however minimal, of Orthodoxy brought into the village through early Russian contact or the more recent influx of Newcomers.

The red covering on the casket and the red star on the headstone were influences from the Bolshevik Revolution. The Yup'ik and Chukchi also mark their loved ones' exit from the world with rituals taken from their own cultures, thereby ensuring their passage to the "other side" and their reincarnation in this world. In Sireniki, Orthodoxy, socialism, and native beliefs surrounding death and mortuary rituals and practice were syncretized. Nevertheless, of all the rituals I saw practiced in Sireniki, those surrounding death most closely resembled the ethnographic past.

Mortuary rituals and the system of beliefs associated with them ensured the passage of the spirit to the other side, the world of spirits, and protected the living from the ill effects of coming into contact with a spirit. After a Chukchi person died, the body was laid on the floor and covered with a white sheet. Elderly relatives kept vigil over the body throughout the first night. The next morning a divination took place. A newly carved walking stick was placed under the head of the corpse. Questions were asked of the corpse, and the stick was lifted. If the head lifted easily, the answer to the question was yes; if it was difficult to lift, the answer was no.

The first questions asked were practical: "Would you like to be buried next to your brother Ivan?" "Should we bury you on Saturday?" "Do you want Sasha to be the director of your funeral?" Once these considerations were taken care of, people asked more personal questions, or asked for predictions. "Will I marry Iura?" "Will I have more children?"[1]

The divination was described differently by different people; by one account, the asking was witnessed only by men, by another, women participated. Bogoraz describes this practice among the Chukchi in detail, including the orientation of the body and the fact that a man's head was lifted with a walking stick, a woman's with a scraper handle. As in the present, the primary questions concerned the "manner in which the body shall be disposed of" (Bogoraz 1904–9:522).

I attended four funerals, two for Yup'ik men and two for Chukchi men. They were very similar. During the vigil for a Chukchi man, relations and friends came with food for the family and the deceased. Each package was opened and a pinch of the contents was placed on a stone that rested on the stomach of the body (sometimes the stone was set at the head of the corpse). The most commonly given items were tobacco or cigarettes, cookies, candy, and tea. The family received fish, meat, canned goods, candy, coffee, tea, and other scarce products. Lying by the body were newly made tools: a walking stick, knife sheath, snow beater, adze, and lasso, as well as a newly made pair of *tarbaza*.[2] People often made a point of noting that in the past an entire suit of clothing would have been prepared for the body out of white reindeer skins, but in this instance the deceased's only new article of traditional clothing was his *tarbaza*.

After the vigil, which lasted approximately twenty-four hours, the coffin was brought in and the body dressed and laid out. The coffin was bound in reindeer lashing, carried from the room, covered with a red cloth, and placed on a trailer to be hauled out to the graveyard. The younger adults walked behind the coffin and the elderly and children rode on the trailer. At the graveyard the coffin was carried up the steep slope and lowered with the reindeer lashings into an open grave. Then all of the lashings were cut into small pieces and buried in a hole at the head of the grave. The newly made tools were laid in the grave, and everyone threw a small rock onto the casket. Then the younger male relatives shoveled dirt into the grave.

After the grave was filled, a cup was broken and placed on top to ensure a well-equipped passage for the soul to the other side. Everyone took a seat on the surrounding ground and proceeded to eat various prepared foods and drink a little vodka. Younger adults and adolescents did not drink, but simply put a finger in the vodka glass and then in their mouths. After eating and drinking, everyone circled the grave clockwise before walking away. In the winter everyone rolled in the snow at the bottom of the hill, and the deceased's *kamleika*, a cloth anorak, was torn to pieces and pushed into the snow. Upon returning to the village, we stepped over a small fire and our clothing was rubbed with reindeer sinew, which was then thrown to the wind.

To my surprise, the appearance of Newcomers at a Chukchi or Yup'ik funeral was very rare. Once the director of the state farm came to the wake of a very prominent Chukchi *brigadir*. The reaction of the participants to his appearance was one of surprised shock. The director's tears at the graveside was a topic of discussion for weeks. This fact speaks not only to the divisions in the community but also to the high degree of structure surrounding the appropriate participants in a funeral. For this reason I attended the funerals of only close friends' relatives or people whom I personally knew well.

The mourners adhered to several cultural practices during the mourning period. Among the Yup'ik, kin were not supposed to drink alcohol until after the funeral, and until three days after the *pominki*, the memorial ceremony held later, they were not supposed to sew, do laundry, or laugh. When people left a house where someone had recently died, they put a commode in the middle of the floor and a suitcase on the bed, so that if the spirit came into the house it would believe someone was there and would leave. One was not supposed to cry, because a spirit who heard someone crying might refuse to leave the village. After a death, people burned a small root, if one was available, and spread the smoke throughout the corners of their apartments to ward off the spirit of the dead.

The Hugheses analyze this process among the Yup'ik as a means of defining the line between the living and the dead.

> The destroying of the personal effects of the deceased, the slashing of cloth-ing and bodily covering, the placing of pebbles to make high mountains, the fumigating of clothing and person in smoke, the ritual washing, and, per-haps as dramatic as anything, the preventing of the deceased soul's seeing homely and familiar actions if he returned to the village on those nights just following death—all these can be seen as actions intended to make unam-biguous the status of the living as opposed to the dead. (Hughes and Hughes 1960)

These basic patterns of mortuary practice were followed by Yup'ik and Chukchi alike, although some of the details differed. The Yup'ik might ask a Chukchi corpse questions but they did not divine with their own deceased, and they had a huge feast in the house as soon as the coffin was carried out. Before Sovietization, the Chukchi funeral on the tundra extended for several days, with a feast, the slaughter of a reindeer to pull the spirit's sled to the other side, drumming, and singing, before finally the corpse was cremated.[3] From oral ac-counts, I gathered that the practice of cremation was discontinued in Sireniki in the 1960s.

Before the Soviets exerted their influence, the Yup'ik laid their dead on the ground, sometimes covering the body with rocks to protect it from foraging animals. In 1990 it was still possible to see skeletal remains of these ancient "burials," which were located a few kilometers from the village. The Yup'ik also left grave goods (beads, pots, tobacco, tea, etc.) to provide the spirit with provisions for its journey to the other side. I assume that the early Russians preferred to have the bodies actually buried, and that was when the graveyard on the hillside near the village was started. Undoubtedly coffins became mandatory at that time, too.

In contemporary Sireniki, the Chukchi revisited the grave seven days after the funeral for *pominki* to "put the spirit to rest": they built a fire, shared a meal with the deceased, and placed a reindeer antler at the head of the grave. The Yup'ik held *pominki* every fall at the graves of all their kin, but they did not place antlers on the graves.

The Chukchi still occasionally held *pominki* on the tundra—they were held in 1988 for a highly respected *brigadir*—but the exigencies of contemporary village life made *pominki* impractical for many families. The timing of the *pominki* was probably an Orthodox Christian tradition that the Yup'ik and

Chukchi had woven into their own practices and beliefs about death and the afterlife. Russian Newcomers held *pominki* nine days after the burial and then again forty days after the burial. This was an old Russian Orthodox practice that survived the Revolution as a "tradition." Newcomers believed (probably correctly) that it was rooted in folk belief.

One of the *pominki* in which I took part was at the grave of a friend's elderly uncle. The party consisted of the deceased's two sisters, mother, niece (brother's daughter), and nephew (sister's son). The women unwrapped the provisions they had brought: *kompot* (canned or stewed fruit), cookies, to-bacco, cigarettes, reindeer meat, *chebureki* (meat pies), bread, candy, tea, and vodka. Two pieces were broken off of each item, one to be placed on a small fire of tundra grasses and the other on the grave. Then the rest of the food was consumed. One of the women worried about how good the food would taste, as it was forbidden to eat any of it until it was shared at the grave—"not even a taste for salt!" After everyone had eaten, a bottle of vodka was opened. A small drop was spilled for the spirits, and then each person drank a glass. As at a funeral, the younger adults simply tasted the vodka from their fingers. Vodka was a very important part of the ceremony; the *pominki* had been postponed a week so they could be held on a weekend, when alcohol was sold.

At the conclusion of the feast, the leftover food was distributed among the members of the party. Everyone circled the grave clockwise and walked away. One of the aunts mentioned as they left that her mother had forgotten a lot of the ceremony. "She should have introduced each of us as we walked up to the grave and wiped our chests and backs as we left." Nina was also disturbed when her mother started to cry at the foot of her sister's grave. "Enough, you shouldn't cry here!" she admonished. If the spirit caught her crying, it would return and be dangerous to the living.

The spirits of the dead, especially one's ancestral spirits, played a part in the people's daily lives. One paid respect to spirits by feeding them, placing a tiny pinch of special food or a drop of alcohol in the woodstove or in the corridor of the house. Whenever a new package of candy or cookies was opened, the first portion was given to the spirits to ensure a good relationship and thus ward off misfortune, such as sickness or untimely death. When a friend heard that I was having bad dreams, she advised me to buy some candy at the store to feed the spirits in my apartment. I followed her advice, and the bad dreams stopped. This practice was so routine among the Chukchi and the Yup'ik that no new food entered a household that was not first given to the spirits.

Bogoraz describes this practice, among both the Reindeer and Maritime Chukchi, as the "zealous" offering of foreign products to the spirits. Such products as "tobacco, sugar, flour, or bread, and even alcohol" were placed as offerings to the spirits (Bogoraz 1904–9:370). Even in contemporary Sireniki, when I gave people some of the foreign supplies I had brought with me—candy, cigarettes, tea, coffee—they immediately opened the package and made a small offering. Not to offer such treats immediately would be dangerous. A group of visitors from Alaska were particularly confused when their *baidara* crew poured what the foreigners thought was very precious alcohol into the sea as an offering to the spirits.

One young Yup'ik woman pointed to this practice as proof that her people were preserving their culture. Upon returning from a trip to visit relatives on St. Lawrence Island, Alaska, she despaired, "They still speak Yup'ik, they dance the old dances, and they sing the old songs. We do none of those things." A few days later, however, she consoled herself with the thought that "they don't pay respect to their dead. They are Christians and they don't feed their ancestors anymore. I guess we have lost some things, but they have also lost."

Individual beliefs about spirits, death, and burial varied. "Every family has their own way of doing things," one woman said in response to a question about funerals. Practices differed among individuals, families, and cultural groups, yet a fundamental system of Yup'ik and Chukchi cultural beliefs persisted. Yup'ik, Chukchi, and Newcomers accommodated Soviet ideology and practice. They covered coffins in red cloth, erected red stars, and buried their dead in the ground. Meanwhile, the spiritual relationship between the living and the dead continued to hold meaning for the Yup'ik and the Chukchi, as their mortuary practices testify.

The Metaphysical World

The world of the Chukchi and Yup'ik was filled with metaphysical presences. As with many traditional beliefs, many younger people chose not to believe their elders' stories about their contact with the creatures of the other world. The young people did not believe stories of giants and giantesses, dwarfs, evil walruses, fire-breathing creatures half reindeer, half human, and miniature mice.

After shamanism was declared a crime against the people, shamans could no longer practice their calling in Sireniki. Now there was no professional negotiator between the human and spiritual worlds. However, this does not mean that shamanistic practices had disappeared, for they had not. Although shamanism as a "technique of ecstasy" in which the soul was believed to leave the body and travel to the heavens or the underworld was no longer practiced,[4] some shamanistic knowledge survived in other people.

Several individuals in the village were called shamans, but what these people practiced resembled more a type of sorcery than shamanism.[5] One elderly woman was renowned for her ability to cure illness or to make people ill.

Her daughter, who was particularly skilled at raising foxes, was rumored to cast spells on the other workers' animals, making them less productive or giving them fatal diseases. Some of the workers on the fox farm sought the advice of another "powerful" woman, who would give them protective incantations to counteract the bad influence.

Amulets and talismans were quite common and were often worn by the herders on their belts or simply kept in the house. Once an elderly Yup'ik woman showed me an amulet that resembled the guardian talisman that Bogoraz pictured. The figure, made of wood, was in anthropomorphic form. When I inquired about the meaning of the figure, she shrugged off the question; either the information was secret or she did not know it. A Russian described to me how the Yup'ik woman had used the figure to cure an illness in her family. Bogoraz described a similar amulet as protecting its wearer or being able to transform itself into a living creature to provide assistance (Bogoraz 1904–9:341–42). A woman told me how a similar figure was used to predict the weather. Her mother would hold a needle on a string above the figure, and the way the needle swung told her what the weather would be.

Although most of the believers in the spirit world were among the older generation, younger people did not scoff at the supernatural. Anatolii Kashpirovskii, a Russian "healer," filled soccer stadiums and huge concert halls throughout the Soviet Union with his followers in the 1980s and early 1990s. With a few passes of his hands he "purified" cups of coffee, glasses of tea and water, and bottles of hand lotion, which were then guaranteed to produce miracle cures. He was so popular that he had a weekly television program. Viewers had only to listen to his hypnotic voice to be cured of whatever ailed them; he could even repair their watches. The villagers devoutly watched his program and then saw with their own eyes the "miracles" he had performed for people in the village. This type of healing, by a power that emanated from the hands, was very popular in Sireniki. A Russian acquaintance, Sasha, visited a healer during his vacation to the Primori'e region and returned with the healer's power to cure with his hands, or so he claimed. He went about the village "healing" everything that ailed his friends.

In the fall of 1990 a spaceship landed in the village. Unfortunately, I was enjoying a cup of tea in my kitchen and missed the entire episode, but according to reports, a spaceship was sighted near the fox farm and a large metallic creature came out of it. When one of the workers approached, the creature returned to the spaceship and flew away. That evening a number of people in the village claimed to have witnessed the landing and for weeks the "visit" was the main topic of conversation among believers and skeptics alike. The elderly began to reinterpret their former experiences with glowing objects on the tundra and the beach as UFO sightings.

The scientific validity of the phenomena I have described is not important here; what is important is the people's interpretations of those events. Even the younger people, trained in scientific empiricism in Soviet schools, chose to interpret various phenomena according to their own culture's conceptualization of the world. I took an informal poll and found that 60 percent of those polled had seen the UFO themselves or believed it had landed, and told stories of how their parents and grandparents had seen such phenomena before the Soviet era. Fully 95 percent believed that Kashpirovskii cured illness and that Sasha had gained the power to cure people with his hands.

The Yup'ik and Chukchi fed the spirits not only out of habit but out of the belief that this practice kept them and their family members from harm. Young adults frequently sought the advice of their elders on proper behavior toward the spirit world. Although the Yup'ik, Chukchi, and Newcomers were educated in the empirical world of Soviet socialism, their own cultural beliefs about the way their worlds were constructed continued to hold meaning for them.

[4]

The Economy: Production
as Cultural Space

> Yesterday a woman from the state farm warehouse came into
> the skinning *kollektiv* and told the women that because they
> had been working so hard, the state farm was going to reward
> them with candy from the warehouse. Everyone was excited
> about receiving the candy, which had not been available in
> the store for some time. The bonus was for the very long
> hours the *kollektiv* had worked skinning the more than forty
> walruses brought in by the hunters. Candy? For women who
> support their families on very low wages? I was personally
> outraged, and approached several women to ask what they
> thought of the proposal. The response was overwhelmingly
> positive; "Candy hasn't been in the store for weeks—what a
> great reward!" Obviously the tenets of a workers' revolution
> don't apply to native women's labor in Sireniki.
>
> EDITED DIARY ENTRY, JUNE 1990

The Formal Economy

In 1928, under the name Udarnik, Sireniki was organized into a hunting artel,
a cooperative arrangement that was the forerunner of the collective farm.
The members of the artel were Yup'ik sea mammal hunters (Providenskii
Rai'onny Gosudarstvennyi Arkhiv [PRGA] 1959). In 1944 a *rybatovarish-
chestvo* (fishing cooperative) was added to the hunting cooperative, and it

became a kolkhoz (collective farm). Its charter officially stated, "The territory of the kolkhoz Udarnik includes: the Provideniia region, occupying the valley of the lower and middle portion of the Kurupka River, and the upper middle portion of the Ioniveem River, including the village of Sireniki. Located on the right bank of the Rakakyrgynveem River, 6 kilometers south of Imtuk Lagoon, 45 kilometers from Provideniia by sea and 50 kilometers by land." By 1959, 50.4 percent of Udarnik's gross income was produced from sea mammal hunting, 24.2 percent from reindeer herding, 8.7 percent from fishing, 1.9 percent from trapping, and 14.8 percent from "other." At that time Udarnik's material assets included "5,116 reindeer, 157 sled dogs, 41 black fox, oil rendering plant, warehouse with refrigeration, fish smoker, three whaleboats with motors, one motorboat, eight *baidary*, eleven dogsleds, and one C-80 tractor," for a population of 338 people, primarily Yup'ik. In the 1960s, with the addition of a fox farm, Udarnik was organized as a sovkhoz (state farm).

The Sireniki state farm as it operated through the early 1990s provided primary infrastructure support to the village. Everyone in the village (except for the few new cooperative workers) officially worked for the state farm and received his or her monthly wage from it. The state farm and its administration operated under a model of paternalism that had its roots in the Soviet belief that northern indigenous peoples were like naive children in the primitive state of precapitalism. The "children" had to be educated in the ways of socialism, which in the 1930s became synonymous with Russification.

The farm director, Slava, a veterinarian from Belorussia, viewed himself as the patriarch and the citizens of the village (especially the native peoples) as his personal wards. Slava was an affable fellow, and many agreed that he had been a "very good veterinarian" for Udarnik; but people complained that now that he was the state farm director, "he promises a lot and delivers very little." Most of the problems the state farm faced were inherent in its structure and had very little to do with who was director at any particular time. All revenues were paid to the state and then allocated to the various regions. The amount the state returned to Sireniki was dwindling as the costs of transportation, material goods, and fuel rose. Other factors that affected the success of the state farm were the state monopoly of the fur industry, which resulted in small revenues for the village; the global increase in synthetic lubricants and cosmetic base materials, which lessened the need for sea-mammal oils; and the rising costs of animal feed and vaccines. Thus Slava's inability to solve the state farm's problems was more a function of the global economy than of his personal character or skills.

Subordinate to the director were the various administrators who managed both the economic and the infrastructure activities—the fox farm, the reindeer herds, the hunters, the school, the hospital, the dairy, the heating plant, the warehouse, the stores, the nursery, and so on. Each of these activities were part of a *kollektiv*. The *kollektivy* created work schedules, organized labor, and provided a platform for workers to voice their concerns to the various administrators about the way the *kollektiv* was managed, its pay scale, its access to products, and the like.

Each *kollektiv* was organized into several brigades. Brigades were the actual working groups. The people who composed a brigade worked together on a daily basis. In the reindeer herders' *kollektiv*, for example, there were three brigades, each with approximately ten to seventeen herders (all male) and 2,000 reindeer. The brigade was headed by a *brigadir*, the person responsible on the tundra for the daily work schedule. *Brigadiry* were older, more experienced herders who had received formal training in Anadyr. A *brigadir* decided when and where to move the herds, which deer to slaughter, when to give vaccinations and medications, the work schedules of the herders, and the timing of the yearly slaughter. He also kept a record of all the reindeer, their births, sex ratios, and losses. Next under the *brigadir* was an apprentice called the *starshii olenevod*, "older herder," and under him were the other herders.

A *brigadir* answered directly to the *zootekhnik*, whose training was in animal economics and veterinary medicine. The *zootekhnik* provided professional advice to the *brigadiry*. In Sireniki the *zootekhnik*, Ivan Lebedev, was a young Ukrainian with considerable empathy for the herders; he often acted as a buffer between them and the state farm system as a whole. Ivan was ultimately responsible for fulfilling the state farm's yearly plan as it concerned reindeer herding.

Other *kollektivy* were similarly organized. The sea mammal hunting *kollektiv* consisted of five brigades, each one headed by a *brigadir*, or *baidara* captain, but record keeping was handled by the state farm economist (number of animals caught, equipment orders, and off-season work assignments). Even the school, headed by a "director" who was subordinate to the state farm director, was organized into a teachers' *kollektiv* that evaluated its members' teaching performances, voiced opinions to the school and state farm director, set the curriculum for each grade in the school, and organized parents' meetings.

The *kollektivy* functioned not only as work organizations but as units for the distribution of scarce goods. When limited numbers of items in great demand became available, such as snowmobiles, television sets, shoes, and washing machines, a certain number were allocated to each *kollektiv*, which then decided how the goods should be distributed. Decisions might be based on a worker's need or length of service; sometimes the *kollektiv* held a drawing.

I observed *kollektiv* distribution on several occasions. Once, for the sake of "fairness," the school distributed shoes on the basis of a random drawing. Each pair was described on a scrap of paper, the scraps were put into a box, and the teachers took turns drawing them out. The result was that single women received size 40 men's boots, married men received size 28 high-heeled shoes when their wives wore size 34, and teachers without children received baby shoes. People eventually took matters into their own hands: friends traded shoes, acquaintances bought shoes from one another, and the rest were traded to anyone in exchange for alcohol or cigarettes. This distribution was typical of the lengths to which villagers went to make sense out of the nonsense of the system.

The *kollektiv* "that one belonged to was intricately bound up with the statuses and rights which were linked to one's nationality" (Anderson 1995:106). Some *kollektivy* in Sireniki had an exclusive Chukchi, Yup'ik, or Newcomer membership, and these *kollektivy* were hierarchically organized within the state farm (Humphrey 1983:433). Although the Soviet ideology did not condone economic stratification, in practice the Russification project inevitably conferred advantage on the Newcomers.

Among the 413 people who were registered by the local government as workers, 51 percent of all Newcomers held professional positions while 49 percent held laborer positions. By comparison, 85 percent of the native population held laborer positions while 15 percent held professional positions. Professionals, or "specialists," included doctors, administrators, accountants, teachers, electricians, nurses, mechanics, chauffeurs, animal technicians, and day-care workers, all of whom required some formal training or degree and often received higher wages than laborers. Unskilled laborers included herders, hunters, and fox farm workers; janitorial, swine, and dairy workers; heavy laborers and utility plant workers.

Of the white-collar professionals (101 in all) there were nine top administrators (director of the state farm, first Party secretary, director of the school, two doctors, hunter and herder administrators, director of the warehouse, and mayor); eight (99 percent) were Newcomers and one, the pediatrician, was a Chukchi woman.

As the figures indicate, some Yup'ik and Chukchi individuals were given opportunities for economic and social advancement through higher education; but when Newcomers controlled the infrastructure (schools, state farm administration, local government, hospital, warehouse, transportation, and supplies), the majority of opportunities open to the Yup'ik and Chukchi were laborer positions or native economic endeavors, such as fishing, trapping, skin sewing, reindeer herding, and sea mammal hunting. Although these positions sometimes paid well (a reindeer *brigadir* was paid more than a schoolteacher), they still had low status.

In contrast, the Chukchi and Yup'ik placed a high cultural value on this type of labor. To be a reindeer herder or sea mammal hunter was in many ways synonymous with being a man. However, although these jobs conferred status within their own cultural systems and were glorified by the slogans of the workers' state, in practice they were at the bottom of the Soviet job hierarchy. This stratification of the economic system reinforced the structural and cultural boundaries between the Newcomers and the Chukchi and Yup'ik peoples.

Reindeer Herding

Reindeer herding was an exclusively Chukchi endeavor.[1] The administrators of the reindeer herding *kollektiv* were the *zootekhnik*, the *brigadiry*, and a spokesperson elected by the herders from their ranks. This organization was decidedly different from the Chukchi's own model of herding. Before Soviet intervention, the economic unit of reindeer herders was the "family." The family might be only spouses with children, or it might be an extended family of brothers, cousins, sons, and sons-in-law.[2] It might also include young men in bride service or poorer men who were working to acquire their own herds (Bogoraz 1904–9:587; Kis' and Lebedev 1978:123–24). This structure was reorganized during collectivization. The Soviet system of reindeer herding, "production nomadism" (*proizvodstvennoe kochevanie*), was juxtaposed to "nomadism as a way of life" (*bytovoe kochevanie*), which was the system in Sireniki before Soviet intervention. This was a distinction made by Soviet social scientists between the traditional form of nomadism among the indigenous herding peoples, in which the entire family moved together and lived with the herd, and the contemporary Soviet form of nomadism, in which the herd was tended by a brigade (Boiko 1987; Vitebsky 1990).

There was an ongoing debate among social scientists in the Soviet Union over the health and welfare of nomadic peoples. V. A. Vasiliev and his colleagues (1966) state that early in the process of collectivization it was believed that the "transition to a sedentary life was one of the fundamental conditions for the building of socialism." It is not surprising that the urban proletariat found it difficult to understand the nomadic lifestyle; except for the Committee of the North, most believed that settling nomadic peoples would greatly improve their standard of living. The dilemma facing these social strategists had been how to balance a settled life with a viable reindeer herd, a valuable economic resource. The suggestions for this transition included such propositions as truck and livestock farming (which proved impossible on the tundra) and the mechanization of herding through the use of tractors and mobile

Reindeer *brigadir* and *starshii olenevod* survey their herd. (Photo by Aleksandr Kalinin.)

homes. "Production nomadism," although originally rejected by herding peoples, was made more palatable by the "shift system" of herding, one month on and one month off. That was the system used by Udarnik.

Social Organization of the Reindeer Brigades

The Sireniki brigades were designated First, Second, and Third, and each occupied a specific range within Udarnik's territory. The First Brigade had fifteen herders and 2,188 reindeer, and was the second in distance from the village. The Second Brigade was the closest to the village, with ten herders and 2,380 deer. Farthest from the village was the Third Brigade, with seventeen herders and 2,305 reindeer. In Sireniki, the brigades consisted primarily of men ranging in age from 16 to 40 years; the *brigadiry* were usually in their 40s or early 50s.

The herders had a special relationship with the reindeer. They lived with them, protected them by spending hours on the tundra watching the herd's movement and scanning the horizon for signs of wolves and bears, and moved their camps in coordination with the natural movement of the herds. The

Pithing a reindeer in a state farm tundra slaughter. (Photo by Anna M. Kerttula.)

herders were responsible for the general welfare of the reindeer. They took this responsibility very seriously, not only as Soviet workers and the protectors of their state farm's ability to fulfill its plan but as the keepers of their culture's wealth.

The reindeer of each brigade were perceived to have their own character, which was attributed in part to their environment. In the two brigades closest to the village, the reindeer were considered to be *dikii* (wild). Their feeding grounds were less than optimal, as the terrain was rocky and the animals had to wander farther to find forage. The herders had less control over these deer and on occasion, when unattended, some reindeer would wander off. Herders were known to spend months recovering lost reindeer.

Some reindeer, many of which were orphaned, had been hand-fed and cuddled since birth. This treatment not only made them more docile but gave them the special status of a herd pet.

Brigadiry were reputed to know every animal in the herd on sight, and before Sovietization, every animal had a name and a genealogy. The original system of naming was based on color variation, antler morphology, and occasional pet names (Bogoraz 1904–9:74–76; Kis' and Lebedev 1978:123–27). During my fieldwork, *brigadiry* admitted to knowing many of the deer but not all. Younger herders knew their own personal deer by their antler morphology and color variations but seemed to have no interest in learning the traditional system of naming. The state farm identified deer by clipping their ears with the sign of the brigade. Before collectivization this method was used to mark family herds (Bogoraz 1904–9:84; Vasilevich and Levin 1951) as well.

There were no explicit state farm or cultural rules that mandated the social composition of the brigade. Herders could choose the brigade they wanted to join, and kinship was a factor in a man's choice. As a result, brigade members tended to be related. Women worked exclusively on brigades where they had kin connections. As we have seen, older women set up their summer *yarangi* near the brigade in which they and their husbands had worked before their retirement or in which their sons and daughters were now working. Young women worked as cooks for their father's or husband's brigade, and one young woman worked year round on the same brigade as her husband. This pattern was a cultural one, resulting from the personal preferences of the women and their kin, as well as Chukchi social rules for appropriate behavior.

The state farm rarely overruled people's choice of brigade, even though brigade composition was ultimately the responsibility of the state farm director. Ivan Lebedev made recommendations to the director, and considered the personal choices of individuals to be a top priority in brigade assignment. His opinion was that, generally speaking, the herders themselves should decide their own brigade composition with little interference from him. Many herders worked on their father's or uncle's (both maternal and paternal) brigade, while others choose to work with brothers and some with school classmates. One Chukchi man, a *vezdekhod* driver, chose to work on the brigade of his deceased father. One woman expressed her desire to have her husband, who was a carpenter and stayed in the village, work as a *vezdekhod* driver on the brigade where she, her mother, and several other kin (male and female) worked in order to create an "all-Chukchi brigade." This was a dream expressed by many of the herders, that they would have their reindeer returned to them, or that they would purchase them from the state, and be able to control their herds themselves. When I returned to the village in 1994 the dream had still not been realized, and it remains unfulfilled to this day.

The brigades also had Newcomer members, but Newcomers did not herd. These men exclusively drove the *vezdekhody*, transporting herders to and from the tundra, supplying the brigades with food and equipment, carrying mail, recreational materials (magazines, newspapers, television sets, videos), and fuel for the diesel generator, and moving equipment and herders to new foraging areas with the herd. The Newcomers refused to work more than the eight hours a day they were being paid for. They did not eat or sleep with the herders. The one Chukchi driver, by contrast, was known to work long hours regardless of pay, presumably because he had a personal (and cultural) stake in the continued success of the herd. The herders appreciated his devotion to the herd; many of them wished they could have only Chukchi drivers.

I became aware of the separation between the Chukchi herders and their Newcomer drivers when I accompanied the reindeer herders to the tundra my first summer in Sireniki. Every evening when the herders prepared for dinner and bed, the Newcomers did not share food with them and slept in their vehicles. Ivan Lebedev was the sole exception; although he was Ukrainian, he ate and slept with the herders and was generally liked. The Newcomers gave various excuses for their self-segregation: the Chukchi undercooked their food (they "might get sick"); they had brought their own provisions; they had brought vodka, but not enough to share. The classist and racist undercurrent of their behavior was not lost on the herders and reinforced the cultural and structural separation of the two groups.

I traveled, ate, and slept as the herders did, and I seemed to be generally accepted and admired for it. On only one occasion did anyone question my presence: a *brigadir* who didn't know me complained at mealtime, "Now the Russian will watch how we eat." Natasha, a friend of mine, spoke up for me: "What are you talking about? She eats meat just like we do." That was the end of the incident, and later the *brigadir* spoke in a friendly way to me.

The factors that controlled a brigade's social structure were complex. An important one was the herders' preference to work in familiar territory and to be in the company of family members. When I asked how they chose a brigade, a herder's most frequent response was "Friendship"; yet out of forty-two herders, over two-thirds had a family connection in their brigade. Of course, many friendship and kinship ties overlapped.

A herder's work schedule was organized into two seasons, summer and winter. In summer, which began at the calving season in late March and lasted until after the main slaughter in October, herders were scheduled to be with the reindeer without break (although they were allowed to take personal leave or vacation time). In order to avoid long family separations, some wives (accompanied by children) and other family members chose to work on the tundra in the summer. Such jobs, which were paid by the state farm, entailed working skins, cooking, and operating radios. This option, however, was open only to women who did not have year-round jobs, such as those with small children who were not required to work, retirees, people with vacation time, and schoolchildren on summer vacation. For women who had full-time work in the village and couldn't afford vacation time, the herders' long extended absence from the village over the summer put a strain on personal relationships. Such stress, as we have seen, was one of the main factors in the reindeer herders' high rate of bachelorhood (Donskoi 1987).

Families highly valued the time they spent on the tundra, and people whose

[89]

jobs forced them to stay in the village envied them. At the end of the school year, many Chukchi children joined their families on the tundra. They were sent off atop a *vezdekhod* amid the pomp and circumstance of the village brass band and waving relatives. Memories of a childhood spent on the tundra were recounted fondly by adults. Lifelong bonds of friendship, often between kin, were created and strengthened by summers spent wandering creek beds, exploring hillsides, fishing, picking berries, and fighting off mosquitoes. Young boys trained to be herders and young girls learned to scrape, tan, and sew skins. Whether they actually became herders or continued to sew skins as adults seemed irrelevant. These group memories, when recounted over a cup a tea or a glass of vodka, were always accompanied by a smile, a warm look, and an understanding of something precious shared by all that participated.

The winter season provided a sharp contrast to the activities of the summer. Families returned to the village, where the children enrolled in school and the women returned to village jobs (if they had them). The elderly returned because life on the tundra in winter was too harsh for them. The state farm administrators viewed winter on the tundra as a hardship both physically and mentally, and indeed it was.

In Sireniki's extreme Arctic climate, where temperatures often reached −60°F, the ground lay under 10 feet of snow, and 50-mile-an-hour winds howled, winter herding was very difficult and often dangerous. The herders in winter were on a rotation schedule of one month on the tundra and one month off in the village—the shift system. Men coming in from the tundra were immediately recognizable by the condition of their faces, blackened by frostbite. Although the skin peals and repairs itself, this condition year after year dried and aged the skin prematurely. Endless stories were told about narrow escapes from the weather, wolves, and treacherous terrain.

Even under such arduous conditions, the rotation system was not always followed. In the winter I rarely saw a *brigadir* or *starshii olenevod* in the village. Although the state farm allowed *brigadiry* to rotate just as the herders did, most felt an intense responsibility to their young and often inexperienced herders, as well as to their reindeer. A *brigadir* might leave for a day or two of respite, but he hurried back long before a month was up.

As in the past, the day-to-day activities of the brigade followed the natural cycle of the reindeer: birthing in spring, nursing newborns, traveling to summer pasture areas, the fall rut, and winter feeding. These activities were punctuated by spring and summer vaccinations and various state farm slaughters. The first slaughter, scheduled for late summer, after the calves had been weaned, provided meat and the high-quality skins needed to make the herders' clothing. The second slaughter was of unhealthy animals who were unable to make the journey back to the corral at Sireniki for the fall slaughter. The fall slaughter, at the village, was for the benefit of the state farm. This slaughter provided meat and skins to be used in Sireniki and to be sold to the warehouse in Provideniia. There the meat was made into sausage and the skins were processed into leather to be resold throughout the region.

A more recent activity, introduced when the relaxation of the borders opened Chukotka to trade, was the collection of the reindeer horns, or *panty*. The ideal time was the spring, when the horn was just beginning to grow and was still covered by a velvety soft fur. Many people in Asia believed this horn was a strong medicine with spiritual powers, and it was in high demand. The main trade in horn was with Korea (via Alaska), where dried reindeer horn fetched up to $40 a pound (Bernton 1993).

The first shipment out of Sireniki was in 1989. The profits from this shipment were brought back in the form of Western goods, which the state farm sold back to the reindeer herders and their families. The herders' exclusive access to these imported goods created some tension in the village.

This was not the reindeer herder's only special privilege. In the village store a *polka olenevoda* (herders' shelf) was stocked with "deficit goods." When products in short supply became available in the store, the herders were on the tundra and couldn't purchase them, so a few were set aside for the herders' return to town. This arrangement may have been reasonable, but some people resented it. The reindeer herders seemed to be getting special treatment, especially when those goods were no longer available for open sale. Some people viewed the shelf as just compensation for the hard and dangerous work the herders did, but the sea mammal hunters believed their work on the ocean was just as dangerous, and nobody was putting anything aside for them. Further, the cashmere sweaters, cigarettes, radios, fine knives, leather jackets, and jeans were displayed openly in the store, a constant reminder of difference.

The goods on the herders' shelf were available to others in the village by alternative means, if not by outright purchase. One could get a herder who was a relative to purchase something, or trade for an item. Also, herders often made gifts of items from the shelf. In fact, the complaints against the shelf came primarily from Newcomers, who had little contact with Chukchi people and so had the least access to the items on the shelf. They complained even though they had access to all of the same items through a pseudo-black-market system. People frequently pointed to that shelf as one of the inequities of the system and as a significant indicator of group differences.

There had been dramatic conceptual and structural changes in the social organization of reindeer herding under the Soviet system. The brigade in 1989–90 reflected a dialogue between Soviet structure, embodied in the hiring policies of the state farm, and Chukchi social structure and culture. Soviet structure redefined the activity of reindeer herding within its own definition of a

[91]

worker state. When this new system was administratively labeled "production nomadism," herders were redefined as workers who had work schedules and were paid a monthly wage by the state farm. Their accountability was no longer to an older relative but to a bureaucrat, in particular to the *zootekhnik* or director. Ultimate decisions concerning the health, reproduction, and feeding of the herd were made by state farm administrators rather than by the herders themselves. Although social relationships on brigades were constructed along kinship lines, kinship no longer formed the elemental structure of the relations of production. Work was rewarded under the Soviet concept of productive labor and fulfillment of the yearly production plan.

In Sireniki the reorganization of a family nomadic herding system into a *kollektiv* brigade system of wage work had been effected over forty years. The contemporary structure had points of flexibility, however, and it was at these points that the Chukchi reworked the system. Most brigades were a loose affiliation of kin ties, and people often worked on brigades that used territory historically occupied by close kin, such as parents, in-laws, or parents' siblings. The location of the herds on the tundra and the reindeer's own natural cycle precluded total control of the herders' movements and activities by the state farm. Herding provided a place where the Chukchi could be Chukchi: speak their own language, work by their own rules, and act in culturally appropriate ways without interference from the Soviets.[3]

Sea Mammal Hunting

Sea mammal hunting, pursued exclusively by the Yup'ik (plus a few related Newcomers), had taken a different form from herding in the state farm structure. Because hunters lived year round in the village, they were under constant surveillance by the state farm. At sea they had an opportunity to cross the border into U.S. waters, so the state subjected them to more regulations than the Chukchi.

The hunting of sea mammals was the first economic activity in Sireniki brought under the Soviet structure. In 1928 the Soviet state created an artel and enticed Yup'ik hunters to join by offering guns, ammunition, food supplies, and later boats and motors. The structure of the artel was based on Yup'ik social structure in that hunting crews, each representing one *baidara*, consisted of related males (Chlenov 1973; Hughes and Hughes 1960; Krupnik 1993; Menovshchikov 1962, 1964).

The difference between the Yup'ik hunting system and the Soviet artel was that, although the mode of production was still Yup'ik, the means of production and the products now belonged to the state. The daily catch was sold to a representative of Moscow rather than distributed to the hunter's family and trading partners. Acquiring Western goods and participating in the global economic system was nothing new to the Yup'ik, as they had been trading with other indigenous peoples, Russian traders, and U.S. whalers for several centuries. What changed was Yup'ik control. The state now determined the hunting schedule, the composition of *baidara* crews, and which animals would be hunted. The Yup'ik became defined as workers and accordingly were subjected to direct state control.

The sea mammal hunting *kollektiv* was organized along the same principles as the reindeer *kollektiv*. It was divided into five brigades and one cooperative (formed in 1990; cooperatives are discussed in more detail later). Each brigade, represented by a *baidara*, consisted of a minimum crew of four men, two *strelki* (shooters), one motorman, and the *brigadir*, who steered the *baidara* and held the position of captain. The ultimate safety of the crew was the *brigadir*'s responsibility. All of the equipment the brigade used (motors, guns, ammunition, fuel, and *baidary*) belonged to the state farm.

Like all other *kollektivy* in the village, hunting crews worked six days a week. The hunters received a monthly wage from the state farm, between 100 and 700 rubles. In addition they received a bonus for each sea mammal brought in.[4] Like other state workers, they received a pension upon retirement, set at age 55 for men (Gurvich 1987). The largest portion of sea mammals' meat was used as food for domesticated foxes, but it was also one of the major sources of food for the people in the village. In 1990 the year's catch consisted of walrus, bearded seal, harp seal, ringed seal, gray whale, and beluga.

As in the case of the reindeer herders, the hunters' activities were still controlled by the natural cycle of the animals they hunted. As we have seen, the terms the Yup'ik used for the months and seasons often described events in the natural cycle of animal life that were culturally and materially significant. The month of March, or spring, was *belok*, which signified that the seals were giving birth. This was when sea hunting started again in the village. Although the Yup'ik hunters knew about ice hunting and could describe how it had been done in the past, they also knew that it was very risky, and they chose not to do it any more. One middle-aged hunter, Nikolai, did walk on the ice, hunting seal in the winter and ducks in the spring, but he was the exception.

The hunters and the village as a whole looked forward to spring with much eagerness. Winter often meant being forced to do menial tasks for the state farm while one waited out bad weather or waited for the animals to migrate. Before Soviet control, hunters spent the winter covering the *baidáry* with new skins, cleaning the hunting equipment, cleaning their cabin, and hunting and trapping on land. They enjoyed these activities even after Soviet intervention, as they fitted within a Yup'ik hunter's conception of appropriate work. It was difficult, however, to keep all of the hunters who worked for the state farm occupied with culturally appropriate tasks, so some of the younger hunters were forced to accept work in other *kollektivy*.

Hunters who had received appropriate training worked at the garage, at the fox farm during the fur harvest, or as drivers; but for most of them, winter meant working at the coal furnaces. Although they had time to play cards and dominoes, gossip, and drink while they waited for the huge furnaces to need tending, this was considered a repugnant job. The furnaces, which provided heat for the entire village, were fueled with a very low-grade brown coal. The dust, the smell, and the soot of the coal permeated everything in the village. The men worked twelve-hour shifts, hauling wet, frozen coal into the furnace room, scraping slag out of the furnace onto the floor, throwing the coal into the fire, and then hauling the slag away in wheelbarrows. It was physically very demanding labor, extremely dirty, and probably dangerous to the workers' health because they could not avoid breathing coal dust.

In addition, the coal was very volatile. In 1990 a pile of brown coal stored outside the furnace room exploded after methane had built up over the winter. The explosion blew out several windows in the village apartments and the school. The entire village shook as though from an earthquake. People in the village recalled such explosions in previous years; one of them had blown a worker apart.

For all these reasons, some hunters preferred to go without wages for a few months in the winter rather than be assigned to the furnaces. It was easy to understand why, after several months of fueling the furnaces, the hunters eagerly awaited the chance to resume hunting.

Spring was anticipated especially by retired hunters. Old hunters scaled the small hill in Sireniki and sat on a bench under the bay windows of the village hospital, scanning the horizon through binoculars in search of the migrating game. They carefully studied the movement of the ice, the winds on the ocean, the clouds, and signs of walruses, seals, and whales, looking forward to the coming hunt. The main topic of discussion on a March day was how good it would be to have the taste of fresh walrus in your mouth again.

For the hunters themselves, the day began with the sun. They got up and went to a window that looked out onto the sea, observed the weather conditions, and decided if it was a good day to go hunting. For this reason, as well as for enjoyment of the view, the Yup'ik always tried to get apartments that faced the sea. People judged each other's apartment on the basis of this criterion. Hunters who did not have a view of the sea complained that they had to get up, dress, and walk down to the beach before they could determine if it was a hunting day or not.

Weather permitting, the men gathered around the hunters' cabin and planned the day's hunt. If a hunt was decided upon, many returned home to dress in warmer clothing, as spring hunting meant from ten to twelve hours on the open ocean in temperatures that were still below zero.

Hunters' clothing consisted of a combination of Yup'ik and Western items. On a particularly cold day, the hunters doned *kuklankas, kamleikas,* sealskin pants, and fur hats. Garments made from skins provided better protection from the cold than the imported cotton and wool clothing.[5] Similar clothing was used by the Chukchi herders, and the state farm had a *kollektiv* of women who sewed these garments from reindeer and sea mammal skins. Because the women of the sewing *kollektiv* were paid by the piece, however, the skins were often poorly stretched and the garments were heavy and cumbersome. Most men preferred garments that were prepared by their own family members.

The mother of my friend Ada demonstrated the difference between *kollektiv* and homemade garments for me. She showed me a *kuklanka* she had worked and sewn herself next to one from the *kollektiv.* When she placed the state farm *kuklanka* on the floor, it stood on its own without support. When she tried this with her own work, the *kuklanka* collapsed into a pile like a silk scarf. As Ada and I stood there laughing, her mother shook her head. If Igor' (Ada's husband) fell overboard in the state farm *kuklanka,* she said, he'd sink like a rock.

Elderly women objected to the state farm garments for another reason: the women who sewed them might be menstruating. Yup'ik once believed that sea mammals found menstrual blood and its odor repugnant. Younger women and men were not concerned about this pre-Soviet taboo, but elderly women contended one of the reasons for the poor hunts of recent years was that the hunters might be wearing clothing sewn by a menstruating woman. Therefore, arthritis-plagued elderly women continued to sew garments for their husbands, sons, sons-in-law, and grandsons.

Once dressed, a crew reassembled at the hunters' cabin around eight or nine o'clock. Hunters collected the equipment, prepared the motor, and went for fuel, constantly checking the weather and the condition of the sea. The pace of activity accelerated. The crews consulted one another about the weather conditions and the best hunting sites. Some carried supplies to the *baidary* lining the beach, while others prepared the *baidary* to be rolled into the water. The artifacts of the hunt had changed—ivory to steel, lances to rifles, *puk puk* (sealskin floats) to plastic floats, sails to motors—but otherwise the scene was much as it had always been. One could see the material changes, but the activity itself, based on the knowledge of the sea, the weather, and the behavior of the animals, remained Yup'ik.

Around ten o'clock the border guard arrived on the beach to check the hunters' passports and list their names. This was an ongoing irritation to the hunters. They complained that the guards refused to get up early and as a re-

Oleg Isakov, Yup'ik hunter, harpoons a walrus. (Photo by Aleksandr Kalinin.)

sult their hunting day started very late. By the time they got to the hunting grounds, it was often past the peak hour for hunting. The practice of checking passports was, officially, to keep track of who was in the boat for "safety reasons," but most believed it was to keep them from crossing over to Alaska.

Once the Soviet formalities were out of the way, the members of the brigades gathered on the beach at their *baidary*. The *baidara*, which had been set on its side to dry after the previous hunt, was righted, loaded with equipment, and then rolled down the beach on floats or pieces of walrus or whale fat, which kept the skin over the keel from tearing on the gravel of the beach. Once it was in the water, two of the hunters lifted the outboard motor into its place in the motor box, and then each hunter positioned himself in the *baidara* for the day's hunt.

The spring hunt concentrated on the migrating walrus herds that had moved north for calving and for feeding in the cool Arctic waters. Although because of its size and value walrus was the main prey, any sea mammal (spotted or ringed seal, bearded seal, or beluga) was fair game. Pulling away from the beach, the *brigadir* headed for the ice floes where the animals were feeding while the hunters searched the horizon for signs.

Baidara crews tie up to discuss
the day's hunt. (Photo by
Aleksandr Kalinin.)

I had always had a great desire to experience the hunting process myself; for various reasons I had never been able to do so in Alaska. So while in Sireniki, I approached a series of *brigadiry* to ask if I might join their brigade on a hunt. At first, being aware of Yup'ik menstrual taboos, I went into lengthy discussions of how I would not participate during my menstrual period. One *brigadir* simply looked at me and said, "Oh, Anna, those are really ancient ideas." Be that as it may, I was able to persuade only one *brigadir*, Viktor Menkov, to let me go on several hunts.

This reluctance may have been due to a combination of reasons: most brigades were composed of related males and close friends and didn't like strangers with them; I would take a spot in the *baidara*, either adding weight or replacing a more productive person; many had been in the navy and had a general feeling that women on a boat were bad luck. Viktor's brigade had many unrelated members and he was fairly young.

Interestingly, women seemed more disapproving of my journeys than men. Their disapproval took the form of mild teasing. I believe this was due to my crossing the gender barrier, rather than any Yup'ik beliefs about women and hunting.

[97]

Carcass of a gray whale on the beach at Sireniki. (Photo by Anna M. Kerttula.)

I was with the hunters one spring morning when a walrus surfaced about fifty yards from the *baidara*. The chase was on! The brigadier tried to anticipate where the walrus would surface next in an attempt to steer close enough for the hunters to have a good shot at it. As the *baidara* moved closer to the walrus, the *brigadir* slapped the water with a piece of metal (rubber might also be used) attached to a handle in imitation of the sound of a killer whale's fin. The walrus turned to face its aggressor. When the *baidara* was close enough, the hunters shot around the head of the walrus to confuse and stun it. They were careful not to kill it, as a walrus has negative buoyancy and will sink if it stops swimming. This was a critical moment in the hunt. The *brigadir* had to get close enough to the walrus to be within harpoon range, but not too close, as the animal might turn on its attacker. A walrus could have easily punctured the skin cover of the *baidara*, or upset it, leaving us in icy water that produces hypothermia in less than fifteen minutes. Finally the hunter threw a harpoon with a float attached into the walrus. It held, and the hunters were free to kill the walrus without fear of losing it.

[98]

Once dead, the walrus was tied to the side of the *baidara* and dragged to the nearest ice floe to be butchered. This was one of the conveniences of spring hunting—by butchering the walrus during the hunt, hunters could get up to four animals into the *baidara*. In summer and fall, the only option was to tie the walruses (again up to four) to the sides of the *baidara* and drag them to shore. The drag of the carcasses in the water made for a long and tedious trip.

At the ice floe, the crew pulled the walrus on the ice and butchered it, removing the skin, fat, meat, and ivory. Only the head and some bones were left to decompose on the ice. After the butchering process the *baidara* was washed of all blood, as it "might be detected by other prey." Then the hunters were off in pursuit of new prey.

The hunting process was very similar for all sea mammals except whales. Seals were not as aggressive as walruses, often hiding in ice floes and changing direction underwater in order to evade their pursuers. Their fat allowed them to float for some time even after they were dead, so hunters could shoot them from a fair distance before getting close enough to harpoon them.

After a successful hunt, the animals were brought to the beach for butchering (in summer and fall) and processing. When the brigades arrived at the beach, the entire village showed up with buckets and knives in hand, hoping to get a choice piece of the day's catch. The hunters had to sell the entire animal to the state farm, but they could purchase meat and fat back from it. The whole process took place directly on the beach in front of the village. The hunters were given first choice, either because they were the first on the beach or because of unstated cultural rules; they frequently chose the breasts of small seals and the flippers of small walruses, both of which were considered delicacies. In 1991 meat was priced at 1 ruble per kilogram, while fat cost 50 kopeks per kilogram. Retirees received 20 kilograms per year free of charge. The meat and fat were weighed on a scale at the beach and the amount of the sale was deducted from the worker's monthly wages.

Meat that wasn't immediately sold was taken to the fox farm for feed. The fat was put in huge pits to be rendered, processed, and sold for machine grease and cosmetics. The hide was turned over to the skin-sewing *kollektiv*. A few walrus hides that would be used as covers on *baidary* were defatted by a specialist, while the smaller sealskins were worked by the *kollektiv* to be made into clothing.

In the summer of 1990, one of the hunting brigades reorganized itself under new legislation as a cooperative. Now it operated as a quasi-private brigade, and the state farm paid a higher price for the sea mammals the brigade brought in. At that time a state farm brigade was paid 80 rubles for each walrus, the cooperative 800. However, the cooperative had to rent its

[99]

equipment, such as motors, and buy gasoline from the state farm, and the members were no longer eligible for pensions. For these reasons, none of the other brigades went co-op. The one that did was made up of young hunters more interested in independence and profit than in security.

Social Organization of the Hunters' Kollektiv

The hunters' cabin, located on one of the hills along the shoreline, functioned as the Sireniki socialist equivalent of a *qashgiq* (men's house).[6] There they stored guns, ammunition, motors, and basic supplies. The hunters gathered at the cabin in the morning to prepare their supplies for the daily hunt. In the off-season they built and repaired the *baidary* there. Meetings of their *kollektiv* were held at the hunters' cabin, and men met there informally to socialize, play cards, and wait out inclement weather. Outside, facing the sea, were several benches where the older men sat watching the ocean for signs of game or just to enjoy the spectacular view.

Although women were not actually forbidden to enter the cabin, there was a general sense that it was male space. Women went there infrequently. One woman who worked for the hunters' *kollektiv*, keeping track of equipment and meat sales, sometimes went to the cabin to socialize with the hunters; seamstresses from the skinning *kollektiv* went to sew the seams for the *baidary*; and occasionally young women went in search of their husbands and boyfriends. Although the cabin was the focus of Yup'ik male activity, it had no ceremonial function.

Entering the hunters' cabin in the winter, one walked into a fury of activity. On one side of the cabin, men were building or repairing *baidary*, repairing motors, and cleaning equipment. Wooden frames for *baidary*, 15 to 20 feet long, were being readied for recovering with newly dried walrus skins. The hunters were compensated by the state farm for each completed *baidara*.

In Sireniki, walruses that the *brigadir* determined to be of the proper quality for covering a *baidara* were marked by a red string sewn through the skin so the women of the sewing brigade who joined in defatting the skins would recognize it as special and leave it to the more experienced workers. Once the fat was removed from the skin, it was stretched on a frame and split in half. Because walrus skin is very thick, it was possible to double its size by splitting it and leaving the two halves connected in the middle; one skin was then large enough to cover an entire *baidara*. It is interesting to note that in Sireniki men were the ones with the skills in skin splitting, whereas on St. Lawrence Island, women split the skins. Each group thought the other was peculiar.

Meanwhile, in other parts of the cabin men were involved in carpentry, motor repair, the spiral cutting of sealskins for rope, and the soldering of har-

A split walrus skin dries in the sun in preparation for being fashioned into a *baidara* cover. (Photo by Aleksandr Kalinin.)

poons. Sireniki's harpoons had a distinctive form that the hunters claimed was superior. According to them, Sireniki was the last village on the coast where hunters still manufactured their own toggling harpoons. Through this and all the previously described activities, the hunters' cabin provided a space for cultural reproduction among men.

Although some hunting brigades had crew members who were not related, the primary organizational feature of the hunting crew remained kinship. Menovshchikov (1962) and the Hugheses (1960) relate *baidara* crews to patrilineal clan structures, but such clans did not seem to play a part in the contemporary composition of crews. As I mentioned earlier, Yup'ik crews seemed to give no preference to patrilineal over matrilineal kin. When I specifically asked about this, the hunters responded, "Anyone who wants to hunt with us can." Yet if one carefully examined the composition of the *baidara* crews, a pattern of kin preference emerged.

Records of the state farm from the 1950s and 1960s revealed that in those years most members of the hunting brigades a were not related (Krupnik 1993). This was undoubtedly a function of the Soviet influence in the structuring of labor in the new state farm. By the 1990s, however, the *baidara* crews were again evolving into kin-based hunting units. It is possible that during the period of intense collectivization, when the collective farm was changing into a state farm based on reindeer herding, men were appointed to crews by the state farm. Such crews were probably based on what the Newcomer director viewed as appropriate criteria, such as age, individual skills, and experience. As time passed and the state farm became less concerned about micromanaging hunting crews, the Yup'ik themselves began to rearrange themselves into crews of their liking. For whatever reasons, by 1991 the Yup'ik hunting crews were based on a more Yup'ik pattern of social organization, rather than the Soviet concept of worker organization.

The ways in which the Yup'ik reclaimed their own cultural space on the hunting crews evidenced their ability to adapt to change without losing their sense of self. The kinship among crew members, the distribution of sea mammals among hunting crews, and the activity of hunting itself gave the Yup'ik some cultural identity within the Soviet system. Although they did not achieve the autonomy of the Chukchi herders, they were still able to maintain core Yup'ik concepts of hunting and the sea.

The Fox Farm

The fox farm was the state farm's second largest enterprise (after reindeer herding). It was started by the state farm in 1958 with black foxes. In 1967 the director decided to switch to silver foxes, as they were more profitable and easier to handle. The fox farm employed thirty-two people year round and several additional workers during the fur harvest season. The workers were primarily women, and only native women worked in laborer positions.

In 1990 Slava, the director of the state farm, claimed that the foxes were not profitable and that the farm was barely breaking even, but that he continued to support it because it provided jobs for the women in the village. It should be noted that the state set the prices for furs, as for everything else. All local fox furs had to be sold to the state fur company in Irkutsk. In Irkutsk the furs were processed into garments, which were then sold in Russian cities or exported to foreign markets for hard currency. The state company kept the price of furs artificially low in order to make a large profit when they were sold abroad. Thus local state farms received an artificially low price for their products.

The women who worked on the farm recognized the inequity of this system of skimping on the costs of producing a natural resource in order to reap manufacturing profits. They did all of the hard physical work of breeding, feeding, slaughtering, and tanning; and just at the point where they could begin to get a just return by sewing garments for sale, the skins were taken by the state. A first-grade, first-size fox fur was sold to Irkutsk for 108 rubles (approximately $18 in 1990). The same fur sold in Anchorage, Alaska, for over $150 retail. This was a difference of over $130 for just the raw fur alone. The profit increased dramatically as the furs became garments. In claiming his benevolence for continuing the "unprofitable" enterprise for "the good of the women in the village," the state farm director was, in reality, minimizing a structural inequity of the Soviet system.

Upon starting her work at the fox farm, each woman was given 85 foxes for which she was responsible. She made all decisions concerning their feeding, cleaning, breeding, and slaughter. Because bonus pay was given to women on the basis of the number of pups born and the number of adults slaughtered, women with more knowledge and facility with the foxes received higher pay. Some women consulted the supernatural world for help with their foxes, and one woman who was uncannily (as some perceived) skilled in the husbandry of foxes was suspected of using spells to kill other women's pups.

Work on the fox farm followed the natural seasons of the animals. Fall was when decisions about breeding were made, winter was for the slaughter, spring was busy with the birthing of the pups, and summer was for growth and vaccinations against disease. These creatures were highly susceptible to disease. The local veterinarian explained to me that they could get colds just as humans did, so nonworkers were discouraged from entering the farm. On occasion an outbreak of rabies occurred, at which point the farm was quarantined.

The fox farm was considered the heaviest work, but the compensation was considered good. The average fox farm worker received approximately 4,000 rubles per year. Meeting the physical demands of the work, however, was very difficult for many of the women.

The farm was a series of long buildings called *korpusa*. A *korpus* held more than a hundred cages of foxes, each representing one male fox or a female and her kits. The *korpus* was supported on stilts, which allowed the fox droppings to fall to the ground under the cages. Each woman had responsibility for seventy female foxes and fifteen males. The foxes were bred in the spring, and the litters averaged between five and ten kits. During October and November, each woman decided which of her foxes to keep for breeding and which to slaughter for their furs. Those from the new litters that she judged would not be productive were slaughtered, along with those foxes past their reproductive years (approximately four to five).

The job required workers to hand-carry numerous buckets of water and food to each cage. In winter they had to chop the meat, primarily walrus and whale, from the frozen carcasses with a hatchet, then add water and grain to make a gruel, and cook it. The women complained about the hard work and

Klava scrapes the fat from a fox pelt. (Photo by Anna M. Kerttula.)

the tremendous toll it took on their health. They blamed the work for back-aches, the flu, colds, and bad health in general; but because the pay was good and they were able to make their own decisions, none was willing to quit.

Although all the furs were sold to the state, each worker was allowed to pur-chase a fur after he or she had worked a certain number of years for the state farm. They paid 150 to 300 rubles, depending on the quality of the fur. The workers might make the fur into a hat, collar, or some other garment for their own use; sell it to pay bills or to purchase something else; give it as a gift; or trade it. Occasionally one heard complaints that a Newcomer had taken ad-vantage of someone while he was drunk and had bought a fur for a 15-ruble bottle of vodka. This was technically illegal, but a formal complaint was rarely lodged with the local council because such complaints were seen as futile. Be-sides, no one wanted to cut off access to the Newcomers' vodka through less one-sided transactions.

The Informal Economy

Several theories have been advanced to explain the informal economy—what was referred to in the Soviet Union, as elsewhere in times of scarcity, as the black market. Katherine Verdery (1991) labels the rationale of the seemingly

Iuliia grades the finished furs before shipping them to Irkutsk. (Photo by Anna M. Kerttula.)

irrational socialist system as the accumulation of "allocative power." According to Verdery, redistibution is the central legitimizing principle of socialism. The socialist system, and therefore the Soviet system, monopolized the means of production and the social product in order to redistribute this product through the bureaucratic apparatus according to Party priorities. So as not to confuse the socialist form of redistribution with other forms designated by anthropologists, Verdery labels this type of redistribution "bureaucratic allocation." Because some sectors of the economy were more strategic than others (heavy industry and armament), they were allocated more of the resources. This system accounted for the immense shortages of resources in nonstrategic sectors, most notably consumer goods, in socialist economies.

Parallel to this allocative economy was the "second" (or informal) economy, which, although not officially sanctioned by the state, was allowed to operate, theoretically to placate and therefore help control the workers / consumers. This second economy, in Verdery's view, functioned as an oppositional space

[105]

within the socialist system. Although the development of the second economy is partially controlled by the formal economy, I propose that in Sireniki the second economy, which consisted primarily of native subsistence activities, was not directly "oppositional" or counterhegemonic but cultural. The second economy in Sireniki was a space in which the Chukchi and Yup'ik could reproduce their cultures within the constraints of the Soviet system.

Personal Reindeer

Each state farm brigade included some reindeer that were the personal property of individuals. This circumstance provides insight into the points of tension between the formal and informal economic systems, or the Chukchi system of reindeer herding and the Soviet state farm system.

Personal ownership of reindeer was part of even the early stages of collectivization. Like the collectivized peasants who were allowed to use some land to grow their own crops, the Chukchi in Sireniki were allowed, as Nadia described earlier, to keep a certain number of reindeer. The state ideology was that these nomads would eventually evolve into a "higher" form of social development, and in the future all reindeer would be held collectively by the state. The Chukchi, however, never "evolved" out of the "stage" of owning personal reindeer. Although the number of privately owned reindeer was small, the system of personal reindeer remained in place.

The size of an individual's "herd" was limited primarily by economic factors. The state farm required 100 rubles per year in compensation for each personal reindeer in a herd, and this amount was automatically deducted from the workers' pay. The payment was to reimburse the state farm for vaccinations, extra feed during the winter, and grazing on state farm lands. Because the average wage in the village was 6,000 rubles, one person could not support very many deer. In Sireniki the largest personal "herd," comprising thirty-six reindeer, was owned by a *brigadir* who received an average wage of 7,500 rubles a year and paid approximately 3,600 rubles per year to support his herd, or 48 percent of his income. He was able to afford that amount because his wife worked and helped support the family. He considered it necessary to have a large herd in order to meet the cultural and social obligations he felt toward his family and friends. Such a large number of personal reindeer was impractical for most people; most families generally kept only one or two animals.

Social factors, too, limited the number of deer any individual could keep. Personal reindeer were still looked after by the herders. The herders refused to look after large numbers of other people's reindeer in addition to the state-owned reindeer. I suspect this was another reason why *brigadiry* had the most personal reindeer. They had more resources, including the influence needed to get herders to help with the herding of their animals.

[106]

The state farm persevered in its attempts to control the system of personal deer through various mechanisms, including Soviet ideology. Some people sold their reindeer to the state farm for 2.81 rubles per kilogram as a sign of their support. One Chukchi woman, the secretary of the regional Communist party who had come from Anadyr for the 1990 fall slaughter, told me that she sold her personal reindeer to the state farm because "it's my duty as a Party member to support the state farm by selling the reindeer I don't need." Party member or not, she retained an emotional connection to the tundra and took part in various Chukchi rituals. It was also very important to her to stay in Sireniki and participate in the fall slaughter. She wanted to contribute her labor to the state farm as a "good Communist," but she also wanted to take part in the slaughter of personal deer as a reconfirmation of her Chukchi identity.

The *zootekhnik* kept copious notes on the numbers and locations of all personal deer in the state farm herds. It was his responsibility to ensure that the state farm herds remained numerically stable, and if reindeer wandered off or died during a winter storm, a percentage of personal deer were assumed to have died as well. If, for example, 10 percent of the First Brigade's herd of 2,188 were personal deer and if 100 deer died during the winter, 10 of those deer were considered to be personal deer.

In such a case, and in consultation with the *brigadir*, the *zootekhnik* canceled ten personal deer from the brigade's listing. If only five personal deer had actually died, the remaining five living deer would be transferred to the state farm's ownership. Most *brigadiry*, having the largest number of personal deer, agreed to take the brunt of the loss. Rarely did someone with only one deer lose it in this statistical accounting process.

Some people, primarily Chukchi herders, were personally attached to their reindeer and were loath to relinquish ownership to the state farm as part of a yearly death calculation. Because the system was based on statistical calculations and had no reference to actual dead reindeer, it was easily manipulated. As long as the numbers and gender percentages of a herd remained stable, the state farm did not concern itself with the actual individual animals.

A few Yup'ik also owned deer, and although they did not recognize their reindeer, they believed that the Chukchi *brigadir* did (which may or may not have been true). The Chukchi thought so too, although they had the added advantage of having kinsmen watching over their reindeer for them. Both groups depended on the *brigadir* for information about and advice on their own reindeer—when their reindeer had given birth, the gender of the calf, whether the reindeer was ill and should be slaughtered, whether it had died. Animosities flared in years when many reindeer died and some Yup'ik families lost all of their personal reindeer. These individuals spread gossip that their reindeer had been unfairly taken away. Yet the gossip never escalated to a formal complaint.

While herders did what they could to maintain the genealogical integrity of the personal reindeer herds, the state farm's system of accounting made it inevitable that some personal reindeer became state farm property. Although it was difficult to synchronize the two systems, they continued to coexist. Through the actions of the herders themselves, the personal reindeer system was preserved within the state farm structure.

Just as the Chukchi made gifts of reindeer among themselves, non-Chukchi people obtained personal reindeer through gifts, trading, and occasionally purchasing from owners (although buying a reindeer was considered not at all the proper way to acquire one). Most "purchased" reindeer were exchanged for Newcomers' vodka. Although such transactions were illegal, the authorities seldom took steps to stop them. I purposely use the word "purchase" rather than "trade" because alcohol commonly substituted for money in the village and was used to purchase many things in short supply, such as furs, cigarettes, and clothing. These commodity exchanges did not imply any kind of social relationship beyond the transactions themselves, whereas trade involved reciprocity and implied a social bond, often the ancestral one of partners who exchanged reindeer products for sea mammal products.

This is not to say that the majority of reindeer owned by Newcomers were obtained through purchase; gifts were exchanged among the Chukchi, the Yup'ik, and the Newcomers. Most Newcomers, however, interpreted reindeer ownership very differently from the way the Chukchi and the Yup'ik interpreted it. Newcomers did not have the intricate social and trading relationships that existed between the Chukchi and Yup'ik. They were unaware of the symbolic and spiritual relationships created through reindeer trading and gifting.

Because several elements of the personal reindeer system were survivals from pre-Soviet days—such as the naming of personal deer and their use in gifting and trade, and the distribution of their meat among kin—one could say that the economy of personal reindeer was an adaptation of the Chukchi culture within the structure of the evolving collective and later of the state farm.

Subsistence Resources and Their Distribution

Although the state farm controlled the primary resources of production, such as reindeer, sea mammals, and farmed foxes, an active subsistence economy survived. Most of the resources of the subsistence economy were gathered, although they included fish, water fowl, and personal reindeer as well. In some areas of the Soviet Union, workers gathered mushrooms and berries for the state farm, but in Sireniki, gathered resources were family property.

The primary resources that were gathered were various greens, mushrooms, and berries. Greens included *nunivakh* (*Rhodsola atropurpurea*), *khu-*

vykhsii (Polygonum triptercarrum), and the root of *petushok (Pedicularis ver-ticillata)*. Most of these foods were gathered in the spring, when the plants were most tender. Small quantities were gathered at a time, mostly by elderly women on afternoon walks. Children in the village learned quite young which plants were edible by accompanying their grandmothers on such outings. Older children might also gather greens for their infirm parents as a special treat.

Greens might be eaten fresh, boiled, or pressed to remove the moisture and frozen for storage. They were eaten as an accompaniment to walrus or fish (which was eaten frozen). They were considered a delicacy, especially by the elderly, and were recognized as a good source of vitamins. Although at family meals everyone might consume the greens, most people reserved them for the elderly because old people found Russian vegetables unpalatable, and tradi-tional greens might be their only source of some vitamins.

While most greens were gathered in a catch-as-catch-can manner, collect-ing mushrooms and berries called for planned after-work or weekend outings by the whole family. Only the Yup'ik and Chukchi ate greens, but everyone enjoyed mushrooms and berries. In fact, Newcomers were connoisseurs of mushrooms and took great delight in gathering and preparing them. During mushroom season the village's obsession with the fungi bordered on fetishism. Everyone talked about mushrooms: when they were going to pick them, where they had picked them, whether there were more this year than last, how they would prepare them and why. Even reindeer were crazy about mushrooms. Herders described the reindeer as "out of their minds" when they came upon a field of mushrooms. The reindeer would charge the field, jumping and frol-icking until an observer could believe the mushrooms had a psychedelic effect on the animals.

Mushrooms were preserved by drying; when they were to be eaten they were rehydrated and then sautéed or put in a vinaigrette and served as a side dish. No holiday table, especially if guests were invited, was considered com-plete without mushrooms.

The most frequently gathered berries were *brusnika (Oxycoccus microcar-pus*, wild cranberry), *golubika (Vaccinium* spp., blueberry), *moroshka (Rubus chamaemorus*, cloudberry), and *chernika (Empetrum ingrum*, crowberry). They might be eaten on the spot, taken home to eat with sugar, sugared and stored in large jars, or made into preserves. The Newcomers, Yup'ik, and Chukchi all prepared berries in the same manner. The Newcomers' favorite berry was the *brusnika*, second only to mushrooms in pleasing the palate; the Yup'ik and Chukchi liked the *moroshka* best. Unfortunately, very few *mo-roshka* plants had survived the destruction of the local tundra environment by the villagers and their motorized vehicles.

The Yup'ik and Chukchi frequently discussed childhood memories of berry picking and preparing *agutuk*, a frozen mixture of whipped fat and berries still prepared in many Alaskan villages. I never saw this dish prepared in Sireniki, although people spoke of it with relish.

Roots and branches were also gathered. *Zolotoi koren'* (golden root, similar to a wild ginseng) was brewed to make a tea or used to flavor vodka. As in other areas of the world, this root was considered to have medicinal qualities and was given with small quantities of vodka to relieve the symptoms of a cold or flu. Another root, whose name I failed to get, resembled a twisted tree stump and was burned to ward off evil. The branches of another small Arctic conifer were burned in the house as an air freshener, especially to overcome the smell of spoiled meat.

Beach grass was gathered and dried to use as a liner for skin boots. The dried grass acted as a wick for moisture, keeping the foot dry and thus less susceptible to frostbite. If it got wet, the grass could be dried and reused throughout the winter. By midwinter, beach grass became quite a valuable commodity; people who had not had the foresight to gather grass in the summer often went among relatives and friends asking to borrow some.

Morskaia kapusta, or kelp, was one of the few resources that still followed a subsistence primary distribution pattern. Villagers gathered it along the beach after a storm; hunters collected it fresh when they took a break from their spring hunting. The fresh kelp was tastiest. The hunter stood on an ice floe holding a long wooden stick with a crosspiece nailed to the end. He thrust the stick to the bottom, twisted it to entangle the kelp around the crosspiece, and brought it to the surface. Hunters gave the kelp to their wives or mothers, who then distributed portions to other family members.

Waterfowl were caught primarily with nets, but a few people caught them with bolos. The only species I personally saw people eat was the crested auklet.[7] It was the most prevalent bird in the rookery near the village.[8] Hunters set nets at the rookery to catch the birds as they emerged in the morning from their tunnel nests. So few birds were caught that they were rarely distributed farther than the hunter's own table. Berries did not need to be distributed because they were so plentiful that anyone who wanted them could collect them. Kelp was plentiful, but fresh kelp, because it was gathered only by hunting brigades, was distributed by the female head of household to family members, trading partners, and friends.

Hunters also visited the rookery to gather murre eggs. These large speckled eggs were highly valued but were very dangerous to collect and were therefore scarce. Hunters scaled the sea cliffs from a *baidara* to collect the eggs, and more than one young man had fallen to his death. Eggs, like greens, were often saved for the elderly, but because of their value they might find their way into the trading system. When eggs were in season, people would subtly remind others of any obligations due.

Mollusks, a favorite treat, were gathered on the beach after a storm. Such delicacies as crabs, sea cucumbers, clams (also extracted from the stomachs of walruses and consumed), and a variety of sea plants that I could not identify were collected by people of all ages.

Salmon, especially salmon caviar, was controlled by the state farm, but all other fish (Dolly Varden and other trout, whitefish, and northern pike) were subsistence resources. Fishing was a passion for Newcomers, Chukchi, and Yup'ik alike. All the villagers enjoyed fishing on the open water in summer and through the ice in winter. Weekend fishing trips were savored as much or more than mushroom outings. The social patterns of fishing, however, differed from the pattern of gathering, which was primarily a family activity for all three groups in the village.

Among Newcomers, fishing was primarily a male activity. Men went fishing with male friends, especially in the summer. The traditional fishing trip was replete with Slavic male bonding rituals, such as the preparation of *ukha* (fish soup), the drinking of liberal amounts of vodka, and storytelling. All were very much savored by Newcomers.

The Chukchi and Yup'ik had a different pattern. It was not uncommon for them to set up a fish camp along the shore of Imtuk Lake (6 kilometers from Sireniki), where pensioners could spend all summer tending nets and casting lines. Their children and grandchildren visited on weekends to resupply the camp, to fish themselves, and generally to enjoy some time away from the village.

Opportunistic fishing was also considered fun. On trips to the tundra, the *vezdekhod* driver might stop near a known fishing stream to let people try their luck. In this instance, a fishing pole was a carved stick about 16 inches long with nylon fishing line wrapped around it and a hook attached to the end. The line was swung over the fisherman's head like a cowboy's lasso and then released into the river. On one such occasion, the Arctic char were so thick that every time the line was thrown into the water, a char would be waiting at the other end. In fifteen minutes three people caught more than twenty char.

All groups went fishing alone. On a summer evening it was frequently possible to see a lone hip-wader-clad figure walking into the village with a knapsack bulging with fish.

Because transportation had to be organized, ice fishing was a group activity. On a clear, cold winter day Imtuk was dotted with *vezdekhody* and snowmobiles (personally owned) pulling sleds, all carrying groups of families and friends to fish. The catches of the day were pike and white-fleshed fish. These trips served to provide not only food but also an escape from the village. After weeks of being held inside by winter storms or work schedules, ice fishing was recognized as a psychological stress reliever.

In villages that were located on salmon streams, it was possible to fish for salmon, but no salmon came to Sireniki's river. Salmon fishing was a state farm activity, and all three groups participated. Salmon fishermen were organized into fishing brigades, which traveled seasonally to other villages. Salmon was available to the Sireniki villagers only through purchase from the state farm or through barter with fishermen, who were allowed to take part of the catch home with them.

Salmon and personal reindeer were the only subsistence resources the state farm took any interest in. As for the rest, the director exerted no direct control over their distribution or use. Indirect control was felt through work schedules, the availability of transportation, and the use of firearms, but these were minimal invasions into the subsistence system.

Subsistence resources were distributed in culturally appropriate ways. The primary pattern of distribution was among relatives. Depending on the availability of a resource, distribution could be expanded or contracted. Distribution started with the consumption unit, or everyone who was invited to dinner; extended to close kin and then to more distant kin; and finally it was extended to friends or to acquaintances in trade.

The few waterfowl that were taken were consumed fresh that day. Rarely were crested auklets frozen for later use. When a hunter brought home auklets for dinner, then, the birds would most likely be eaten by anyone who showed up at the hunter's home that evening. If there was only one or two, a hunter was likely to give them to the oldest adult female of his kin group (probably his grandmother), as auklets were a delicacy and people understood how much the elderly yearned for traditional foods. The general feeling was that younger adults, being accustomed to Russian foods, didn't require native foods for variety, and didn't appreciate them as much.

Because most kelp harvests were so large, a hunter would give his share to whichever family member came to the beach to collect the family's share of meat. That person would deliver it to the hunter's mother or the oldest capable female relative, and she would distribute it in a culturally equitable way, as she did most subsistence resources that were plentiful enough to share. Once the kelp was secondarily distributed, it was shared further among trading partners and friends. Fresh kelp was available at every Yup'ik and Chukchi table in Sireniki. Since most Newcomers did not view native food as food, Newcomers were rarely part of the distribution patterns.

The state farm system had no interest in the distribution and use of subsistence resources because they were not defined as production. The only interference in the subsistence economy came from the central government and concerned those resources listed in the Krasnaia Kniga, the Soviet version of the endangered species list. The people in Sireniki were familiar with the Krasnaia Kniga and for the most part avoided taking the species listed. This general lack of interest by the state farm and the Soviet system as a whole in controlling subsistence resources allowed the system of distribution to be defined in Chukchi and Yup'ik ways. Subsistence hunting, herding, and gathering formed a vital part of Chukchi and Yup'ik practice and were an integral part of their cultural reproduction and identity, which were intimately associated with food and food production.

The Newcomers' disdain for native foods was one of the ways they distinguished themselves as "civilized" and thus different from the Yup'ik and Chukchi. My Newcomer friends constantly admonished me for indiscriminately eating foods that were "bad" for me. The Newcomers were determined to classify native foods as inedible. One winter I became quite ill with stomach cramps and was taken to the village hospital. The Newcomer doctor immediately assumed I had eaten mollusks and poisoned myself. She ignored my insistence that I had not eaten anything harmful and gave me medication to induce vomiting. In the end, I was proved right when she discovered that I had broken some ribs, but only after several harrowing days of misdiagnoses and hectoring for my deplorable eating habits.

Blat

Everything that was not produced in Sireniki was brought in, either on cargo ships from Vladivostok, or by helicopter from Provideniia. Domestic goods were ordered by the administrator of the state farm warehouse; she stored them at the warehouse until they were sold in the two village stores (which were also part of the state farm). One of the stores sold produce and meat; the other sold household items, electronics, and clothing. In the eighteen months that I lived in Sireniki, fresh produce (lemons, apples, cabbage, chickens, and onions) arrived only a few times. When it did arrive, the store was so crowded that it was not unusual to wait several hours to buy three lemons or one chicken. The first time I waited in line for four hours in a village of 700 people to buy three lemons, I insisted on speaking to the director of the state farm. During our meeting I expressed my view that they should set aside a few hours to sell nothing but the specialty product, at a set price. Then everyone who wanted that item could come to the store at that time and the line would move more quickly. The director all but patted me on the head. "*Nu*, Anechka, where are you in such a hurry to get to?" My suggestion was never accepted because, my friends explained, time was not viewed as a commodity, as it is in Western industrialized cultures. Time was viewed as something everyone had plenty of.

These experiences taught me a great deal about waiting in line. It was a great place to talk to people, and I learned a lot about who controlled the goods and why not everyone in the village had to stand in line.

Because goods were shipped into Sireniki from Vladivostok only in summer, the warehouse contained all of the goods, both food and clothing, that were necessary for the following year. The administrator decided, sometimes in counsel with the state farm director, the chairman of the local council, and the state farm economists, when and in what quantity goods would be imported and sold. The cargo shipments were vital to the survival of the village, bringing everything from the year's supply of coal for the village furnaces to livestock feed. A particularly poignant episode that shows how dependent Sireniki was on these shipments occurred in the fall of 1990. Because of one mishap after another, the potato shipment arrived frozen, and Sireniki was without potatoes—the main staple of a Russian kitchen—for an entire winter. This was a grave situation because no other fresh vegetables or starches were available, and the canned food selection was minimal.

This was a particularly interesting case because of the layers of insight it provides into the Soviet delivery system. It was September when the ship arrived early one Sunday morning off Sireniki's shore. The captain called the warehouse administrator to ask for assistance in unloading the potatoes. The administrator was on a business trip to Provideniia, so the captain spoke to her husband, who stood in her place. Unfortunately, the night before was P'ianaia Subbota and the director's husband had a very bad hangover. He refused the captain's request for help. The captain was left with no option but to sail north with his cargo and supply the other coastal villages, then stop again in Sireniki on his return south. By the time he returned it was late October and the remaining potato cargo was frozen.

With a warehouse full of thawing and rotting potatoes, the state farm called upon every *kollektiv* for volunteers to help in sorting out the spoiled potatoes. For the extra work, people were given the incentive of being allowed to purchase a deficit item, such as jeans, a sweater, or chocolate, from the warehouse. The more days one volunteered, the more coveted an item one could purchase.

The villagers' reactions to this situation ran the gamut of their responses to the more obvious Soviet incompetencies. The older Party members, mostly Newcomers, thought it was a disgrace to have to bribe people to volunteer for such work. In *their* youth they had done such work for the "the good of mankind and the good of the Party." The next level of reaction was more practical. People drawn by the incentive wanted certain items in the warehouse and saw volunteering as a way to get them. The intelligentsia refused to play what they saw as a typical Soviet game. They intellectualized the situation, viewed the offering of goods as ludicrous, and thought the system had created the shortages

to extort labor from the workers. They were willing to forgo the goods to uphold their principles. Some adolescents and children went with their parents
to help and some refused—not out of loyalty to principles but out of apathy
or capriciousness.

It is difficult to conceive of the underlying current of frustration that was felt
in the village and undoubtedly all over the Soviet Union over situations like this
one. People in positions of responsibility were irresponsible, and the consequences for poor judgment or incompetence were nil. The situation was de-
moralizing, especially among the talented and highly educated. I spent hours
listening to confessions of frustration from people drunk and sober.

The warehouse was a long, tall building at the end of the village. It held
salt, sugar, flour, butter, rice, canned goods, dried fruit, tea, candy, chocolate,
frozen meats, storable vegetables (potatoes, cabbage, carrots, onions), barrels
of salted cabbage and carrots, much alcohol, cleaning fluids and soaps, furniture, appliances, china, throw rugs, towels, utensils, cooking pots, batteries,
toys, electronics, and clothing. All of these items were stored for sale in the
produce store and the household store.

In Sireniki, as all over the Soviet Union, access to material goods was determined by, and also created, a certain amount of social influence and power. In
areas where goods were scarce, one of the most powerful positions was that of
the warehouse administrator; in Sireniki, this position was held by a Russian
woman. Either through favors, social connections, or political position, certain
people (almost exclusively Newcomers) had access to warehouse goods outside
of the state-sanctioned channels. It was not unusual to be invited to a dinner
at the state farm director's house and be served food that had never been available in the store.

Some goods, such as sugar and alcohol, were rationed by the local council
and required a coupon for purchase. Other goods were sold only on special
holidays, such as International Women's Day (March 8), Revolution Day (November 7), and New Year's. Holiday goods—chocolate, canned meat, Indian
tea, hard candy, and sweetened condensed milk—were generally distributed
through the *kollektivy*. The packages were made up according to the number
of people in a worker's family. When the *kollektivy* did not distribute the
goods, or if an individual did not belong to a *kollektiv*, then the goods could be
bought at the *klub*.

It was hard to describe the frenzy that accompanied these sales. At least one
person from each family in the village showed up at the *klub* at 5:00 P.M.,
rubles in hand. The place was a mob scene—hundreds of pushing bodies, children yelling and running around, people shouting about who had stolen whose
place in line, and salespeople's complaints about people who held up the line
because they didn't have the exact change. Afterward gossip circulated about

who had behaved badly and who had gotten more than their share. Even though people complained about the system and how long the process took, no one tried to improve it because in the end, again, "Where are you in such a hurry to get to?"

Other goods were sold on a first come, first served basis, which gave an advantage to those who had social connections either in the warehouse or in the store itself. Here most native people had the advantage, because most of the stockers and sales clerks in the store were natives. They told relatives and friends when a particular item was scheduled to be delivered to the store for sale, or they held specialty items under the counter until selected people showed up.

The spirit of *blat* (connections, pull) permeated the economy. The electrician would repair the warehouse administrator's light fixture or the plumber would put in a bathtub in return for access to the goods in the warehouse— goods that were unavailable to others, or just inconvenient to buy because of the long wait in line at the store. People with *blat* got better apartments, or first access to new telephone service, or novocaine (denied to others) when they had their teeth worked on. Sometimes *blat* was as simple as showing up at the dentist's office toting a bottle of good cognac and a salami; at other times it might be getting customs officials to look the other way when you loaded a cargo plane with several tons of caviar to be sold in western Russia. This type of activity was endemic all over the Soviet Union. As Verdery (1991) points out, *blat* was allowed to operate because it provided people with goods and kept them from rebelling against the system.

At one point the regional government in Provideniia sent out the new head of the Party to investigate and control the corruption in the village. This individual said that the corruption was quite severe, but rather than arrest people, he preferred to have them set the system straight. Such investigations would scare people enough to stop their activities for a while, but in a matter of months, when Provideniia forgot about it, they started anew.

Although many goods were extremely scarce in Sireniki, others were much more readily available there than in the western parts of Russia. A certain number of goods were allotted to the northern regions without regard for the fact that their populations were considerably smaller than those of the western regions. As a result, Newcomers bought some items and shipped them out to family members in the West to furnish their retirement homes or to be sold on the black market for a considerable profit. This activity exacerbated the animosity between Newcomers and native people. Local people complained that the Newcomers not only had better access to scarce goods but were supplying their families in the West with products meant for Sireniki people.

Liuda, a Newcomer, had worked for over thirty years in the North and would point to her years of service to win a spot at the top of her *kollektiv*'s distribution list. It seems that over the years Liuda and her husband had managed to secure so much furniture and so many washing machines and other appliances that people joked that her family included the entire population of Russia west of the Urals. Of course everyone assumed she was selling for profit much of what she bought. The ideology of socialism was quite strong among many local people, and profit-making ventures were certainly antisocialist. Because Liuda held herself up at every public meeting as a Party member and model Communist, local people considered her a hypocrite, and she was the butt of many jokes and much gossip.

One day Liuda stopped Tania, a young Chukchi woman, on the street to admonish her for purchasing more than one set of scarce linen sheets at the store. Tania, who was preparing for her wedding, said to me, "I told her I would be sleeping on these sheets in this village, not sending them back to Ukraine." This was the reaction of most native people to the Newcomers' practice of buying deficit products in Sireniki and sending them to their relatives for resale at a healthy profit. By 1991, in an attempt to control this type of trade, the government passed a regulation making it illegal to send certain items to the West. Thereafter all packages sent out of the local post office were inspected for "contraband."

The Newcomers' positions enabled them to make fuller use of *blat* than the Chukchi or the Yup'ik could. Because contact among the three groups was somewhat circumscribed, Newcomers' control over the formal economy and certain aspects of the informal economy led to open animosity.

Alcohol: Commodity and Control

Alcohol was in such demand as a commodity that it had become a pseudo currency. Its distribution and use dramatically illustrate the more subtle aspects of the Soviet system's mechanisms of control.

Mikhail Gorbachev was determined to curb alcohol abuse throughout the Soviet Union, and he instituted tight control over the sale of all alcoholic beverages. They were sold only by coupon and only once a month, on a Saturday from 6:00 to 8:00 P.M. Alcohol was so valuable as a medium of exchange that during the week before P'ianaia Subbota every adult in the village personally signed for a coupon issued by the local council, whether they drank or not. When my birthday approached, one of my roommates called a friend who arranged for us to purchase several bottles of champagne directly from the warehouse. It wasn't until much later that I realized my roommate had used *blat* to get them.

[117]

Customarily, a coupon allowed one to buy two bottles of wine or champagne and one bottle of cognac or vodka. But like everything else, alcohol was also accessible through connections.

The people of Sireniki had an uneasy relationship with alcohol. The social scene at the store on the evenings it was sold was considered unsavory, especially by Newcomer women. After receiving their ration, some individuals immediately started to drink, and the area outside the store became filled with intoxicated people fighting, vomiting, and cursing. For this reason Newcomer women had their husbands or male friends present their coupons and make the purchases on their behalf.

Native people generally felt that the Newcomer women were "hypocrites"—that they didn't come to the store personally so as to give the impression that they didn't drink, when "everyone knew" they'd be drinking as much as everyone else once the alcohol was brought home.

The Newcomers, Chukchi, and Yup'ik exhibited very different drinking behaviors. Although I believe that true clinical alcoholism was no higher in Sireniki than in any other region of the Arctic, it's true that almost every adult under the age of 50 engaged in binge drinking on P'ianaia Subbota. Nearly all of them, including Newcomers, drank until they passed out. This practice fueled myriad other socially debilitating behaviors—public brawling, spouse abuse, promiscuity, rape, suicide, and murder.

The marked difference between Newcomers and the Yup'ik and Chukchi was that Newcomers drank in the privacy of their homes, while many native people, especially young men, walked from apartment to apartment, bottle in hand and often quite intoxicated, sharing their ration with friends. The Yup'ik and Chukchi made no effort to hide their drinking, so their behavior was more likely to be remarked upon by all three groups.

A frequent question asked by Newcomer, Chukchi, and Yup'ik alike was "Do you think the Chukchi and Yup'ik have a lower tolerance for alcohol than the Newcomers?" People in the village, including Newcomers, believed that Newcomers were genetically predisposed to resist the effects of alcohol. Anyone who has spent time in Russia knows, at least anecdotally, that alcoholism or binge drinking is prevalent in all these groups. Not having researched this subject specifically, I can only state from my observations that all three groups got equally intoxicated, but each exhibited a distinctive kind of behavior when they drank, as one could predict for different cultures.

Gossip was one of the main mechanisms of informal control used to curb drunken behavior. After P'ianaia Subbota the village was abuzz with stories of who did what to whom and with whom. Poor behavior was talked about and incurred the wrath of spouses and parents, but for the most part alcohol was seen as the cause of the behavior and thus the behavior was excusable.

Russia in general has a greater tolerance for drunken behavior than most

Western European counties. The drinking behavior of Russians has been under world scrutiny more frequently than it used to be; before Gorbachev, Soviet leaders were rarely seen outside of the Soviet Union, and the world was unable to comment on their drinking habits. The spectacle of an intoxicated President Yeltsin grabbing a conductor's baton and directing the orchestra at the Oktoberfest in Munich, as well as his debacle in Ireland in 1994, brought this whole issue to the world's attention. International gossip put pressure on Russian diplomats to curb their drinking abroad.

In Sireniki, even the mechanism of alcohol distribution led to gossip. A woman who went to the store to purchase her allotment always raised eyebrows because "cultured women do not drink." The mayor seemed to take particular pleasure in personally handing out the bottles; people in the village thought that was her way of being "in control"—knowing exactly who came for the alcohol and who didn't.

Although everyone complained about the ill effects of alcohol, especially the Newcomers, the state farm distributed alcohol to its workers. Every worker who participated in the fall reindeer slaughter received a bottle of vodka or cognac. Alcohol was not the only thing offered as a labor incentive, but its use brought up a number of ethical issues about state incentives and control.

Because Soviet ideology was based on Marx's economic theory, many of the state's most aggressive social policies were presented as economic measures. The original members of the Committee of the North questioned the applicability of collectivization to northern indigenous hunting and herding peoples, but it was a blanket policy applied throughout the Soviet Union. By the 1960s collectivization had dramatically reorganized the social structure of Sireniki.

Through collectivization, regulation, population resettlement, and in-migration, the Chukchi and Yup'ik economic systems were irrevocably changed. The formal state-sanctioned economic activities of the villagers had conformed to the Soviet model of the worker state. That model, based on a theory developed from the study of an industrialized workforce, did not fit the subsistence-based economies of the indigenous populations of Sireniki. Regardless, local people adjusted to the demands of the Soviet model.

Chukchi herders and Yup'ik hunters became Soviet workers, with defined work schedules, yearly plans, *kollektivy*, brigades, and monetary and in-kind compensation for their labor. Women too became workers for the state system, using their skills in skinning, tanning, sewing, and cooking. Their once familial contributions were now incorporated into the Soviet economy. A system devised to remedy the alienation of workers from the work process under capitalism now alienated men and women from their labor and their production through a state-controlled economy.

Collectivization created a new identity for the Yup'ik and Chukchi: instead of contributing to their families' economies, their labor was viewed as a contribution to the *kollektiv*, and thus the primary economic and social responsibility was to the state. The resulting alienation of Yup'ik and Chukchi workers from their production ultimately alienated them from aspects of their own system of social organization and culture.

Chukchi herders worked on brigades ideally formed on Soviet conceptions of labor and took orders from a Ukrainian *zootekhnik* rather than an elder kinsman. Yup'ik hunters conformed their hunting schedules to Soviet border patrol regulations and gave up their right to hunt whales directly. Women worked in nonkin groups with caged foxes, an activity totally foreign to them.

These changes affected the Chukchi's and Yup'ik's relation not only to their production but also to the resources themselves. Yup'ik hunters no longer paid homage to the spirits of the sea mammals; Chukchi herders did not endeavor to learn the system of naming for their herds; and women paid no attention to the strict menstrual taboos of the past. These changes, based on the alienation of production, reached to the very core of Yup'ik and Chukchi culture, changing the very way in which these people conceptualized their universe and themselves. Nevertheless, although collectivization and Stalin's other policies had altered the cultures of the Chukchi and Yup'ik of Sireniki, those cultures were not extinguished.

The Soviets' concern was primarily the formal economy, represented in Sireniki by reindeer herding, sea mammal hunting, salmon fishing, and fox farming, as this economy gave the system the allocative power it sought. Meanwhile, the informal economy grew, relatively unhampered by state restrictions. This unrestricted space became cultural space in which the Chukchi and Yup'ik created, recreated, and preserved their own cultural perceptions and behaviors.

By continuing to hunt and herd with their kin; by continuing a pattern of primary distribution of subsistence resources and to some extent of state farm resources; by slaughtering personal reindeer in the Chukchi way; by the culturally defined separation of labor by gender; by defying Soviet law to take young boys hunting; and by paying respect to the spirits of certain animals— through these and other behaviors, the Chukchi and Yup'ik continued to construct and reconstruct their own cultures within the Soviet state structure. Although the Yup'ik and Chukchi interpreted many of their formal economic activities in their own uniquely Yup'ik and Chukchi ways, it was the informal economy that gave continuity to Yup'ik and Chukchi culture. The dialectic between structure and agency had created a space in which the Yup'ik and Chukchi were able to reproduce their own cultures.

[5]

The Cultural Construction of Other

"I'm going to the tundra," I said timidly. Ol'ga looked up at me in acknowledgment of my having spoken, then took another drag on her cigarette. I was apprehensive about the response I would receive, because until now I had spent most of my time with Yup'ik companions and I instinctively knew my decision would be questioned.

We were sitting on the gravel beach as we had done every day that spring during our breaks from scraping the walrus and seal hides brought in by the hunting brigades. Our breaks provided the much-needed opportunity not only to stretch our back muscles, which had become tight from the strain of our labor, but to discuss the day's events, what would be sold in the store when it opened at three, and whether a concert or a film would be on TV that night. Such collective moments always occurred over a cup of tea and a cigarette.

Ol'ga fixed her stare on the horizon where the sea intersected the sky and responded, "You know what we say. You're at home on the sea but on the tundra you are a guest." "It's OK to be a guest once in awhile," I asserted. She simply looked at me in disbelief—a look I frequently saw whenever I made a statement that unequivocally made sense to me but was at absolute odds with what my companions knew to be true.

EDITED DIARY ENTRY, JUNE 1990

Reaching the top of the mud-sodden trail leading from the beach to the village, I was approached by an older Chukchi man, and we exchanged smiles. I had been released by the *brigadir* from the usual duties of hauling and butchering the day's kill. It was my first time on a hunt, and the *brigadir* could see I was exhausted from the eleven hours I had spent

in the *baidara*, but mainly I was told to go home because I
was a woman. Although I had been given special dispensa-
tion to participate in and observe the sea mammal hunters'
daily activities, I could tell that to stay would be pushing my
privileges. I was too tired to argue.

The man stopped in my path and asked, "Have you been
hunting?" "Yes," I said triumphantly. "On the ocean?" he continued. I again said yes but with some reluctance, unsure as
to where he was leading and perceiving a sudden change in
his mood. "Then you love only Eskimos and not Chukchi!" he
retorted, and walked on toward the beach.

EDITED DIARY ENTRY, MAY 1990

They can't survive without us. They don't have the knowledge or training to do what we do. They can't even run the
electrical plant. Let them kick us out, they'll be begging us to
return.

PAVEL, NEWCOMER TEACHER

Metaphors and Symbols

These passages cited from my field notes and diary serve to illustrate fundamental discursive cultural differences between the Chukchi, Yup'ik, and Newcomers. Analysis of these differences will show how each collective group's
own boundaries become more salient through interaction with the other two.
The Soviet state created a physical as well as social landscape that encouraged
the articulation of "otherness" in ways that were previously unknown.[1] By
changing the social and physical proximity of these three groups to one another, the state encouraged the development of a language of difference,
based in and on prior cultural and symbolic texts.

The contemporary village of Sireniki was a Soviet phenomenon, created
through village closures and relocations, collectivization, and in-migrations of
young nonnative professionals. Here three fundamentally different cultures
were artificially brought together to create a pluralistic community. Sireniki
had become the point of intersection between tundra and sea, Chukchi and
Yup'ik, native and Newcomer, tradition and progress.[2]

The Chukchi culture was oriented to the tundra, the Yup'ik culture was oriented to the sea, and the Newcomer culture was oriented toward socialist pro-

duction. The root metaphors and many of the associated symbols of the Chukchi and Yup'ik were drawn from the features of the tundra and the sea, respectively.[3] Because of their cultural diversity, the Newcomers did not easily lend themselves to this type of characterization. Although Sovietized, Newcomers had diverse cultural and geographic backgrounds. The orientation they collectively shared, however, was rooted in their Russified Soviet history. By first focusing on the Chukchi and Yup'ik and their constructions of themselves as well as of each other, we can begin to understand how all three groups created social interaction and community across symbolically and culturally defined spaces of difference.

To say that the Chukchi were oriented toward the tundra and the Yup'ik toward the sea may seem to be a very superficial observation; one would expect reindeer herders to be most familiar with and thus have an affinity for the tundra and sea mammal hunters to have an affinity for the sea. The relationships between these cultures and their environments, however, were not purely materialistic. The tundra and the sea were root metaphors within the Chukchi and Yup'ik symbolic worlds. As such, they formed one of the ways in which the Chukchi and Yup'ik conceptualized their world as well as their experiences of one another. The tundra was a metaphor for the Chukchi, who were connected materially as well as spiritually to the land, and the sea was a metaphor for the Yup'ik, who were materially and spiritually connected to the ocean.

This was not to say that tundra and sea were oppositional, certainly not emically so. They were, in fact, complementary. The Chukchi and Yup'ik depended upon the resources of both the tundra and the sea. In the past they created trading partnerships in order to ensure access to each other's resources in a classic symbiotic trading relationship between two ecological zones.[4]

Before Soviet intervention, the Chukchi were nomadic reindeer herders whose settlements consisted of mobile family encampments. The Yup'ik had permanent villages, but their villages were limited in size to the *yarangi* of several extended family groups. The village of Sireniki, besides being considerably smaller than it is today, had an exclusively Yup'ik population. Contact between the Yup'ik village of Sireniki and the mobile Chukchi encampments was limited to a few days of circumscribed, very structured trading scenarios.[5] Before the Revolution, contact with nonnatives was limited to a few Russian traders, government representatives, and foreign whalers. It was not until collectivization (1930–60) that the indigenous peoples in the Sireniki region had sustained contact with Newcomers. During my fieldwork, this interaction was limited to the village.

The village marked where the sea ended and the tundra began—or, as the Chukchi saw it, where the tundra ended and the sea began. It was the space where all three groups, Chukchi, Yup'ik, and Newcomers, interacted and formed their perceptions of one another. The village was the focal point of intergroup dialogue in a literal as well as a symbolic sense. The three groups' unique concepts of themselves and their relationship with the natural environment created a tripartite structure to this dialogue of difference. In order to unwrap this package more fully, it is necessary to look at each of its elements independently: tundra, sea, and village.

The Tundra

Before Sovietization, the Sireniki Chukchi lived continuously on the tundra, coming to the seashore to give their herds relief from the menacing black flies that plagued the reindeer in the summer and to participate in the yearly trading event with the Yup'ik. In the early 1990s the Chukchi participated in reindeer herding for the state farm and continued to live and work on the tundra, although, as we have seen, to a diminished degree.

The Chukchi associated strongly with the tundra; it was their point of physical, cultural, and symbolic reference. They went to the tundra not only to work but for vacations, afternoon walks, and weekend picnics. They traveled to the tundra to relax, "find peace" in the open spaces, and escape the drinking that was unavoidable in the village. (Women often confided that they wished their husbands or sons would return to the tundra so they would stop drinking.)

Young herders talked of their yearning for the tundra during the difficult isolation of their military service. Upon returning to the village, they returned to the tundra and continued to find solace there in its "openness and cleanliness." The Chukchi attributed the richness of the tundra environment to its distance from the "dirt" (*griaz'*) of the village. This was only one of the ways they distinguished the tundra from the village.

For them the tundra had fewer people to "spoil" its pristine spaces. It was true that, as one traveled the 300 kilometers to the inland tundra, the environment became devoid of telltale signs of "civilization"—no abandoned fuel barrels, no artificial pools of melting permafrost to mark the passage of *vezdekhody*, no piles of human refuse. More significant, however, was that when the Chukchi spoke of "dirt," they were describing a condition not only of the physical environment but of the symbolic environment as well. The tundra to the Chukchi was by definition "pure." For them, to foul the tundra was like desecrating a church. The village was "impure."

Newcomers received most of the blame for the actual physical contamination. The Soviet state had shown blatant disregard for the environment, and the low priority that the government gave to the problems of pollution fostered a similar attitude in many of its citizens. On every trip made to the tun-

Yaranga on the tundra. (Photo by Aleksandr Kalinin.)

dra, people pointed to the muddy pools of melted permafrost and complained, "Look at all the tracks, they're everywhere! Why can't these drivers [all Newcomers] stay in the same ones? They drive anywhere they want without thinking about the effects. Look at how the tundra is weeping!" Use of the word "weeping" is significant: the tundra was a spiritual being and was actually weeping to see the lack of respect and the offensive behavior of the Newcomer drivers. It should be noted, however, that once a *vezdekhod* had torn up the tundra, the huge mud pools created by the melting permafrost made it impossible for drivers to follow the same tracks without getting irretrievably stuck: they were forced to make new tracks in order to avoid getting mired in the mud of the old ones. With each new track came new pools of water and new symbolic tears.

Before the Chukchi's relationship with the tundra can be fully understood, it is necessary to understand their relationship with their reindeer. This relationship, which was both material and symbolic, can best be understood by contrasting the two systems of reindeer herding, the state farm herd and the personal herd. Personal reindeer filled a material, cultural, symbolic, and metaphysical niche in the lives of the Chukchi that could not be filled by the state farm reindeer.

In Sireniki reindeer were still a measure of wealth. People proudly mentioned that they had reindeer. A number of women in the village (primarily over the age of 50) had facial tattoos, and before the Revolution one of the reasons for tattooing had been to indicate the size of one's father's herd.[6] Older women teased younger men who owned reindeer, saying that the size of the young man's herd should attract a good wife. A further indication of this principle was that reindeer were butchered reluctantly, especially large, healthy adults. Several years before, herders and women support workers living on the tundra starved for almost a month because supplies from the village warehouse had not been delivered on time. When I was first told this tale, it seemed unlikely to me, because I knew that reindeer were a perfect source of food. When I mentioned this to a friend, she was horrified that I could suggest such a thing. "State farm reindeer are not yours to butcher, and no one would butcher their own deer just to eat. Who would destroy their own wealth?" she asked. But reindeer were more than a material resource or an indicator of social status; they were an integral part of the Chukchi spiritual world.

Bogoraz (1904–9) wrote of the Chukchi belief that reindeer were created of fire, and that there was a spiritual relationship between the Chukchi and their reindeer. He described how during the memorial feast for the dead, the Chukchi painted certain members of their family with the blood of a newly slaughtered reindeer. He explained that body painting was a representation of the spirit of the deer. I recorded in my diary a similar scene among the Chukchi and Koriak of the village of Achavaiam in Kamchatka in 1992:

> Upon finishing her grandson's anointing, the grandmother of one of the families with whom I had come to the tundra motioned for me to come to her. I stood there over the carcass of the slaughtered reindeer as she carefully painted my hands and face with its blood. When she had completed her work I asked, "What does this mean?" The old woman gave me an incredulous look and said, "You are a reindeer." Then as she pointed to the blood streaks on my body and clothing she began to recite the parts of the reindeer—"antlers, eyes, nose, mouth, throat, hoofs, and vagina." At that moment I was indeed—a reindeer.

Although Kamchatka is several thousand kilometers from northern Chukotka, many of the Chukchi who lived there were the descendants of people transplanted from the Chukotka region. This was the ritual the Chukchi in Sireniki described to me.

The Chukchi believed they were the human incarnations of reindeer. The blood painting not only symbolized the juncture at which humans became reindeer and reindeer became human, but actually caused, in the metaphysical sense, a human being to become a reindeer. As I mentioned earlier, before Sovietization the Chukchi cremated their dead, and in some villages in Kamchatka they still did. Cremation completed the ritual cycle: fire to reindeer to human to fire—from fire to fire.

But not only human death illustrated the relationship between the reindeer and the Chukchi. The death of the reindeer itself gives clues to the nature of this complex symbolic bond. A comparison of the slaughter of personal reindeer with the slaughter of state farm reindeer, two economically and symbolically very different animals, will clarify the cultural meaning of reindeer to the Chukchi.

Personal reindeer could be butchered any time the owner requested, but those moments were limited by logistical factors, such as how and by whom the carcass would be brought in from the tundra herd. Most of the personal reindeer were slaughtered at the same time as the state farm reindeer, with a few exceptions during the summer when meat and skins were needed. The most dramatic distinctions between these two events happened during the fall slaughter. At that time, the actual method of slaughter was determined by the identity of the reindeer, personal or state farm.

When the reindeer were herded toward the village for slaughter, reindeer owners or family members went out on a *vezdekhod* to meet the herd a few kilometers from the village. These people told the herders the number of their own personal reindeer that they wanted to slaughter. The herders then wandered among the herd, lassoing those specific reindeer and killing them by stabbing them in the heart.

After the deer died, the animal was skinned with care so as not to create holes in the hide. The hide was removed, the abdomen was sliced open, and the internal organs were removed intact. The contents of the stomach and intestines were cleaned onto the ground and the intestines were stuffed with fat from the thoracic cavity, creating what was locally known as *Chukotskaia kolbasa* (Chukotkan sausage). After this process, the organs were returned to the abdomen, and the carcass, with the head and antlers removed, was covered and tied in its own skin. When one observed a field after the slaughter of personal deer, all that could be seen were the small piles of intestinal contents and a few drops of blood.

A significant part of this butchering activity was its social aspect. All butchering of personal reindeer was done by kin groups: sisters; mother's sister and sister's daughter; husbands and wives; mothers and daughters; mothers and sons; mother's brothers and sister's sons; or brothers (I did not record any unrelated Chukchi or Yup'ik working together at that time). This arrangement stands in marked contrast to the state farm slaughter, which was done by working partners. The partners were both kin and nonkin, chosen primarily on the basis of skill and friendship. No Newcomers undertook this labor. The elements of the state farm slaughter differed markedly from those of the personal reindeer slaughter:

Yesterday I worked with the reindeer. Two older women showed me how to do the work. We got up at 5 A.M. and rode out on the *vezdekhod* to the corral. Two young women let me walk out with them to chase the reindeer into the corral. At the end, I was running right into the reindeer holding a cloth or burlap fence over my head. When they got the reindeer into the corral, they started lassoing some to be butchered. Earlier, several men threw lassos at the reindeer to keep them in a bunch. When they started to run, we waved our arms wildly to keep them in a circle, a lot like cattle. The few that broke away were shot. The reindeer were in the corral around 9 A.M. The first reindeer taken by lasso were stabbed in the heart and processed by various family groups. The area for processing was as follows: on the western side of the [slaughtering] shed women were processing the stomachs, old women were stuffing fat from the inside [of the abdomen] into the intestines. On the eastern side of the shed the reindeer processed had been chased into a chute, hit on the head with a sledgehammer, and decapitated with an ax. These deer were then dragged out to female working pairs to be skinned.

EDITED FIELD NOTEBOOK ENTRY, OCTOBER 1989

Clearly the slaughter for the state farm was structurally very different from the slaughter of personal reindeer. No Chukchi would chase a personal reindeer into a chute or hit it on the head with a sledgehammer. If the state farm animal did not die immediately, it was pithed with a knife placed at the base of the cranium behind the antler. The deer were then dragged out of the corral to working pairs of women who skinned the reindeer. Because women were paid by the number of deer they processed, these partners chose each other according to their skill in skinning. Therefore, both kin and nonkin, Chukchi and Yup'ik, worked together during the state farm slaughter.

While the women worked to remove the hide, two men came and chopped off the head. A spray of blood shot into the air and covered the entire work area. After the hide was removed, men dragged the carcass into a shed and hung it by its hind legs to facilitate the removal of the internal organs. The prized organs (liver, heart, and kidney) were inspected for flukes and worms and either kept for sale or, if contaminated, discarded. The carcass was then placed on a meathook and hosed down with cold water to keep the meat from spoiling. The workers repeated this process until all of the deer were slaughtered.[7] Once the slaughter began, it could not stop, because when the deer were corralled they did not stop running. This activity builds up lactic acid in the muscles and could eventually spoil the meat.

The contrast between state farm and personal butchering was visually very dramatic. During a personal reindeer slaughter, the reindeer's death was ritualized and very peaceful. After the skinning and butchering, almost no evidence of the event remained. After the state farm slaughter, the ground was a pool of blood. Workers were covered with it and were standing in it. The un-

Final preparation of the reindeer carcass at the state farm slaughter. (Photo by Anna M. Kerttula.)

skinned, unprocessed heads were discarded into a pile, with only the antlers and tongues removed. There were hundreds of steaming barrels filled with blood and internal organs, and reindeer were crying and writhing on the ground awaiting death.

The personal reindeer were butchered by kin groups, the state farm reindeer by working partners. This difference first came to my attention in 1989, when people refused my help while they butchered personal reindeer in the morning but eagerly accepted my help in the afternoon, during the butchering of state farm reindeer. Then in 1990 I was invited to slaughter with the family of one of my main Yup'ik hosts. They extended an invitation to me as fictive kin; besides, they believed me to be a skilled butcher after the time I had spent with the Chukchi on the tundra.

Although the reindeer's eyes and facial muscles were delicacies to the Chukchi and they savored the ones they removed from their personal reindeer, no one ever removed them from the pile of discarded heads after the state farm slaughter. This practice was wasteful and contrary to Chukchi principles, since they believed that to waste usable parts of a reindeer (and virtually every part of a deer was usable) was spiritually dangerous. The Chukchi's obligation to waste nothing from the reindeer extended only to their own personal deer.

Chukchi sisters dress their personal reindeer. (Photo by Anna M. Kerttula.)

This practice was recorded historically among the Chukchi as well. Bogoraz notes that "among both the Reindeer and the Maritime people it is forbidden to throw away crumbs and remnants of food . . . if a reindeer bone is not entirely gnawed up, the reindeer will be stricken with some disease" (Bogoraz 1904–9:493). When the Sireniki Chukchi ate reindeer on the tundra, they stripped the bones of meat, sinew, and ligaments, leaving it completely clean. This operation took skill with a knife and strong teeth. I had difficulty getting the knack of it; people who were close to me would pick up the bone I had left and finish it, or they would say tactfully, "Since you're not Chukchi, you can't be expected to clean the bone completely."

When given a choice, and when not constricted by time, the Chukchi chose to slaughter even state farm reindeer in a way more closely resembling a personal reindeer slaughter. One fall on the tundra when the state farm workers slaughtered deer that were too lame or too sick to make the trip back to Sireniki, they did so in a way very similar to the slaughter of personal reindeer. They lassoed the reindeer, and although they pithed them rather than stabbing them in the heart, so as not to ruin the hide, they removed the stomach con-

Personal reindeer bundle
ready to be taken home.
(Photo by Anna M.
Kerttula.)

tents and the hide with great care, and they cleaned and saved some of the intestines. After this slaughter of state farm animals, the ground had very little
debris and almost no blood.

One young Chukchi man, on summer vacation from technical school and
participating in a tundra state farm slaughter, noticed halfway through his first
reindeer that he had instinctively started butchering in the "Chukchi way." He
shouted out, "Oh, no, I've started it our way!" and laughed with embarrassment. He had been away from the village so long, he explained later, that he
had forgotten the need to butcher the state farm reindeer differently. The
"Chukchi way" was ingrained, even among young adults who had had years of
Soviet indoctrination.

A controlling element of the Chukchi slaughter was its location: it took place
on the tundra. To butcher the reindeer there as they did in the village would
be doubly offensive—to the reindeer and to the tundra. Such carnage and
spilling of blood on the tundra were unthinkable. The village, however, was already symbolically polluted, so it demanded no such careful treatment.

Both the Chukchi and Yup'ik were unable to objectify the differences between the two slaughters. When I asked why personal deer were treated in
a particular way, they always answered that it was their "tradition." They preferred to lasso the reindeer and to stab it in the heart. They felt this procedure

[131]

was more humane to the animal, and more respectful. The state farm did not allow its reindeer to be stabbed in the heart; it spoiled the hide by leaving an entrance wound, and besides, "It takes too long."

When questioned about the state farm methods, people said they preferred the Chukchi way, but they accepted the economic reality of the state farm slaughter, which necessitated speed. Thus, under certain circumstances, cultural practice fell victim to Soviet economic expediency. The state farm system had forced the Chukchi to categorized its reindeer as different from their own. As such, they commanded less respect, and "mistreating" them was not considered "dangerous." By maintaining their own herd within the state farm system, the Chukchi were able to maintain the meaningfulness of reindeer within their own cultural system.

The interrelatedness of people and reindeer as a basic cultural principle can be seen in other Chukchi practices. To waste reindeer meat or skins was considered spiritually dangerous. A young Chukchi woman, a teacher in the village, confided to me that she was very nervous about some reindeer meat she had let spoil. When I asked what would happen if she threw the meat out, she was uncertain, but she was sure it would be "bad"; perhaps "someone" (the inference being a close relative or friend) would become ill. She sought the advice of another woman who had an elderly mother. The older woman was reputed to know a lot about Chukchi tradition, and she advised the young teacher to burn the meat (again the theme of fire). Such finer points of Chukchi traditions were not common knowledge among younger people, and they frequently sought advice from their elders.[8]

When the Chukchi ate reindeer meat, they cleaned the bones of all flesh, cartilage, and sinew. On the tundra the proper way to dispose of the bones was to burn them. In the village, however, many people considered burning too much trouble, so they simply threw the bones into the garbage bins. Eventually the bones ended up at the village dump, on the tundra some distance from Sireniki. The important thing was that they were not thrown into the sea. A few of the older women in the village, both Chukchi and Yup'ik, collected the hairs that fell from the reindeer skins while they were working on them and burned them on the tundra when they went out to pick berries or mushrooms, or just on an afternoon walk.

We have seen other indications of the symbolic significance of reindeer: the Chukchi gave reindeer or their meat at key life events, such as birth, marriage, and death; reindeer carried the spirit of the deceased to the other side; and cremation of the dead symbolically completed the Chukchi life cycle—from fire to reindeer to human to fire. Although in Sireniki cremation was replaced by a small campfire beside the grave, this act still provided symbolic closure and thus meaning for the Chukchi.

Reindeer were not only a sign of wealth but also a sign of one's Chukchiness. The slaughtering of personal reindeer was very carefully calculated for specific material and cultural needs. Reindeer were killed and butchered according to specific cultural practices, which protected the reindeer and the tundra from offense and ensured the bounty of the resources as well as Chukchi culture itself.

The Chukchi maintained their relationship, both material and spiritual, with their reindeer through their practices. By continuing to travel to the tundra to herd reindeer, by continuing to respect the reindeer in life and in death, and by respecting their common tundra home, they ensured the meaningfulness of their culture for the future generations of Chukchi.

The Sea

A Yup'ik and a Chukchi were arguing about whose job was more dangerous. The Chukchi man said that the herding of reindeer was much more dangerous than the hunting of sea mammals. One had to follow his animals across the tundra and protect them from wolves, subject oneself to the dangers of grizzly bears, climb steep cliffs, cross deep rivers, clothe oneself against the bitter cold of winter, and fortify oneself against starvation. His work was definitely more dangerous. The Yup'ik man nodded calmly as his Chukchi comrade spoke and then invited him to go hunting. The next morning they went out hunting in a *baidara*. The Chukchi was very frightened, never having been in a *baidara* before. At the end of the day's hunt the Chukchi admitted the Yup'ik man's work was harder: "On the tundra my feet can always touch solid ground. In your work you have only the icy ocean. I prefer the safety of the land."

YUP'IK ANECDOTE

The Yup'ik were people of the sea. They lived on the seacoast, the sea provided them with their food and material needs, and the sea was a root metaphor for their lives. Unlike the Chukchi, however, who gained independence from the Soviets by traveling to the tundra, the Yup'ik were faced with daily Soviet intervention. Because over half of the state farm economy (food, fox feed, and technical oil production) was dependent on the sea mammals brought in by the hunters, this aspect of Yup'ik life was heavily controlled. Therefore, the spiritual relationship between the sea mammals and their hu-

[133]

man hunters had, in many respects, fallen victim to the economic necessities of the Soviet-directed system.

Yup'ik hunters were aware of the "ancient ways" concerning the proper treatment and disposal of sea mammals, but chose to ignore many of them. As illustrated by the reaction of the *brigadir* to my request to go hunting, the spiritual and symbolic relationship that once existed between the Sireniki Yup'ik and the sea mammals they hunted was retained only in the memories of the elderly.

As we saw earlier, older women were very concerned about the improper treatment of the sea mammals. As they walked the beach littered with the bones and rotting flesh of dead walruses, seals, and whales, tears rolled down their cheeks. "These animals are truly dead to us," one woman told me. Many elderly residents accounted for the poor hunting of recent years by the failure of the younger hunters to dispose of the remains of the animals properly. The hunters agreed that they should probably drag the bones out to sea, as their traditions dictated, but the general consensus was that the job took too much time and energy when "the fall storms do it" for them.

Yet the younger Yup'ik did not act with total disregard for the animals. They kept the bones of sea mammals they had eaten separate from reindeer and other bones. They might throw them on the garbage pile (occasionally they returned them to the sea at the prodding of an elderly parent), but these bones were never burned. Even the young considered it anathema to burn them. Once I placed a weathered seal bone that I had collected on the beach near the wood stove of a friend. She became very excited and screamed at me: "Don't burn the bone!" It would be "very bad" if it caught fire. "Someone might get sick."

The beautifully weathered and water-rolled bones of walruses, seals, and whales were always very aesthetically appealing to me. Their alabaster color and intricate patterns made them resemble carefully sculptured pieces of art. However, I never felt comfortable about bringing them into the house. Whenever I brought a particularly captivating specimen home, my Yup'ik friends always looked at me askance. "Bones from the beach are better left on the beach." No one would say it was wrong or dangerous to gather bones from the beach, but they were uncomfortable when I did so. These feelings related to the Yup'ik belief that because sea mammals are of the sea, their remains belong there.

Although many practices showing proper respect for sea mammals had been discontinued, the relationship between the Yup'ik and the sea and its creatures remained. The Yup'ik spent their free time at the shore. They went there for quiet contemplation. A trip in the *baidara* was considered a wonderful adventure.[9] They relished a picnic on the beach or a holiday outing in a *baidara*.

A whaleboat heads to Provideniia loaded with passengers and gear. (Photo by John Echave.)

The Yup'ik coveted apartments that overlooked the sea, not only because of the convenience to the hunter of being able to judge the day's weather from his morning bed but also for the calming affect they believed the ocean had on them.

Many Yup'ik considered dreams about the sea or the shore to be prophetic. One Yup'ik woman told me about a dream of walking on the beach in traditional Yup'ik dress and then being swept away to Alaska. The next day she borrowed a *kamleika* and went for a walk on the beach in order to fulfill her dream. She was not swept away, but the dream came true just the same: several months later she was able to visit her relatives in Alaska.

Several people told me that the orca was the protector or helper of their families. Hunters generally revered the orca as a helper, and when they hunted walrus they slapped the water in imitation of the orca, a natural enemy of the walrus. Hunters described how on many occasions the orca helped them by chasing game close to the beach. One woman told me that an orca saved her husband from drowning. But more than a material helper, the orca was a spiritual helper, keeping evil at bay.

[135]

Just as reindeer herding was the culturally appropriate work for Chukchi men, sea mammal hunting was the culturally appropriate work for Yup'ik men. Although other work was available, many young Yup'ik men continued to choose sea mammal hunting as their profession. When inclement weather made hunting impossible, hunters were assigned other jobs at the state farm. Many hunters consider these alternatives so distasteful that they would rather go without pay than accept such work. Some young men tried working on the tundra, but complained that it was "hard to be away from the ocean and the freedom of hunting." One Yup'ik man who had worked with his father-in-law on the tundra told me he had missed the sea so much that he spent many hours wandering along the various tundra rivers just so he could "be near water." A young Yup'ik woman confessed that when she went to visit a relative in Bilibino (a tundra city to the north), she and her daughter spent most of their time walking the riverbed because they missed the water.

The roots of this cultural orientation lie in an ancient lifeway of sea mammal hunting, and specifically whale hunting, that dates to at least the Old Bering Sea and Okvik archaeological cultures (500 B.C.) Intensive whaling in Chukotka dates back to the Punuk period (ninth to fifteenth centuries) (Arutiunov and Fitzhugh 1988; Dikov 1989; Rudenko 1947). Krupnik concludes that because of the large numbers of bowhead bones found in archaeological sites in Chukotka and "from folklore and oral tradition and from numerous findings of whale amulets, sculptures and rock paintings," as well as the "brief accounts of native whaling festivals and rituals from the late 18th and early 19th century, the symbolic role of the bowhead whale seems to have been extremely important in both Eskimo [Yup'ik] and maritime Chukchi cultures" (1987:21).

In the pre-Soviet period, or what Krupnik labels the "traditional period," the Sireniki Yup'ik, following ancient practices, took one or two bowheads a year. Through oral history and historical records it was known that before Sovietization the Chukotka whaling complex consisted of the following social characteristics: "high prestige [of] boat captains and of the whole crew who first harpooned a whale; fixed norms for whale meat and baleen distribution among eight crews (a symbolic number) based on the role of each in the hunt; potlatch-like festivals organized by a captain or by his crew in the case of a successful hunt; communal whale festivals at the beginning and conclusion of the whaling season; and ritual treatment of some parts of the whale" (ibid.:24–25).

Throughout Sireniki stood the jawbones of bowhead whales taken in the past. These bones were erected as monuments to the spirits of the whales taken and to ensure the whales' future abundance. After the government appropriated the right to hunt whales, the jawbones remained as ghostly monuments to a fading ritual. The Yup'ik of the village took their last bowhead whale in 1972, and people still relished the memory of the sweet taste of *mangtak* (skin and attached subcutaneous fat; what is commonly referred to as blubber).

Mature hunters recounted with delight how they used to prepare for the hunt, then sneaked up on the sleeping whale, stabbed it in the heart or lung, and quickly moved to get away from its thrashing. The elderly yearned for the taste of the *mangtak*; the gray whales brought in by the whaling cutters are "less tasty." Krupnik concludes that the bowhead is "still very important to their national self-consciousness and to the conservation of cultural and linguistic traditions" (1987:29).

Perhaps the most devastating blow to Yup'ik symbolic and ritual life was the state control over the hunting of whales. The bowhead whale was the center of their ritual world. Starting in the 1960s the Soviet government began sending official whaling vessels to Chukotka to hunt whales for the coastal communities. This was an economically rational decision made by Soviet bureaucrats. According to Krupnik, the Soviets used the high rate of unproductive losses among village sea mammal hunters (estimated at 30 percent) as their reason for ending aboriginal whaling (ibid.:27).

The ramifications of this decision spread through all layers of the social and cultural landscape in Sireniki. Hunting brigades were no longer allowed to hunt the whales themselves but only to drag the carcasses from the whaling cutter to the shore. The Soviet cutters provided only gray whales, forcing the local population to accustom themselves to a resource they previously fed only to dogs. Because walruses were so numerous and relatively easy to catch, they became the species taken by the state farm brigades to provide food for the villagers, hides for the *baidara* covers, and, most important, feed for the foxes. The transition from whale hunting to walrus hunting for the state farm disrupted not only the transference of practical knowledge about how to hunt whales but also the associated ritual knowledge. Also changed were many of the social relationships that surrounded the proper distribution of whale meat and *mangtak*, and the high social status accorded a successful captain and crew.[10]

Although Soviet interference severed much of the relationship between the Yup'ik hunters and the sea mammals they hunted, the Yup'ik kept the sea as their main point of reference. Just as the Chukchi related to the tundra, the Yup'ik viewed their relationship with the ocean as one of their defining features. When Mikhael Chlenov, a Russian ethnologist, asked a Chukchi man and a Yup'ik man to draw the village of Sireniki, the Chukchi drew the view of the village from the tundra and the Yup'ik drew his view from the sea (Nikolai Vakhtin, personal communication, 1990). Young men continued to hunt sea mammals; people separated sea mammal bones from reindeer bones to keep them from contaminating each other and offending the spirits of those animals; fresh *mangtak* from a bowhead whale was remembered with relish; children were taken to the ocean shore and on *baidara* outings; and hunters were relearning from their Alaskan relatives the skills necessary to hunt the bowhead. It was the fundamental perspective of themselves, as intimately tied to the sea, and their seagoing practices that continued to make the sea meaningful to generations of Sireniki Yup'ik.

The Village

It seems reasonable to think of the Newcomers as oriented to the village, but it was not quite so simple. Because Newcomers were more urbanized, the village was their natural sphere of operation; but this village was only a temporary place of residence for almost all Newcomers. Even though some people in this group had actually been born in Sireniki and others were married to local people and chose to build their homes there, for most Newcomers "home" continued to be their *rodina* (birthplace) or the *rodina* of their parents. Some Newcomers were attached to the village for ideological reasons, believing they were bringing the benefits of socialism to a primitive region that lagged behind the civilized West. Most Newcomers, however, thought of Sireniki as a means to a sound economic future. Their ideology was production. They perceived themselves as building their futures by taking advantage of the high pay and professional positions the state offered in the northern regions.

Among the government's goals was the exploitation of the North's resources. The Newcomers were interested in resources that had monetary value (minerals, fish, and fur) and the most expedient ways to extract and put them to use. Ecological disasters were simply the cost of building the new productive socialist life.

I must admit that this is a very simplified statement about the very complex relationship between the government apparatus and the industrial complex. Paula Garb (1993), in analyzing environmental thinking among the Russian environmental intelligentsia, points out that Russians feel that they are very "close to nature" but that industrialization has "destroyed [their] consciousness." The biocentric view of nature for its own sake prevalent in the West does not exist among the Russian environmental community. In their more anthropocentric view, technology can remedy past abuses of the environment and resources must be managed to optimize sustainable yields.

At an international conference on environmentally sound practices for oil development in the Arctic sponsored by the U.S. Department of Energy in Alaska in 1995, it became clear that the U.S. and Russian contingents had differing perceptions of the environment. The U.S. participants spoke about the environment as something to be protected, and offered technology for "safe" exploration and extraction of oil in the Arctic. The Russians, by contrast, spoke of the environment as something to be overcome; they were looking for technology that would make extraction of oil in the Arctic environment easier.[11]

The experience of the conferees supports my assertion that the Newcomer community was production-oriented. Although their discourse was filled with romantic images of nature and their relation to nature, their actions were heavily biased toward technology and production. Their priorities allowed the Newcomers to strip-mine without reclamation, recklessly extract oil and ignore leaky pipelines, and clear-cut forests with no plan for reforestation. In Sireniki they drove *vezdekhody* indiscriminately and destructively across the tundra, ordered the mass slaughter of sea mammals to provide feed for the state farm's foxes, abandoned used fuel barrels on the tundra, permitted the groundwater to become contaminated, and stripped roe from salmon to sell as caviar and discarded the flesh. A young Yup'ik woman expressed her distress in this way:

> I worry about what's happening here, the huge number of walrus we kill to feed the foxes. Earlier we never questioned, when the government commanded we just did what they said. [She pantomimed marching.] This year the hunters brought in too few walruses to provide enough feed, so the *kitoboi* [government whaling ship] brought in whales to make up the difference. We never used to kill females or pups. Now they take everything. This should not be done! These actions are destroying our bonds with the animals and eventually they'll destroy the spiritual base of our culture.

Clearly the Newcomers were not oriented to Sireniki and its environment.

In Sireniki, as all over the Soviet North, Newcomers were blamed for the poor physical upkeep of the village and the general deterioration of the area's ecology. Local people said that Newcomers "come and they go, and they just leave garbage dumps on the tundra." Newcomers themselves admitted that the Soviet system had had a disastrous effect on the local ecology. "This is a land without a master," they frequently said, meaning that they knew they would leave before they came and therefore didn't bother to take care of the land.[12]

Some individuals were concerned about the effects of their own behavior on their environment, and might complain about the fuel barrels on the tundra and the garbage dump at the edge of town, but most felt powerless to make a change. Occasionally someone would take action; in order to stop the stench of rotting whale carcasses from permeating the village, Kolia, a young *traktorist* (tractor driver), dragged the carcasses off the beach and hauled them up the side of the nearest mountain. This move created a rather surreal scene for anyone taking a hike along the mountain trail. Sun-bleached whale crania, vertebrae, femurs, and pelvises lined the path, reminiscent of an ancient Inuit ritual site.

Kolia effectively removed the odor from the village but completely ignored the spiritual consequences of abandoning sea mammal remains on the tundra. Those skeletons provided a fitting symbol of the Newcomers' attitude toward the natives' beliefs and their lack of concern for the native spiritual environment.

The Soviets' classification of elements of the natural environment according to their contribution to economic production was in such radical contrast to the indigenous cultural relationship with the natural environment that it stood out as one of the defining features of the Newcomers' orientation. Their perception of the natural environment was rooted in a conception of utilization. These perspectives permeated the interaction between Newcomers and natives and inhibited dialogue between the two groups.

Another reason one cannot associate Newcomers exclusively with the village as one can associate the Yup'ik and Chukchi with the environment is that the village also served as a reference point for the Yup'ik. The Yup'ik were oriented not only to the ocean but to the very old pre-Yuit archaeological site on which the village was built. The group most closely attached to the village, then, historically and culturally, was the Yup'ik.

Although the village was now the product of many Soviet-induced material changes, the Yup'ik believed the village to be theirs. Their personal identification with the physical site of Sireniki, coupled with the rate of Yup'ik exogamy and the long history of contact between Yup'ik and Newcomers, blurred for them the distinction between what was Yup'ik in the village and what was Newcomer.

The affinity the Yup'ik felt for the village was shared, to a degree, by the Newcomers. Although most Newcomers did not call Sireniki home, they were more comfortable among its stuccoed apartment buildings, warehouses, hospital, schools, and *bania* than they were on the open tundra or ocean. This familiarity with the physical form of the village created a subtle understanding between the Newcomers and Yup'ik that eluded the Chukchi. The Yup'ik were more "acceptable" to the Newcomers and the Newcomers were more "understandable" to the Yup'ik than the Chukchi were to either.

This is not to say that the Yup'ik were becoming Newcomers. Indeed, the differences remained immense. By being physically located in the village, however, the Yup'ik had been more inundated by Soviet-implemented change; and by identifying with the village they had more easily built a social and cultural dialogue with the Newcomers. The village was common ground for the Yup'ik and Newcomers; the Chukchi did not share it. As we shall see, the understanding between Yup'ik and Newcomers had elevated the Yup'ik within the Soviet system, giving them an advantage over their Chukchi neighbors.

The village was alien to the Chukchi. Whether it was defined as Yup'ik, Newcomer, or Soviet, it was definitely not theirs. As Soviet citizens they knew that they had as much right to live there as anyone else, but they did not feel an affinity for it. The village embodied everything that was not Chukchi: the sea, the Soviet system, alcoholism. Therefore, the Chukchi separated themselves from the village and pointed to the tundra as their place, a pure place away from the influences of the village and ultimately from the Soviet system.

When a Chukchi man went to the tundra from the village, he was advised to beat himself with a snow beater made of antler and to say, "I remove all the bad [spirits, events, and memories] from my body and put in the good." When he returned he must say the reverse in order to remove the spirits of the tundra so they would not be contaminated by the village. This practice, which I observed only once, may have served as a spiritual nexus between what the Chukchi conceptualized as two very different worlds. From the point of view of the Chukchi, the tundra was distinct from the village because the village was on the seacoast and was essentially the domain of the Yup'ik. The Yup'ik view was the opposite.

Just as the Chukchi avoided the sea as perilous, to the Yup'ik the tundra was a dangerous place filled with quicksand and evil spirits. Stories were told of how people had fallen asleep on the tundra without properly securing their garments and *cherviaki* [worms] had eaten the flesh from their bodies. People were said to have set out on dogsleds and become hypnotized by *cherti* [devils and evil spirits] to wander for days in circles. Another tundra being, according to the Yup'ik, was a fire-breathing creature, half human and half reindeer, that could overtake and kill the unsuspecting traveler. As my Yup'ik friend Ol'ga said, "On the tundra you are a guest."

The Yup'ik, culturally and spiritually tied to the sea, viewed themselves as fundamentally different from the Chukchi. We have seen the differences many times, most obviously in the types of animals associated with the Chukchi and Yup'ik: reindeer and sea mammals, respectively. Even the bones of reindeer and sea mammals were kept in separate containers before they were disposed of—separately.

Newcomers distinguished mainly between locals and nonlocals, but there was a second level of distinction, reflected in the marriage patterns of the three groups. Newcomers considered the Yup'ik more understandable and therefore more acceptable partners than the Chukchi. They explained that the Yup'ik, being a sedentary people, had more exposure to Newcomers, so "we're used to each other." The Chukchi, being relatively recent "immigrants" to the village, were considered more different and less understandable. After an argument with his young Chukchi wife, a young Yup'ik man said in frustration, "Sometimes I just don't understand her. Maybe that's because she's from the Bilibino region, on the tundra far inland?" The Newcomers' distinction between the two local groups conferred certain advantages on the Yup'ik. They had increased access to goods via their Newcomer spouses; and even though children were most often officially ascribed the nationality of the native spouse,[13] they had relatives on the "mainland" where they could visit and be exposed to broader Soviet life.

Although there were several arenas of intergroup dialogue (one's class in school, friendships, working partnerships), dialogue alone was unable to counteract the structural and cultural categories in place. The aspects of "otherness" that were based in symbolic systems and on social structures that magnified difference informed group and individual discourse in Sireniki and ultimately led to the creation of distinct cultural collectivities within the social system as a whole.

Baidara on the Tundra: The Gift as Dialogue

> When I was little I remember how my father used to take us
> fishing on the lake near where the Third Brigade is today. He
> had his partner in Sireniki make him a *baidara* and he hauled
> that *baidara* all the way out here on the tundra. We would
> float in it on the lake and catch the best fish. I wonder what-
> ever happened to that *baidara*.
>
> NATASHA, A CHUKCHI WOMAN, 1990

The symbolic and structural boundaries between the three groups were not impermeable. They could be penetrated by friendship, working partnership, Party membership, and exogamy. One of the most significant ways in which the three groups attempted to create social dialogue was through gift exchange.

Marcel Mauss theorized that gift exchange was a system of prestations and obligatory counterprestations between social groups ("moral persons"). Mauss's contribution to exchange theory was to recognize the inalienable character of goods exchanged as gifts, as opposed to the alienable character of gifts exchanged as commodities. "Prestations which are in theory voluntary, disinterested, and spontaneous are in fact obligatory and interested" (Mauss 1967:1). It was his contention that exchange was one of the fundamental structuring elements of "archaic" social systems. In Sireniki, each group exchanged gifts with each of the others. The gifts stimulated social dialogue.

Not surprisingly, Chukchi, Yup'ik, and Newcomers interpreted gift exchange differently. Newcomers gave and accepted gifts among themselves on birthdays and holidays. Such gifts helped to sustain the networks of *druzhba* (friendship) that were necessary if one was to maintain a household in the Soviet Union.

Druzhba was particularly important to Newcomers in the north because they lived without extended family ties and therefore must rely on *druz'ia* (friends) for support. *Druz'ia* provided each other with material support (food, drink, the use of a motorcycle or a car, a loan, or clothing), mutual assistance (child care, shopping, or mechanical repairs), and "the possibility to display one's true personality" (Markowitz 1993:106). Only with *druz'ia* you knew to be trustworthy could you talk openly about the daily hardship of Soviet life and your growing suspicion of the Soviet state.

These friendships were solidified through the sharing of food and drink; hospitality was highly valued among Newcomers. *Druz'ia* were frequently found at each other's apartments conversing over tea after the workday, or on weekends (especially when alcohol was sold) organizing an evening party of drinking, eating, and singing to the guitar. *Druz'ia* were a respite from the severity of Soviet life, and these relationships were carefully nurtured through gift exchange. My Russian friends who have immigrated to the United States lament that friendship here is different. They complain about the time constraints of the work-oriented U.S. society; there is not enough time for friends. The few and infrequent times we have gotten together for a holiday, sat together, reminisced together, drunk and eaten together, and sung together, everyone has exclaimed how wonderful it has been, the way it used to be in the Soviet Union.

For the Newcomer, trust was an integral part of *druzhba*, and because the Chukchi and Yup'ik were so different from them and therefore by definition untrustworthy, *druzhba* between Newcomers and Chukchi and Yup'ik was almost impossible. Therefore, gift exchange between Newcomers and Chukchi and Yup'ik was very rare.

The Chukchi and Yup'ik were also noted for their hospitality. Among the Chukchi, giving was a cultural imperative. Strangers were treated to the finest hospitality and always given gifts. Their generosity was always a problem for me. My economic circumstances, even as a student, were so far above those of most people in the village that I always felt guilty accepting gifts from my various hosts. And I frequently embarrassed my hosts by bringing chocolate, or some other gift I thought appropriate, to dinner parties. When I returned to Sireniki in 1994 with gifts for my friends, Ada gently chastised me. "Stop, you're embarrassing us! We're the ones who should be giving you gifts."

Bogoraz describes the gifting imperative among the Chukchi he studied. He describes a fall slaughter ceremony among the Chukchi that included "Eskimo" guests whose every request would be granted. "To refuse such a demand was dangerous, because the guest might take offense, and bewitch the host" (Bogoraz 1904–9:375). One of my housemates, Lida, always gave a portion of her reindeer meat (from her own animals or from a relative's animals) to her Newcomer housemates, and she always said, "Now you can't say I don't give you anything." The Newcomers were vastly annoyed. What a grudging way to give! In actuality, she was fulfilling an obligation to give. Not to have shared her reindeer could have had consequences for her or her family. "Someone might get sick," she would explain. By fulfilling her perceived obligation to give, she ensured the health of her family.

The Yup'ik were equally generous and hospitable. It was unthinkable to refuse a request, especially by a relative. As among the Chukchi, in the Yup'ik community material goods were cycled and food was shared. Relatives "borrowed" clothing, tools, books, and other items from one another, and as we saw earlier, when special foods (seaweed, eggs, fish, auklets) were brought home, they were frequently distributed among related households. The imperative of giving was unquestioned among the Yup'ik. I once joked with an elderly friend that I was a frequent visitor for dinner at her house. She became very upset. "Don't ever talk like that! Never say 'I've been eating here too many times,' or 'You're always feeding me.'" Her concern was for more than etiquette; she was worried that such a statement might have supernatural consequences.

The morality of giving was a basic cultural principle among both the Yup'ik and the Chukchi, but gift exchange in Sireniki occurred at many levels; gifts were given not only at life cycle events (birth, marriage, and death) but on national holidays as well—International Women's Day, the New Year, and various workers' holidays. Everyone received a gift on national holidays—coworkers, peers, friends, and family members. These gifts generally consisted of factory goods, such as clothing, books, games, needles, and candy. Many *kollektivy* drew names from a hat to determine which co-worker would buy a gift for whom. When Newcomers and natives worked together, gifts were exchanged between the three groups. Although these gifts could create ties between people, because these holidays were Soviet holidays (by definition artificial), the gifts given depended on the nature of the social relationship and not vice versa. Therefore, these gifts were for the most part alienable and were not infused with the reciprocal obligations of gifts given at life cycle events. Gifts given on holidays did not entail extended social interaction unless they were given to people with whom one had other social ties.

In contrast to gifts given on national holidays, gifts given at life cycle events were given between people with strong social obligations, often by family members. Such gifts were exchanged between Yup'ik and Chukchi who were connected through the reciprocal gifting of reindeer and sea mammals.

The exchange of reindeer for sea mammals was particularly important because of the symbolic properties of these animals. [14] People and families who participated in such an exchange were bound together by a moral obligation of reciprocal gift giving. Such gifts were generally offered at life cycle events.

For example, certain gifts given during a mortuary ceremony were given not only to the family but to the spirit of the deceased. These gifts showed respect to the family and the individual and protected the health of the village by ensuring a quick and easy passage of the spirit to the other side. When they could, the Chukchi sacrificed a live reindeer on the tundra to carry the spirit of the deceased to the other side.

Gifts given at weddings not only constituted an economic contribution to the new household (china, glassware, furniture, carpets, and cutlery) but also solidified relationships between families and created new distribution networks. On two occasions I heard a Chukchi uncle promise a favorite niece to contribute a reindeer to her wedding. And at one Yup'ik wedding the couple was given a reindeer by a close relative.

It should be noted that many Yup'ik own personal reindeer, although not so many as Chukchi do. Because of their availability and the Yup'ik's familiarity with the Chukchi system of giving, the Yup'ik also give reindeer at life cycle ceremonies as a gift of great value. Consider an incident that took place in the winter of 1989–90: A dozen or more reindeer showed up on St. Lawrence Island, Alaska. Everyone assumed that they had crossed the ice from Chukotka. Amid much joking about how the reindeer wanted to visit America just like everyone else, people saw their appearance as symbolic. The people in Sireniki took this phenomenon as an appropriate start to the new openness between Alaska and Chukotka. Yup'ik people told their St. Lawrence relatives to keep the reindeer as a gift and a symbol of the many exchanges to follow. Thus, for the Yup'ik, reindeer too became an appropriate symbol of the solidification of a newly recreated dialogue with Alaska.

Gifts to the family of a newborn were given by close friends and family members and made significant the arrival of the new group member. Among both groups a close family member might give a reindeer to the newborn.

Before Soviet intervention, the Yup'ik's trading relationship with the Chukchi provided them with reindeer meat, but more important were the skins from which they made bedding and the *kuklankas, tarbaza*, and leggings that were so necessary to their survival on winter hunts. The seal oil the Chukchi received provided necessary dietary fat and fuel for their lamps. Sea mammal products also provided sealskin ropes for the Chukchi's lassos and waterproof soles for their *tarbaza*, as well as walrus skins to cover their *polog*.

Several Chukchi and Yup'ik families in the village continued their pre-Soviet trading relationships, but the items traded had changed. Now reindeer products were exchanged for *tuutaq* (fermented walrus),[15] and Chukchi now gave living reindeer as gifts, something never done in pre-Soviet days. They frequently gave live reindeer to members of their own families and occasionally to a member of a Yup'ik family with whom the Chukchi family had had a trading relationship for two or three generations (Bogoraz 1904–9:53; Vdovin 1965:54–61). "Our grandfather always gave them walrus," a Yup'ik man explained, "and their grandfather always gave us meat." This was a classic trading relationship across two ecological, territorial, and cultural zones for mutual nutritional, material, and social benefits; but more important, the relationship crossed a symbolic boundary with the very symbols themselves: reindeer to the sea and sea mammal to the tundra. In Sireniki today, such exchanges usually take the form of reciprocal gifts rather than trade and create a dialogue across a symbolic boundary of difference. Because of the significance of reindeer and the need to provide for their proper physical and spiritual care, however, most gifts of live reindeer stayed within the Chukchi community.[16]

Live reindeer were given on special occasions to family members to mark a life cycle event or in appreciation for some previously received aid. Hopeful men gave young women reindeer, friends gave reindeer to one another, and individuals presented reindeer to favorite relatives. Although the system of giving was not so all-pervasive as it is among some peoples, it could not be called haphazard; the receiver might have initiated the gift giving, or the giver might have sensed a need.[17]

I have heard people complain that others, especially family members, had several reindeer while they had none, but such complaints were rare and always made presumably in jest, so as not to be offensive. Just as frequently, however, I have heard people express their hopes that their reindeer would give birth in the spring so that when the fawn was weaned, they could give it to a relative who had no reindeer.

The obligation to reciprocate a gift of a reindeer was strong. Failure to do so might lead to gossip, but because of the small size of the village and the far-reaching family ties, the social relationship would not be completely severed.

The Chukchi's gifts of reindeer to Yup'ik and Newcomers were intended to engage the other two groups in the cultural dialogue of reciprocal gifting and thus to make them more "understandable." When Lida gave reindeer meat to her Newcomer housemates, she was not only ensuring her health; she was attempting to create a deeper social relationship with them.

This strategy rarely succeeded with Newcomers, because they saw reindeer as a commodity (an alienable article of exchange). Although owning reindeer had a different meaning for Newcomers, it still conferred status. I have heard Newcomers brag about their reindeer. The socially sanctioned way to obtain reindeer was as a gift or in trade. Some people received gifts from Chukchi friends or colleagues, but some "bought" reindeer with alcohol. The latter practice was illegal, so no one would publicly admit to doing it; and it was an insult to suggest that someone had received reindeer in that way.

Of all the nineteen live reindeer transferred between 1989 and 1990, eleven went to relatives (Newcomer, Chukchi, and Yup'ik), five were given by Chukchi to Yup'ik friends, two went to the *vezdekhod* drivers, and one was bartered. Other than the gifts to the drivers, no reindeer were given by an individual Chukchi to a Newcomer. One Newcomer received a reindeer from a Yup'ik, but they were related through marriage. Because a live reindeer was a spiritually powerful gift that bonded two people or families, it was not surprising that few Newcomers were trusted with this responsibility. Unlike the Newcomers, the Yup'ik knew the appropriate actions and participated in the system of reciprocal gifting with the Chukchi to the satisfaction of both groups. Therefore, gifts of live reindeer between Yup'ik and Chukchi were more common than between Newcomers and Chukchi or Yup'ik.

In 1989–90 the state farm recorded the transfer of five reindeer to Newcomers. Two of these transfers were to sons-in-law, two were given by the reindeer herders to their *vezdekhod* drivers (for their "good work"), and one was "bought" for a bottle of vodka. One of the two *vezdekhod* drivers who received reindeer was married to a Yup'ik woman and therefore participated in the exchange system through her. The other man interpreted his gift as a work bonus. And so it was, in a way. The man never socialized with the herders on his trips to the tundra. He refused to eat with them, slept in his *vezdekhod* rather than on the sleeping benches with everyone else, and never shared the alcohol he brought except with other Newcomer drivers. The herders were mildly insulted by his behavior, but because he was a hard worker and would drive even when the workday was officially over, they gave him a reindeer in appreciation.

As most Newcomers were ignorant of the native social obligations that follow the gift of a reindeer, such gifts generally put the Chukchi giver in a negative reciprocity relationship. Among the Chukchi and the Yup'ik, the gift of a reindeer created a future social relationship through anticipated reciprocity. The Chukchi giver was giving not only a reindeer but his (or a relative's) services to tend to the Yup'ik's reindeer on the tundra. In exchange, the Yup'ik would give fermented walrus, seaweed, eggs, and other ocean products complemented by store-bought goods (given at weddings, births, and funerals). The entire family of the receiver was expected to participate, and often it took extended family members to fulfill the obligation.

The gift of a reindeer to someone who was not a family member not only created a social obligation but acted as a public token of a social relationship between two people not otherwise connected. The Yup'ik woman who attended the pominki for a Chukchi *brigadir* (Chapter 3) brought gifts of candy,

Ceremonial whale mandibles, moved from their original position near a yaranga, stand near the owner's apartment. (Photo by John Echave.)

cookies, *papirosy* (Russian-style cigarettes), tea, and fish for the deceased and his family. She had worked with the *brigadir* during her internship on the tundra as an animal technician, and at the end of her internship he had given her a reindeer; they had maintained their friendship until he died. She told me he had given her the reindeer because he wanted to start a sexual relationship with her. She refused, but she kept the reindeer, gave his family gifts, and never refused his requests for alcohol. Her funeral gifts were graciously received and a portion was placed on the body as an offering.

When the same woman attended the funeral of a young Chukchi man with whom she had grown up but had had very little daily contact, several Chukchi women questioned her motives. I knew they were personal and sentimental, but the Chukchi women speculated about her relationship with the deceased and concluded that her actions were inappropriate.

The Chukchi community interpreted these two signs of friendship in different ways. The woman's relationship with the *brigadir* was socially recognized and had been solidified by the reciprocal exchange of reindeer and gifts. In the second case, her feelings were strictly personal. Because she had had no

Whale crania abandoned on the tundra near Imtuk Lake. (Photo by John Echave.)

formal, public relationship with the man, the Chukchi misinterpreted her actions: either she was satisfying some voyeuristic tendency or she had had a clandestine sexual relationship with the deceased. Neither was true.

Soviet intervention in Sireniki created a need for a common understanding among three disparate groups. The Chukchi and the Yup'ik discovered a common language in their traditional trading and gifting and through these practices forged their new relationship. In some cases similar relationships were formed with Newcomers. In Sireniki the form of the dialogue had changed from the traditional exchange across ecological zones for the mutual physical survival of both groups to a moral exchange that began with the spiritually empowered gifts of live reindeer and sea mammal products. Gift exchange among the Yup'ik and Chukchi of Sireniki was a morally empowered dialogue across an existing structural and symbolic space of otherness.

Throughout this analysis I have attempted to describe and analyze some of the cultural knowledge that provided meaning and order to Yup'ik, Chukchi, and Newcomer social relationships. Each group relied on their own cultural perceptions to interpret each other's differences and maintain internal group cohesion within the evolving Soviet structure. My intent here has been not to replace structural relationships with native models but to provide some of the cultural and symbolic background for the way in which each group constructed itself, and thus the others, in the context of Sireniki.

[149]

Native discourse of otherness was informed by cultural symbols, which in turn informed native practice — the separation of reindeer from sea mammals, low rates of exogamy, choices of employment, and mortuary practices, to name only a few. Newcomers are much more difficult to characterize. They were the foreigners, the outsiders, the representatives of the Soviet economic, political, and ideological system. Newcomers' discourse revolved around their transient status, their economic goals, and their social position. These aspects of Newcomers' identity defined their difference to themselves as well as to the Chukchi and Yup'ik.

The personal and social relationships the three groups managed to create despite their differences were very tenuous; although they were important to the individuals involved, they failed to breach the boundaries created by strong collective group identities.

Proximity: Structural and Symbolic Spaces

> They're different from us. They can be joking with very serious faces; don't believe everything they say.
>
> YUP'IK WOMAN, SPEAKING OF THE CHUKCHI

> They're different. They're meaner. We are a quiet and shy people.
>
> CHUKCHI WOMAN, SPEAKING OF THE YUP'IK

> How can you spend so much time with them? They're so slow. You're an educated person, what could you possibly have to say to one another?
>
> RUSSIAN TEACHER, SPEAKING OF THE YUP'IK
> AND CHUKCHI

Social scientists have applied such labels as "nationality" and "ethnicity" (Anderson 1995; Balzer 1983; Bromlei 1973; Gellner 1992; Schindler 1992; Tishkov 1992; Vakhtin 1993) to the growing movement toward formation of exclusive group identities among indigenous peoples of the former Soviet Union. Although these labels are often useful in efforts to analyze subordinate group identity vis-à-vis the dominant majority, they carry with them decades of definitional baggage and usage, and ultimately do little to expand our knowledge of the evolving conflicts between the local indigenous groups themselves.

It is possible to infer from the way they talk that the Yup'ik, Chukchi, and Newcomers had a developed sense of otherness. Before Soviet intervention in the 1950s, the Chukchi and Yup'ik of Sireniki had limited contact. The Chukchi lived a nomadic existence on the inland tundra and the Yup'ik occupied settled coastal villages. Contact between these two groups was either for trade or for warfare, with the occasional herdless Chukchi man coming to the coast to serve as *baidara* crew (Bogoraz 1904–9; Krupnik 1993; Vdovin 1965a). Frederick Barth states (1969:16) that the maintenance of collective group boundaries during cultural interaction depends on the structuring of intercourse through agreed-upon prescriptions for dialogue, which "need not extend beyond that which was relevant to the social situation in which they interact." Between the Chukchi and Yup'ik, trade and warfare were highly structured forms of social interaction, often almost ritualized (Bogoraz 1904–9:53–69). Because their interaction was so highly structured, it is reasonable to assume that at that period in their history the Chukchi and Yup'ik had a very restricted sense of one another as other, and that their sense of the other that exists today is a manifestation of the contemporary setting.

Before the Revolution, contact with outsiders was limited to a few Russian traders and the foreign whalers. It was not until collectivization that indigenous peoples of either group in the Sireniki region had sustained contact with Newcomers. In the early 1990s this interaction was primarily limited to the village. It was the space where all three groups, Chukchi, Yup'ik, and Newcomers, interacted and more fully formed their perceptions of one another. Each group's own collectivization became more salient through interaction with the other two. The Soviet state created a physical and social landscape that encouraged them to articulate otherness in ways they had never done before. By changing the social and physical proximity of these three groups, the state encouraged the refinement of a language of difference.

The Evolving Discourse of Otherness

It is not possible to discuss collective identity formation without addressing the issue of interest. Researchers examining the questions surrounding group identity frequently point to economic, political, or psychosocial interest as the motivations for group cohesiveness. Abner Cohen, using a resource-competition model, argues that ethnicity is a "communal organization that is manipulated by an interest group in its struggle to develop and maintain its power" (1981:325).

Such interest-based models help us to understand competition among groups vis-à-vis state resources and they provide insight into the evolving politicization of discourse in Sireniki among the Yup'ik, Chukchi, and Newcomers. Group interest alone, however, cannot account for the divisions between these three groups. Collective identity formation was based on cultural and symbolic constructions, not perceived group interests.

Ronald Cohen (1978:393) suggests that "ethnicity and occupational stratification enhance one another, with the lower status ethnic groups restricted to lower regarded and poorly paid economic positions." The interests created by social stratification and access to scarce resources did play a role in Sireniki. Newcomers filled most of the jobs in the infrastructure, in schools, warehouses, transportation, and administration, leaving few of these economically and socially advantageous positions to the Yup'ik and Chukchi peoples.

Because the Soviet system had its basis in Russian social structure and culture, Newcomers were inherently advantaged. In Sireniki, however, Newcomers interpreted their social and economic status in the system as a sign of their cultural and intellectual superiority to the Chukchi and Yup'ik. Brackette Williams points out that "members of the ruling race / culture / nation often assume a superiority based on their alleged innate intellectual capabilities" (1989:437). This attitude of superiority was intensified by the physical separation of the three groups, both at their place of work and in their free time. As we have seen, very few Newcomers had anything but superficial contact with Chukchi or Yup'ik. This lack of interaction hindered meaningful dialogue between the Newcomer and native groups and structurally reinforced their separation.

Newcomers were identified as nonlocal, literally "in-comers." They frequently spoke of the Chukchi and Yup'ik, who were "local," as primitive and uneducated. Newcomers pointed to basic cultural differences as proof: dietary preferences, the smell of the natives' fur garments and drying foods, the high incidence of childbirth among unwed mothers, and natives' "choice" of jobs. The actual work the Yup'ik and Chukchi people did, such as slaughtering reindeer and sea mammals, was repugnant to many Newcomers. As evidence of Yup'ik "primitiveness," a teacher told of a child who didn't cry when his brother died and in fact played basketball the afternoon of the tragedy. What the teacher didn't know was that the Yup'ik consider it unsafe to shed tears over the dead, as their spirits might hear your sadness and refuse to leave the village. The Newcomers had no understanding of Chukchi and Yup'ik ways. In the Newcomers' structural and cultural constructions of the Chukchi and Yup'ik we see the classic we / they dichotomy that for many anthropologists defines an ethnic group.

In Sireniki, as elsewhere in the former Soviet Union, the destabilization of the centralized state authority opened a new arena for public dialogue, and this dialogue was increasingly politicized. In this new context, the Yup'ik and Chukchi increased their demands for a stronger voice and more local control. Native demands reflected interests of class (better working and living conditions), culture (preservation of language and ritual), and politics (territorial autonomy). The viewpoints of the Chukchi, Yup'ik, and Newcomers conflicted and often competed. In Sireniki each group's definitions of the others were constantly being negotiated. The discourse of otherness was never publicly expressed, however, until 1990, when the Regional Society of the Eskimo of Chukotka organized a conference in Provideniia.

Taking advantage of newly enacted legislation adopted by the USSR on April 26, 1990, titled "Unhindered Ethnic Development of Citizens of the USSR Who Live Outside Their Ethnic Areas or Have No Such Areas Within the Territory of the USSR," the Yup'ik started to organize into political associations based on "nationality" (Vakhtin 1993b:12). One such organization was the Regional Society of the Eskimo (now Yup'ik).

The political demands of this association had been circulating in Sireniki since the winter of 1989–90. They were primarily class concerns about poor pay, especially for the women who worked skins; difficulty in obtaining apartments; Newcomers' complaints about the smell of traditional foods and garments; and lack of access to prized resources, such as salmon and caviar. However, native people also expressed concern over the loss of their language and "cultural deterioration," exemplified by the dwindling numbers of people who were "pure Eskimo." [18]

Because the association was formally organized and its members had a high level of political consciousness (in comparison with the average Chukchi and Yup'ik), its agenda dominated the Provideniia conference. The issues of greatest concern to the members were the formation of native associations, the international park between Chukotka and Alaska, and the possibility of national villages.

Various groups expressed their views of national villages and separate native associations during a town meeting in Sireniki several months after the Provideniia conference. Regardless of the Yup'ik's intent in raising the issue of national villages, the Chukchi interpreted it as an attempt to push them out of Sireniki. Rumors to this effect were rampant and polarized the Yup'ik and Chukchi community, giving the discourse of difference a decidedly nationalist tone.

My wife is Chukchi, I am Eskimo, where will my children live? This is a stupid idea. You can't split a community in half.

PANAUGE, YUP'IK HUNTER

Why do we need a separate association? We should all be in one together, Russians, Chukchi, and Eskimos.

NATASHA, CHUKCHI WOMAN

You're creating a Nagorno-Karabakh! You have your association and we'll have ours.

ZAVINA, YUP'IK STATE FARM ECONOMIST

These comments reflect the various reactions against the perceived separatist thinking of the Eskimo Association. Some Chukchi took great offense and recounted other instances of Yup'ik discrimination against them. Many, however, were genuinely confused as to why the Yup'ik would want them out of the village. The Soviet ideology of a brotherhood of workers and social equality still influenced public opinion. These people were very hurt by the suggestion that they should be excluded. Some people repeated Soviet rhetoric about brotherhood and equality, and insisted that the Newcomers were Chukotkans as well. (These statements were made in public forums by native people who had administrative positions, so it was difficult to determine if they genuinely believed the Soviet doctrine or considered it politically expedient to say so.) And still others, those of exogamous marriages, worried about the fate of their dual-nationality children.

Newcomers' impressions were fairly nondescript. Because they considered themselves indispensable to the continued operation of basic services in the village and because they had always intended to retire to their homelands, most felt that the desire for national villages and associations was a "passing phase" for local peoples.

The discourse after this incident was couched in terms of otherness. In fact, as Vakhtin (1993b:13–19) describes, after the breakup of the centralized state, economic reorganization of the former Soviet Union began along ethnic lines. In Chukotka, according to Vakhtin, many of the people felt that the state farms should be reorganized and land should be transferred to the indigenous communities. Unfortunately, the reorganization legislation was so vague that the very definition of "indigenous" was open to debate. Vakhtin concludes that "dealing with economic issues on ethnic lines can lead only to ethnic conflict." In fact, in 1992 the Council of People's Deputies of the Chukchi Autonomous Area "appealed to all local councils, the local administration, supervisory bodies, the mass media, and political movements and parties to refrain from extreme and ill-considered measures, which would exacerbate an already difficult economic and social situation in Chukotka and were liable to ignite conflicts of an inter-ethnic nature" (Vakhtin 1993b:18).

Although Vakhtin was not discussing Sireniki specifically, it is not hard to understand how the situation there could have escalated to inter-ethnic conflict. The discourse of difference heard at the town meeting was expressed in other situations as well. During parent-teacher conferences Yup'ik and Chukchi parents were sharply divided over the issue of native language instruction. Each believed the other group to be receiving better instruction than their own. The Chukchi complained that there were more Yup'ik lessons than Chukotkan, and Yup'ik parents complained that the quality of the Yup'ik lessons was substandard.[19]

Each group accused the other of favoritism toward their own group in the matter of access to material goods. The saleswomen in the stores were primarily Yup'ik and therefore they were accused of holding special goods for Yup'ik customers and denying them to Chukchi. The Yup'ik pointed to the *polka olenevoda* as irrefutable evidence that the Chukchi were given special privileges.

This dialogue escalated in the summer of 1990 when the reindeer herders sold *panty* (horns) to a Korean middleman in Alaska in exchange for American goods (food mixers, clothing, VCRs, and tape player–recorders). These goods could be purchased through the state farm, but only by the reindeer herders. The Yup'ik hunting brigades became angry because they claimed to have helped the herders in the preparation of the *panty* for shipping. The Chukchi countered by saying that the Yup'ik had the special privilege of visa-free visiting to Alaska, where they had access to the very same goods through their relatives. These forms of the dialogue of difference were interest-based; in some instances very gross material interests were being argued. What was interesting was that the Yup'ik and Chukchi chose to focus their discourse on each other and not on the Soviet system. The system's inefficiencies and overregulation aroused anger among the Yup'ik and Chukchi (among the Newcomers, too), but very few people were able to objectify their positions within the system. Therefore, they chose as the focal point of their dialogue the familiar— each other.

By reinforcing differences through social and economic stratification, the Soviet system was a divisive force in the community. By limiting access to resources and controlling group economic activities, the system structured intergroup dialogue in such a way as to facilitate the emergence of separate cultural collectivities. The boundaries between Newcomer, Yup'ik, and Chukchi became more clearly defined and the differences between the three groups were magnified. As Barth suggests, ethnicity "organiz[es] interaction between people," and in Sireniki collective identity served as a backdrop against which to understand the new context of interaction. What were earlier conceived of as cultural and symbolic differences became solidified as political ones. In Sireniki, the very system that sought to control and homogenize difference reinforced it.

I want to avoid the proverbial chicken-and-egg argument—which came first, political domination and economic subordination or collective identity? These were not mutually exclusive phenomena, and in Sireniki they were both basic to the evolving discourse of otherness. Although these issues provided a focus for political discourse, they were not the impetus for collective group formation. Collectivities were formed on the basis of prior cultural, social, historical, and symbolic conceptualizations. The Chukchi, Yup'ik, and Newcomers had a distinct understanding of each other's otherness. In the context of the Soviet restructuring of local economic, political, and social systems, each group used its familiar cultural texts to make sense of the Soviet world. As they did so, their sense of self and therefore their sense of other became more salient and defined.

The Yup'ik and Chukchi did not organize themselves as collectivities solely for interest-based political and economic gains. If social and economic equality were a reality, the Chukchi, Yup'ik, and Newcomers would still fundamentally not understand each other very well. Yup'ik husbands would have continued to be confused by the actions of their Chukchi wives, and Chukchi wives by those of their Yup'ik husbands; Chukchi herders working in the village would still yearn for the tundra, and Newcomers would continue to romanticize their lives in their home republics.

All the same, it should be clear that the emergence of collective identities and the resulting conflicts were not expressions of unconstrained, ancient "ethnic rivalries." Collective identities emerged among the Chukchi, Yup'ik, and Newcomers in their efforts to understand one another against the backdrop of the economic and social restructuring of the Soviet system, and so to construct and understand themselves.

EPILOGUE

Post-Soviet Sireniki

In the years since I first set eyes on Sireniki, the village that became my second home, much has changed; some might say everything has. From the global perspective, the greatest change was that in December 1991, ten months after the completion of my fieldwork, the USSR ceased to exist. From the local perspective, the greatest change was that all of the Soviet-era social programs and subsidies have ended, leaving Arctic villagers stranded without jobs, wages, schools, medical care, or, in a growing number of cases, basic food, fuel, and clothing.

As the structure changed in western Russia, in major urban areas it was replaced by increasing personal freedoms—freedom of speech, access to Western imports, and at least for some people access to Western jobs and Western salaries. In the remote regions, there was nothing to replace the lost structure. Because the Soviet-era infrastructure in the Far East and the Arctic was a subsidized and artificial construct of the Soviet system, today those regions, with the exception of such major cities as Vladivostok, Khabarovsk, and Iakutsk, are in total disarray. The politically and physically disenfranchised people who inhabit those remote villages and tundra encampments are facing an unprecedented challenge for simple physical survival.

My colleagues and I read national press articles and listen to reports of Russian structural chaos and pending winter starvation, trying to glean a morsel of information about the regions in which we lived, hoping to gain some insight into the lives of the people we worked with, many of whom we consider close friends. I am fortunate enough to be able to correspond with many of the people of Sireniki through intermittent flights between Alaska and Chukotka.

Their letters offer little solace, however, as their tone and content become increasingly and uncharacteristically filled with despair.

When I left the Soviet Union in 1991, the exchange rate was 6 rubles to the U.S. dollar; by January 1998, inflation had robbed the ruble of so much of its value that the Russian government issued new rubles worth 1,000 times less than the old, and by the spring of 2000 one of those new rubles was worth roughly 3 U.S. cents. Inflation has made most people's savings and pensions virtually worthless. People express intense disillusionment about the years they spent in the North with the understanding that they could retire at home with a healthy pension. With hyperinflation, the destruction of supply lines to the northern regions, and the elimination of the northern wage coefficient, Newcomers have no incentive to stay, and so they are leaving for their home republics in search of better living and economic conditions. By 1999 the population of Sireniki had dropped from approximately 700 inhabitants to under 500. This decline follows the general trend for Chukotka as a whole, whose population decreased 49 percent between 1989 and 1998.

Out-migration has given rise to very serious concerns. Most serious is the lack of skilled professionals to teach in the schools and provide medical services in the northern regions. So many teachers have left Sireniki that the middle school had to close; currently only seven years of schooling are provided. A child can attend the Russian equivalent of high school only at a boarding school in Provedeniia. Thus the old system of educating children away from their families and so away from their language, symbols, and culture has returned. The future of these children is in question, not only because of the alienation they will feel but also because of the questionable education they are receiving. As resources dwindle, even in the most populated regions of Russia the ability to maintain high academic standards is in jeopardy; in the remote regions standards have most assuredly slipped. Even if students excel, their families are unlikely to have the resources to send them on to the university.

The picture is not much different in local medical facilities. Many village hospitals are no longer staffed by doctors. If they have any health professional, they do not have the resources to purchase the necessary medicines to provide even the most minimal relief for minor illnesses. The Red Cross reported in its official assessment of Chukotka in 1999 that life expectancy in the region could be as low as 34 years. Many physicians have become so despondent about their inability to provide rudimentary care or even immunizations for children that they have quit their jobs in despair or turned to alcohol for solace.

Other changes of significance are the increased unemployment in the village and the tremendous decrease in access to material goods. Inflation has pushed the prices of the few goods available so high that most families cannot buy them. The state pensions intermittently paid to retirees, pitiful and unreliable as they are, have become the main source of cash for most families.

None of the hopes of commercial independence for the reindeer brigades or the sea mammal hunting brigades have been realized. The one hunting cooperative was the only work group that gained independence from the state farm. Today the state farm is all but defunct. The fox farm has been closed; the reindeer brigades are functioning only at a subsistence level and their production has ceased to have commercial value; and the hunters now hunt to feed the village, not to provide walrus to the state farm for a wage.

The situation has been exacerbated by very harsh winters and a lack of state farm support for the reindeer herds. Lack of wolf control because helicopters are too expensive, lack of access to vaccines, lack of supplemental feed, and the decreasing number of *vezdekhody* to provide supplies to the herders have left the brigades with a shortage of men willing to go to the tundra. These conditions in turn shrank the state farm herd from an estimated 5,000 in 1991 to under 500 in less than ten years.

The deterioration of the state farm and the lack of economic support from the Russian government have forced villagers to become increasingly dependent on subsistence resources. Although the impetus for the resurgence of a subsistence economy is the breakdown of the infrastructure, subsistence practices are being embraced not only materially but culturally. The knowledge of how to gather and hunt is traditional and therefore is strengthening Yup'ik and Chukchi traditional cultural practices. Along with increased dependency on subsistence activities has come increasing interest among younger Yup'ik and Chukchi in learning about hunting and gathering from their grandparents. Contact with their relatives in Alaska has contributed to the resurgence in things Yup'ik and Chukchi.

In 1989, with the lifting of the "ice curtain," Sireniki was the site of the first joint whaling festival in over forty years. This festival reunited the Russian and Alaskan Yup'ik and Chukchi peoples and created a series of summer visits among the coastal communities of Chukotka and Alaska. After this contact came a resurgence of interest in hunting the bowhead. Modern technology has become available to Sireniki through contacts with Alaska, and young Sireniki hunters want to learn how to hunt whales before this knowledge is completely lost to the community. In addition, they have actively pursued their rights to hunt whales in the international arena. Aided by Inuit and Yup'ik in Alaska, in 1997 the Chukotkans successfully lobbied the International Whaling Commission (IWC) for quotas of seven strikes of bowhead whales and 120 gray whales landed.[1]

The native people of Chukotka have not been allowed to hunt polar bears since 1956. After six years of negotiations, the United States and Russia had still not finalized a treaty that would allow Chukotkans to hunt a certain number of polar bears as well.

When I returned to Sireniki in 1994, under the tutelage of their Alaskan relatives, the local hunters were actively pursuing whale. Yup'ik hunters had been given exploding harpoons and had learned some things about the behavior of the whales from their Yup'ik relatives. The Alaskan Yup'ik's whaling activities had not been disrupted, so they have preserved the knowledge needed to hunt these animals. That summer, the cooperative brigade took a small bowhead whale.

One of the young hunters, Oleg, became quite a hero when he brought in the first bowhead to the village since the 1970s. The last whale was taken by a boat crew in 1972 (other coastal villages quit hunting bowheads in the 1950s: Krupnik 1987:28). People relished the story of how he had succeeded in taking the whale, and it was recounted to me with great animation and joy every time I visited a new friend. No one tired of retelling the story of how Oleg had spotted the whale sleeping, how he had steadied the harpoon, and how he released the harpoon directly into the whale, barely escaping from its startled thrashing. Then a second *baidara* approached and Panauge dealt the whale its death blow.

Although it was another man's harpoon that actually killed the whale, it was the first strike that the Yup'ik traditionally honored, and the whale was considered Oleg's. People said that villagers wept on the beach as they cut and ate the *mangtak*. The importance of the event and the emotion with which the story was told, even after several months, indicates that the meaningfulness of the bowhead to the Yup'ik people of Sireniki is very much alive.

An additional bright spot in the international arena is an agreement signed in 1990 between President George Bush and President Gorbachev that allows the indigenous peoples of North Alaska and Chukotka to travel between the two countries without visas. This agreement has greatly facilitated summer travel, especially between the Yup'ik of Sireniki and Novoe Chaplino in Chukotka and the Yup'ik of Gambell and Savoonga on St. Lawrence Island in Alaska.

The ability to travel relatively unconstrained has greatly improved the cultural and social connections between these two peoples. In the summer, *baidary* set out from Sireniki and Novoe Chaplino several times for "visiting." This practice is recreating not only the historical social ties but the economic and linguistic ones as well. The lingua franca of St. Lawrence is the Yup'ik language, and a number of Yup'ik from Sireniki have relearned their native language as a result of their contact with their families on St. Lawrence Island.

Marriages have taken place between the two regions, solidifying the ties. Under the current conditions in Chukotka, people's ties with Alaska have been

Ada and author on the beach at Sireniki, 1994. (Photo by John Echave.)

their lifeline. Missionary groups have responded to the intense poverty throughout Chukotka. Reports of children with distended stomachs are more and more frequent. I was told that a family walked from Sireniki to Provideniia in winter to find food because none was available in the village. Many families are sending their children to the hospital in Provideniia because there they are assured at least of being fed.

The summer visits to St. Lawrence provide not only social connections but material goods. In the winter of 1999 alone, Christian and secular humanitarian aid groups provided over $1 million in food, clothing, and equipment. Despite continuous pleading with the Red Cross and the U.S. Department of Agriculture, no federal aid was directed toward this region. Its only lifeline was and continues to be Alaska.

In 1993 the government rescinded Gorbachev's restrictions on the sale of alcohol and even allowed the importation of alcohol from the United States. When I returned to Sireniki people were drinking 190-proof grain alcohol straight from the bottle. P'ianaia Subbota was no more; people had access to alcohol any day of the week, and many people were heartily sorry. A temperance movement has received support from the many missionaries coming to the region.

Evangelical churches have won members not only by their promise of eternal salvation and their message of sobriety but also by distributing food and clothing. People have taken to Christianity with varying degrees of commitment. Some local people are committed to the newfound religion and hold regular prayer meetings and sobriety meetings even in the absence of a pastor or priest. Some complain about the religiosity of friends and family members who refuse even to talk to nonbelievers.

Christian converts no longer feed their ancestors or believe in reincarnation. When a formerly very traditional woman refused to name her newborn daughter after her dead grandmother, she caused a rift in the family, for now the grandmother had no path for rebirth to this world. I do not know how widespread these practices are or what the missionaries are teaching, but the degree to which people are accepting the new religion is an indication of the people's search for answers to the crisis in which they find themselves. As a friend told me about the conversion of her mother, previously a very traditional Yup'ik woman, she said that perhaps the new religion could provide answers for the new world. We can only hope she is right.

Notes

Prologue: Fieldwork in Sireniki

1. The Yup'ik are more commonly known as the Eskimo or Inuit. Yup'ik is an ethnonym, or the term of reference that people use to describe themselves, as in "I am a Finnish American." When speaking Russian, people in Sireniki used the term "Eskimo," but that is a foreign word, introduced by Europeans to designate primarily the people who live in the Arctic coastal areas. Among some groups of Inuit, "Eskimo" is a pejorative term. I have chosen to use the term "Yup'ik" because it is the term of reference people use when speaking their native language.

2. *Priezzhii*, literally "in-comers," is the term used for nonindigenous residents, primarily from western Russia. Researchers doing work in the former Soviet North have in most cases translated the term as "newcomers."

1. The People of Sireniki

1. For additional information see Dunn and Dunn 1963; they have reviewed the Soviet literature that documents these events of relocation, consolidation, and in-migration as a general pattern for the entire northern region. For more recent ethnographic information see Vakhtin 1994.

2. For additional information on the dynamics of Yup'ik settlement and social organization see Chlenov 1973; Chlenov and Krupnik 1983.

3. According to Bogoraz (1904–9:11), the name Chukchi is a derivative of the Chukotkian word *chau'chu*, meaning "rich in reindeer."

4. Since the Chukchi in Sireniki were the descendants of Reindeer Chukchi, I will not discuss Maritime Chukchi social and cultural organization in any detail.

5. At the Columbia University Conference on Soviet Cultural Studies (1992) it was suggested to me that these anecdotes constitute not a negative image of the Chukchi but instead an image of "natural wisdom" against which the failed logic of the Soviet system could be projected. The intelligentsia may have understood the anecdotes in this sense, but for the average citizen these anecdotes fostered cultural divisions and misunderstandings. I mentioned to some Russian friends, for instance, that similar anecdotes were told in the United States about Polish people.

They were amazed. "Why would you tell such stories about Poles? The Poles are intelligent and sophisticated businessmen, not at all like the Chukchi." I rest my case.

6. The following information on the Kurupka Chukchi was provided by Igor Krupnik in personal communications, 1997.

2. The Social Context: Relatives, Residence, and Space

1. Included in the definition of nuclear families are single women with children and single men with children.

2. In 1988–89 life expectancy among the indigenous population was 54 years for men and 65 years for women vs. 64.5 years and 74.4 years, respectively, among Newcomers. These life expectancies were considerably longer than those Aleksander Pika (1996) found for the same populations in 1978–79. At that time native men and women had life expectancies of 44.5 years and 54.1 years, respectively, whereas their Slavic peers could expect to attain 61.7 years and 73.1 years. The pattern was much the same over the entire Soviet Union. So many men were killed during the Second World War and Stalin's purges that the number of men in the grandparental generation was disproportionately low (Anderson 1983:482). That was why there are so few elderly men in the village: the rest had either been killed in the war or died before they reached 50.

3. Vakhtin (1993a:22) points out that in a survey done in 1979, "out of 24 children born in Sireniki in 1975–1979 to Eskimo mothers under the age of 30, two-thirds were to unmarried mothers (for mothers under 24, the proportion was three-quarters)." These statistics can be attributed in part to the fact that a "high proportion of the incoming population are unattached males."

4. See Hughes and Hughes (1960) for a full discussion of pre-Christian marriage practices among the Siberian Yup'ik.

5. The relationship between alcohol abuse and domestic violence has been well documented (Shinkwin and Pete 1990). The Monday after P'ianaia Subbota (Drunken Saturday) (in Chukotka and the Far East, alcohol was sold only on Saturday during Gorbachev's short-lived efforts to control drinking) many women could be seen with bruises on their faces. Women reported that these altercations started during an argument about infidelity, but alcohol was probably the main cause of the abuse.

Data on domestic violence and infidelity were gathered by observation and informal interviewing. I broached with local people the idea of doing a more formal survey on this topic and was advised not to. People admitted to the problems of drunkenness and domestic violence but did not want to discuss either one formally. When foreign journalists wrote about these problems, people became upset because it seemed to them that outsiders always focused on the negative aspects of the village. Many people viewed me as the village chronicler, and people expressed the hope that my book would be positive. "You will tell the outside world what really happens here." To collect formal data on behavior they were not proud of would have been difficult.

6. The high rate among Newcomers is accounted for in part by the fact that many Newcomers, aside from military personnel, came to the region already married.

7. Data collected January 1990.

8. Most of the women doctors were general practitioners and pediatricians, while the surgeons, hospital administrators, and heads of medical departments were men. All the nurses and physicians' assistants were women.

9. I was in an officer's apartment only once; it was similar to other apartments in the village. The apartment I saw consisted of two very small rooms, each occupied by a family.

3. Life Cycle and Ceremony

1. These were actual questions asked by people in Sireniki, or so I was told. I never actually witnessed a divination.

2. I never witnessed a woman's funeral. My hosts told me that the items given to her would be her sewing kit, pots and pans, or other household items associated with the woman's work.

3. Cremation was a Chukchi practice. Because there are no trees on the Arctic coast, the Sireniki Chukchi lit a grass fire next to the grave (Igor Krupnik, personal communication, 1996).

4. For more information see Anisimov 1963; Eliade 1964; Tein 1994; Vitebsky 1997.

5. Because of the highly secretive nature of this information, I was not able to collect data on it systematically. What I present here is anecdotal evidence from brief observations.

4. The Economy: Production as Cultural Space

1. For comparison, see Stern et al. 1980 for reindeer herding among Alaskan Inuit.

2. Bogoraz (1904–9:537–44, 612–16) states that in "the Chukchi system of relationship the paternal line is markedly preponderant over the maternal." In describing domestic groups, however, he uses only such gross terminology as "brothers and cousins," without distinguishing between paternal and maternal kin.

3. A final way in which the Chukchi reworked the Soviet system, through the personal ownership of reindeer, is discussed in more detail in the section on the informal economy.

4. In 1990 the bonus was 80 rubles for a walrus, 60 rubles for a bearded seal, and 30 rubles for a small seal. The money was shared equally among the crew; the *brigadir* received 10 rubles more per animal.

5. Children and adolescents preferred the more stylish imported clothes and were often embarrassed to dress in Yup'ik or Chukchi garments. Grandparents were frequently heard admonishing them, "Don't laugh at the cold! The cold doesn't laugh!" In other words, the cold is nothing to laugh at.

6. See Oswalt 1967 for a description of the men's house among Alaskan Inuit and Yuit.

7. Other waterfowl taken for subsistence included ducks, geese, and on occasion puffins (when other species were unavailable).

8. This was one of the main Chukotkian rookeries, occupied by more than 100,000 crested auklets (Nikolai Koniukhov, ornithologist, personal communication, 1990).

5. The Cultural Construction of Other

1. It should be noted that before Soviet influence the Chukchi and Yup'ik had been in conflict. Bogoraz points to numerous episodes of warfare between the two groups (1904–9:16). Although there was contact and conflict between the two groups, the Soviets brought it to a new structural level, forcing the Yup'ik and Chukchi to redefine their relationship within the new context.

2. This separation was specific to Sireniki. Other seaside villages had been occupied by the Chukchi since prehistory, and there this dichotomy between tundra and sea did not exist (Peter Schweitzer, personal communication, 1993).

3. The tundra and the sea as symbols within the Chukchi and Yup'ik cultural systems fit Sherry Ortner's categories of both summarizing and elaborating symbols. As summarizing symbols, tundra and sea "synthesize . . . complex experience," and as elaborating symbols they provide "cultural orientation" as well as strategies for the "ordering of action" (Ortner 1973).

4. Several of these trading partnerships were inherited and many persist today.

5. In other areas, Chukchi expansion physically displaced Yup'ik populations on the coast (Menovshchikov 1962; Vdovin 1961). However, this was not the case in Sireniki.

6. Both Yup'ik and Chukchi women were very shy about their tattoos, which were placed on their hands, cheeks, and noses when they were children (see Bogoraz 1904–9:255 for illustrations of tattoos). I asked many people what they meant, and most said they didn't know. Those who did know, or were willing to tell me, said they were an indication of one's father's wealth in reindeer (among the Chukchi) or part of a curing ceremony.

7. I participated in four state farm and three personal slaughters. The maximum work recorded in a slaughtering period was approximately 1,200 state farm reindeer in 17 hours.

8. I was unable to determine if the lack of knowledge of this type of information was due to acculturation under the Soviet system or if this sort of information was age-grade controlled. Igor Krupnik pointed out to me that some people in the community who in 1991 were considered "traditional" were earlier considered "modern / innovative." I suggest that as these individuals became older, their interest in and need for traditional knowledge increased, and so they sought it out.

9. Many Chukchi refused to ride in *baidary*, and they told tales of the wild adventures they had endured when they were forced to do so. Their fear reinforced the separation of sea and tundra.

10. I am speaking here about the importance of the whale symbolically and socially. Even in prehistoric times walrus contributed more to the Yup'ik diet than whale, but it was not nearly so important culturally or symbolically (Krupnik 1993).

11. Michael Champ, Texas A&M University, personal communication.

12. Schindler (1992) makes a similar point.

13. More than 90 percent of all dual-nationality children were registered as belonging to the native nationality. *Natsional'nost'* was designated on the internal passport issued to every Soviet citizen.

14. Note the symbolic significance of exchanging reindeer for sea mammal—tundra for sea.

15. Vera Kaneshiro, personal communication, 1992.

16. Bogoraz made the point that because of the close relationship of the reindeer and its spirit to the family and their herd, live reindeer were never given, only meat and skins. Once a reindeer was slaughtered and its spirit released, the meat and skins were prized gifts. The belief in the affinity of Chukchi and reindeer accounts, at least in part, for their reluctance even today to give live reindeer to anyone but Chukchi.

17. The system of gift exchange in Sireniki was not nearly as rigid as the one Kaut (1961) described in the Philippines. The Tagalog system of *utang na loob* (a debt stemming from personal volition) required that even though a person clearly needed help, no one would offer what was needed unless the person indicated that the "gift" would be accepted, thus accepting the obligation to reciprocate.

18. The local people absorbed this idea from academic texts by Soviet anthropologists who claimed that there were very few "genetically pure Eskimo" families left.

19. The general quality of instruction in the Yup'ik language was poor. Instruction was based on pedagogical methods learned at state institutes, and many Yup'ik teachers who had been able to complete institute training, and thus to gain a job at the local school, did not speak their native language fluently. Most Chukchi teachers could speak Chukotkan because their language loss was a generation or two behind language loss among the Yup'ik.

Epilogue: Post-Soviet Sireniki

1. The IWC is an international commission composed of all whaling nations. Every five years they meet and set the quotas for the number of whales that can be caught. For some species, such as the bowhead whale, the limits are on number of strikes regardless of whether the hunters land the whale. Other quotas, such as for gray whales, apply to the number of whales actually landed.

Glossary

artel   a self-constituted collective of workers or artisans; in Sireniki, a hunting collective

babushka   grandmother

baidara   traditional Yup'ik boat made from walrus skin

bania   Russian steam bath

belok   white seal pup

blat   connections; pull

brat   brother

brigadir   foreman; chief herdsman

buran   blizzard; snowmobile

bytovoe kochevanie   nomadism as a way of life

chebureky   meat pies

dedushka   grandfather

detskii sad   kindergarten

diadia   uncle

dikii   wild

Dom Kul'tury   House of Culture; a community center

druzhba   friendship

druz'ia   friends

glava   head of household

gor'ko   bitter

griaz'   dirt

grubye   rough

iasak   traditional fur tribute to the tsar

internaty   boarding schools

kamleika   cloth anorak worn over a *kuklanka*

kirkir   a child's one-piece garment

klub   club; nickname for the Dom Kul'tury

kollektiv   a worker's subdivision by specialization, such as the hunter's *kollektiv* or the carpenter's *kollektiv* on a state farm

kolkhoz   collective farm

komandirovka   a work assignment that entailed travel

kompot   canned or stewed fruit

Komsomol   Young Communist League

korenizatsiia   nativization; early postrevolutionary policy of recognizing local native languages and cultures

korpus (pl. **korpusa**)   one of several buildings in a complex

krasnyi, krasnaia   red

Krasnaia Kniga   Red Book, the Soviet version of the endangered species list

krasnye yarangi   literally, red tents; the early postrevolutionary program that brought socialist education to the Chukchi living on the tundra

kuklanka   traditional reindeer parka

kulaks   wealthy peasants

kul'tbazy   cultural bases

mangtak   skin and attached subcutaneous fat, what is commonly referred to as blubber

materik   mainland; Far Easterners' term for the western regions of the USSR

morskaia kapusta   kelp; literally, sea cabbage

mylo   soap

Narkomnats   Narodnyi Komissariiat Natsional'nostei: People's Commissariat of Nationalities

odnoklassniki   classmates

panty   reindeer horns

papirosa   Russian cigarette, basically a cardboard tube tipped with cigarette paper filled with a small amount of tobacco

parilka   steam room in a *bania*

pel'meni   meat dumplings

P'ianaia Subbota   Drunken Saturday; the day alcohol was sold in stores

Pionerskii Lager'   Pioneer Camp; basically summer camp for children

polka olenevoda   herder's shelf

polog   sleeping bench in a yaranga

pominki   memorial ceremony

praktikum   internship

priezzhii   Newcomers

proizvodstvennoe kochevanie   the system of reindeer herding instituted by the Soviets; literally, production nomadism

puk puk   sealskin floats

rabfak (rabochii fakul'tet)   workers' department; a postrevolutionary school organized by a university to train workers for management positions

rodina   motherland; birthplace

rodstvennik   relative

sadik   diminutive of *detskii sad*

sem'ia   family

sestra   sister

sladko   sweet

sovkhoz   state farm

strelki   shooters

svidetel'   godparent; literally, witness

tarbaza   skin boots

tetia   aunt

varat   Chukchi kin group

veniki   birch branches soaked in warm water and used in the *bania* to beat oneself in order to heat up the skin

vezdekhod   all-terrain vehicle, the main form of transportation in Chukotka

yaranga   the Chukchi and Yup'ik reindeer skin dwelling

zootekhnik   a veterinarian with education in economics who acted as the top administrator of the reindeer brigades

References

Ackerman, Robert E. 1984. "Prehistory of the Asian Eskimo Zone." In *Handbook of Native North American Indians*, vol. 5: *Arctic*. Washington, D.C.: Smithsonian Institution Press.

Anderson, Barbara A. 1983. "Estimating Russification of Ethnic Identity Among Non-Russians in the USSR." *Demography* 4(4):461–89.

Anderson, David. 1995. "National Identity and Belonging in Arctic Siberia: An Ethnography of Evenkis and Dolgans at Kantaiskoe Ozero in the Taimyr Autonomous District." Dissertation, University of Cambridge.

Anisimov, A. F. 1963. "Cosmological Concepts of the Peoples of the North." In *Studies in Siberian Shamanism*, ed. H. N. Michael, pp. 157–229. Toronto: University of Toronto Press.

Antropova, V. V. and V. G. Kuznetsova. 1964. [Russian original 1956.] "The Chukchi." In *The Peoples of Siberia*, ed. M. G. Levin and L. P. Potapov, pp. 799–835. Chicago: University of Chicago Press.

Arutiunov, S. A. 1988. "Chukchi, Warriors, and Traders of Chukotka." In *Crossroads of Continents*, ed. William Fitzhugh and Aron Crowell, pp. 39–41. Washington, D.C.: Smithsonian Institution Press.

Arutiunov, S. A., and William Fitzhugh. 1988. "Prehistory of Siberia and the Bering Sea." In *Crossroads of Continents*, ed. William Fitzhugh and Aron Crowel, pp. 39–41. Washington, D.C.: Smithsonian Institution Press.

Balzer, Marjorie. 1983. "Ethnicity Without Power: The Siberian *Khanty* in Soviet Society." *Slavic Review* 84(4):840–67.

Barth, Frederick. 1969. Introduction. In *Ethnic Groups and Boundaries: The Social Organization of Cultural Difference*, ed. Frederick Barth, pp. 9–38. Boston: Little, Brown.

Bender, Donald R. 1967. "A Refinement of the Concept of Household: Families, Co-residence, and Domestic Functions." *American Anthropologist* 69:493–504.

Bernton, Hal. Jan. 17, 1993. "Season of the Horn." *We Alaskans: The Anchorage Daily News Magazine*, 7–14.

Bogojavlensky, Dimitri. 1993. "Changing Patterns of Mortality and Fertility in the Russian North." Paper presented at the 92nd Annual Meeting of the American Anthropological Association, San Francisco.

Bogoraz, Vladimir. 1904–9. *Memoirs of the American Museum of Natural History*, vol. 11: *The Chukchi*. New York: G. E. Strechert.

———. 1930. "Elements of the Culture of the Circumpolar Zone." In *Annual Report of the Board of Regents of the Smithsonian Institution*, pp. 465–82. Washington, D.C.: Smithsonian Institution.

Boiko, V. I. 1986. *Kul'tura narodnostei severa: Traditsii i sovermennost'*. Novosibirsk: Nauka.

———. 1987. *Problemy sovremennogo sotsial'nogo razvitiia narodnostei severa*. Novosibirsk: Nauka.

Bromlei, Iu. 1973. *Etnos i etnografiia*. Moscow: Nauka.

Chlenov, M. 1973. "Distinctive Features of the Social Organization of the Asiatic Eskimos." Paper prepared for distribution in advance at the Ninth International Congress of Ethnological and Anthropological Sciences, Chicago–Moscow.

Chlenov, M., and Igor Krupnik. 1983. "Dinamika Areala Aziatskikh Eskimosov v XVII–XIX vv." In *Areal'nye issledovaniia v iazykovnanii i etnografii*, ed. N. I. Tolstoi, pp. 129–39. Leningrad: Nauka.

Cohen, Abner. 1974. "Introduction: The Lesson of Ethnicity." In *Urban Ethnicity*, ed. Abner Cohen, pp. ix–xxiii. London: Tavistock.

———. 1981. "Variables in Ethnicity." In *Ethnic Change*, ed. Charles F. Keyes, pp. 307–31. Seattle: University of Washington Press.

Cohen, Ronald. 1978. "Ethnicity: Problem and Focus in Anthropology." *Annual Review of Anthropology* 7:379–403.

Dikov, N. N. 1989. *Istoriia Chukotki s drevneishikh vremen do nashikh dnei*. Moscow: Mysl'.

Donskoi, F. S. 1987. "Obespechenie ratsional'noi zaniatnosti narodnostei severa." In *Problemy sovremennogo sotsial'nogo razvitiia narodnostei severa*, ed. V. I. Boiko, pp. 82–94. Novosibirsk: Nauka.

Dunn, Stephen, and Ethel Dunn. 1962. "Directed Culture Change in the Soviet Union: Some Soviet Studies." *American Anthropologist* 64:328–39.

———. 1963. "The Transformation of Economy and Culture in the Soviet North." *American Anthropologist* 1(2):1–28.

Eliade, Mircea. 1964. *Shamanism: Archaic Techniques of Ecstasy*. Princeton: Princeton University Press.

Freed, Stanley A., Ruth S. Freed, and Laila Williamson. 1988. "Capitalist Philanthropy and Russian Revolutionaries: The Jesup North Pacific Expedition (1897–1902)." *American Anthropologist* 90:7–24.

Garb, Paula. 1993. "Environmental Thinking Among Environmental Leaders in Russia." Paper prepared for the conference "Critical Masses: Public Responses to the Environmental Consequences of Nuclear Weapons Production in Russia and the United States," Kaluga, Russia.

Gellner, Ernest. 1992. "Nationalism in the Vacuum." In *Thinking Theoretically about Soviet Nationalities: History and Comparison in the Study of the USSR*, ed. Alexander J. Motyl, pp. 243–54. New York: Columbia University Press.

Gurvich, I. S. 1961. "Directions to Be Taken in the Further Reorganization of the Economy and Culture of the Peoples of the North." *Sovetskaia Etnografiia* 4:22–31.

———. 1975. "Izuchenie etnogeneza narodov severa v Sovetskii period." In *Izuchenie etno-*

geneza i etnicheskaia istoriia narodov severa, ed. N. N. Miklukho-Maklaia, pp. 5–42. Moscow: Akademiia Nauk SSSR.

———. 1982. *Etnicheskaia istoriia narodov severa*. Moscow: Akademiia Nauk SSSR.

———. 1987. *Etnicheskoe razvitie narodnostei severa v Sovetskii period*. Moscow: Nauka.

Gurvich, I. S., and V. O. Dolgikh. 1970. *Obshchesvennyi stroi u narodov severnoi Sibiri*. Moscow: Nauka.

Honnigman, John, and Irma Honnigman. 1965. *Eskimo Townsmen*. Ottawa: Canadian Research Center for Anthropology.

Hughes, Charles C. 1964. "The Eskimos from the Peoples of Siberia." *Anthropological Papers of the University of Alaska* 12(1):1–13.

———. 1965. "Under Four Flags: Recent Culture Change Among the Eskimos." *Current Anthropology* 6(1):3–69.

Hughes, Charles C., and Jane M. Hughes. 1960. *An Eskimo Village in the Modern World*. Ithaca: Cornell University Press.

Humphrey, Caroline. 1983. *Karl Marx Collective: Economy, Society and Religion in a Siberian Collective Farm*. Cambridge: Cambridge University Press.

Kaut, Charles. 1961. "Utang Na Loob: A System of Contractual Obligation among Tagalogs." *Southwestern Journal of Anthropology* 17:256–72.

Kis', P. Ia., and V. V. Lebedev. 1978. "Nekotorye aspekty izucheniia traditsionnogo olenevodstva Chukotki." In *Polevye issledovaniia Instituta Etnografii*, pp. 120–27. Moscow: Akademiia Nauk SSSR.

Kolarz, Walter. 1969. *The Peoples of the Soviet Far East*. Hamden, Conn.: Archon Books.

Kouljok, K. E. 1985. *The Revolution in the North: Soviet Ethnography and Nationality Policy*. Uppsala: Almqvist & Wiksell International.

Kovalenko, Svetlana. 1986. *A Stride Across a Thousand Years*. Moscow: Progress.

Krupnik, I., and M. A. Chlenov. 1979. "Dinamika etnolingvisticheskoi situatsii u Aziatskikh Eskimosov." *Sovetskaia Etnografiia* 2:19–28.

———. 1997. *Survival and Contact: Asiatic Eskimo Transition 1900–1990*. Smithsonian Institution Press.

Krupnik, Igor. 1983. "Gray Whaling off the Chukotka Peninsula: Past and Present." *Report of the International Whaling Commission*, no. 33, pp. 557–62.

———. 1987. "The Bowhead vs. the Gray Whale in Chukotkan Aboriginal Whaling." *Arctic* 40(1):16–32.

———. 1993. *Arctic Adaptations: Native Whalers and Reindeer Herders of Northern Eurasia*. Trans. and ed. Marcia Levensen. Hanover, N.H.: University Press of New England.

Krushanova, A. I. 1987. *Istoriia i kul'tura Chukchei*. Leningrad: Nauka.

Lantzeff, George F., and Richard A. Pierce. 1973. *Eastward to Empire: Exploration and Conquest on the Russian Open Frontier to 1750*. Montreal: McGill–Queens University Press.

Lebedev, V. V. 1988. "Siberian Peoples: A Soviet View." In *Crossroads of Contintents: Cultures of Siberia and Alaska*, ed. William Fitzhugh and Aron Crowell, pp. 314–18. Washington, D.C.: Smithsonian Institution Press.

Leeds, Anthony. 1965. "Reindeer Herding and Chukchi Social Institutions." In *Man, Culture, and Animals: The Role of Animals in Human Ecological Adjustments*, ed. Anthony Leeds and Andrew Vayda, pp. 87–128. Washington, D.C.: American Association for the Advancement of Science.

Liber, George. 1991. "Korenizatsiia: Restructuring Soviet Nationality Policy in the 1920s." *Ethnic and Racial Studies* 14(1):15–23.

Markowitz, Francine S. 1991. "Russkaia Druzhba: Russian Friendship in American and Israeli Contexts." *Slavic Review* 50(3):637–45.

———. 1993. *A Community in Spite of Itself: Soviet Jewish Emigrés in New York*. Washington, D.C.: Smithsonian Institution Press.

Marx, Karl. 1977. *Selected Writings*. Ed. David McLellan. Oxford: Oxford University Press.

Mauss, Marcel. 1967. *The Gift: Forms and Functions of Exchange in Archaic Societies*. Trans. Ian Cunnison. New York: Norton.

Menovshchikov, G. A. 1962. "O perezhitochnykh iavlenniakh rodovoi organizatsii u Aziatskikh Eskimosov." *Sovetskaia Etnografiia* 6:29–34.

———. 1964. "The Eskimos." In *The Peoples of Siberia*, ed. M. G. Levin and L. Potapov, pp. 836–50. Chicago: University of Chicago Press.

Muller, Gerhard F. 1967. *Voyages from Asia to America*. Bibliotheca Australiana, no. 26. New York: Da Capo Press.

Murdock, George P. 1949. *Social Structure*. New York: Macmillan.

Novozhilova, V. M. 1987. "Sovershenstvovannie narodnogo obrazovaniia v raionakh prozhivaniia narodnostei severa." In *Problemy sovremennogo sotsial'nogo narodnostei severa*, ed. V. I. Boiko, Iu. P. Nikitin, and A. I. Solomakha, pp. 185–93. Novosibirsk: Nauka.

Okladnikov, A. P. 1965. *The Soviet Far East in Antiquity: An Archaeological and Historical Study of the Maritime Region of the USSR*. Ed. Henry N. Michael. Toronto: University of Toronto Press.

Ortner, Sherry. 1973. "On Key Symbols." *American Anthropologist* 75:1338–46.

Oswalt, Wendell. 1967. *Alaska Eskimos*. San Francisco: Chandler.

Pika, Aleksandr. 1996. "Reproductive Attitudes and Family Planning Among the Aboriginal Peoples of Alaska, Kamchatka, and Chukotka: The Results of Comparative Research." Ed. Pam Stern. *Arctic Anthropology* 33(2):50–61.

Providenskii Raionnyi Gosudarstvennyi Arkhiv (PRGA). 1959. Provideniia. Op. 1, f. 1, d. 1.

Puchkova, M. V. 1993. "The Legal Position of National Minorities in the Former USSR." *Coexistence* 30:45–55.

Reed, Evelyn. 1972. "Introduction." In *The Origin of the Family, Private Property and the State*, by Frederick Engels. New York: Pathfinder Press.

Rudenko, Sergei I. 1947. "Drevnie nakonechniki garpunov Aziatskikh Eskimosov." Akademiia Nauk SSSR, Institut Etnografii, *Trudy*, n.s. 2:233–56.

Schindler, Debra L. 1991. "Theory, Policy, and Narody Severa." *Anthropological Quarterly* 64(2):68–79.

———. 1992. "Russian Hegemony and Indigenous Rights in Chukotka." *Inuit Studies* 16(1–2):51–74.

Sergeev, D. A. 1962. "Perezhitki ottsovskogo roda u Aziatskikh Eskimosov." *Sovestskaia Etnografiia* 6:35–42.

Shinkwin, Anne, and Mary Pete. 1990. "Alaskan Villagers' Views on Problem Drinking: Those Who Forget." *Human Organization* 41(4):315–22.

Slezkine, Yuri. 1991. "The Fall of Soviet Ethnography, 1928–35." *Current Anthropology* 32(4):476–84.

———. 1992. "From Savages to Citizens: The Cultural Revolution in the Soviet Far North, 1928–1938." *Slavic Review* 51(1):52–76.

Slezkine, Yuri, and Galya Diment, eds. 1993. *Between Heaven and Hell: The Myth of Siberia in Russian Culture*. New York: St. Martin's Press.

Stern, Richard O., Edward Arobial, Larry L. Maylor, and Wayne C. Thomas. 1980. "Eskimos, Reindeer, and Land." University of Alaska, Agricultural Experiment Station, *School of Agriculture and Land Resources Management Bulletin* 59.

Tein, Tassan S. 1994. "Shamans of the Siberian Eskimos." *Arctic Anthropology* 31:117–125.

Tishkov, Valery A. 1991. *Use and Allocation of Natural Resources in the Chukotka Autonomous District.* Anchorage: University of Alaska, Institute of Social and Economic Research.

Vakhtin, Nikolai B. 1984. "K sotsiolingvisticheskomu opisanii Chukotskogo poluostrova." In *Istoriko-tipologicheskoe izuchenie raznosistemnikh iazikov*, pp. 69–73. Moscow: Akademiia Nauk SSSR.

———. 1992. *Native Peoples of the Russian Far North: A Minority Rights Group International Report.* London: Manchester Free Press.

———. 1993a. "Perevaritel'nyi otchet: O pabote v ekspeditsii transsibering-Longines." Unpublished manuscript.

———. 1993b. "Indigenous People of the Russian Far North: Land Rights and the Environment." Paper presented at the United Nations Consultations of Indigenous Peoples, Kabarovsk, Russia.

Vasiliev, V. A., Iu. V. Simchenko, and Z. P. Sokolova. 1966. "Problems of the Reconstruction of Daily Life Among the Small Peoples of the Far North." *Sovetskaia Etnografiia* 1: 63–87.

Vasilievich, G. M., and M. G. Levin. 1951. "Tipy olenevodstva i ikh proiskhozhdenie." *Sovetskaia Etnografiia* 1:63–87.

Vdovin, I. S. 1961. "Eskimoskie elementy v kul'ture Chukchei i Koriakov." In *Sibirskii Etnograficheskii Sbornik* 3. Moscow: Akademii Nauk SSSR.

———. 1965a. *Ocherki istorii i etnografii Chukchei.* Moscow: Nauka.

———. 1965b. V. G. "Bogoraz—Issledovatel' iazikov i kul'tury narodov severo-vostoka Sibiri." *Sovetskaia Etnografiia* 3:70–78.

Verdery, Katherine. 1991. "Theorizing Socialism: A Prologue to the 'Transition.'" *American Ethnologist* 18:419–39.

Vitebsky, Piers. 1989. "Perestroika Among the Reindeer Herders." *Geographical Magazine* 6:22–25.

———. 1990. "Centralized Decentralization: The Ethnography of Remote Reindeer Herders Under Perestroika." *Cahiers du Monde Russe et Soviétique* 31:345–55.

———. 1997. "What Is a Shaman?" *Natural History* 106(2):34–35.

Vucinich, Alexander. 1960. "Some Ethnographic Studies of Cultural Change." *American Anthropologist* 62:867–77.

Williams, Brackette F. 1989. "A Class Act: Anthropology and the Race to Nation Across Ethnic Terrain." *Annual Review of Anthropology* 18:401–44.

Yanagisako, Sylvia Junko. 1979. "Family and Household: The Analysis of Domestic Groups." *Annual Review of Anthropology* 8:161–205.

Index

Index

CPSIA information can be obtained
at www.ICGtesting.com
Printed in the USA
LVHW092121131120
671654LV00004B/273